HIRE
WITH YOUR
HEAD
USING
POWER
Hiring®
TO BUILD
GREAT COMPANIES

Second Edition

Lou Adler

John Wiley & Sons, Inc.

To Chuck Jacob who got me started;
my wife Lorraine, who kept me going;
my son Keith, who keeps me inspired;
every hiring manager who wants to build a great team; and
all those great candidates who didn't get the job they deserved.

Foreword

Since the early 1990s, I've been advising business leaders in organizations ranging from JC Penney to JP Morgan Chase on how to leverage talent to meet their business objectives. One piece of advice that is a slam dunk is this: Buy a copy of Lou Adler's *Hire with Your Head* for yourself, read it, and then buy copies for every hiring manager, every recruiter, and every human resources professional in your organization. Why? Because this book offers a systematic approach to performance-based hiring and that is the most important thing you'll ever do to build your team.

As much as things change in the business world from week to week and year to year, there is one fact that isn't going to change: Talent is the number one asset in every organization. That has always been true, but the value of talent is even more important in the changing economy than ever before.

Organizations in every industry are trying to increase productivity and quality and they cannot rely on technology alone to achieve those objectives. As employers cut waste, introduce new technologies, and streamline operations, they put even more pressure on individuals to "add value" on a daily basis. Every operation nowadays must be lean, flexible, and high performance. Every supervisor is under pressure to get more work and better work out of fewer people. That means those few people had better be really, really good.

High performance under pressure is what the *real new economy* is really all about. Technology implementation will continue, organizations will become even leaner, the pace of change will get even faster, competition will be even more intense, businesses will become even more customer focused, expected response times will get shorter, and productivity expectations will grow. The whole game is moving to a higher level.

That's why there is a growing premium on people—at all ends of the skill spectrum—who can work smarter, faster, and better. You want your people to be innovative (within guidelines), passionate (within reason), and armed with sufficient discretion to make mistakes (as long as they are not too big). In lean, restructured companies, the best employees are handling more responsibility, using greater technical skill, and applying more precious human judgment than ever before. Every individual, like every business, has his or her own value proposition to offer employers in the free market for talent, which simply means: "Here's what I can do." And that value proposition is strictly business. One really good person is worth a whole pile of mediocre people. Really good people "can do" real things (very well and very fast) that add real value to your bottom-line. And they know it just as well as managers know it.

We're talking about that senior executive talent who can turn around a division in 18 months. The programmer who can write two lines of code for every one that an ordinary programmer writes. The call center operator who can dazzle every customer, gather market research on the front lines, and routinely suggest improvements in the whole system. The salesperson in the field who can sell anything to anybody and who also monitors warehouse inventory and the production schedule from his palm computer. The warehouse manager who knows everybody by name and also knows the new database inside and out. The nonphysician health professional delivering care previously reserved only for doctors. And the soldier operating a laptop computer mounted on a tank in the midst of battle who turns around, as soon as the battle is won, and plays the role of peacekeeper.

Regardless of fluctuations in the labor market, demand for those great people is going to outpace supply for the foreseeable future. And hereafter, in the real new economy, there's going to be a perpetual struggle in the marketplace to leverage the value of labor. How do *you* go about sourcing, attracting, and selecting the best people?

Business leaders, managers, and hiring professionals who fail to take a long-term strategic approach to hiring in today's rapidly changing business world, will face a perpetual staffing crisis. You may be understaffed one day and overstaffed the next; the problem is, you won't be intelligently staffed with the right people in the right places at the right times.

If you want to be intelligently staffed, you have to hire with your head. Seize control of your talent supply chain, just as you have with other critical resources. That means you need the kind of systematic approach Lou Adler offers in this book.

Throughout most of the industrial era and until recently, the dominant staffing model for most employers was based on long-term full-time on-site employment relationships. But in today's quickly changing marketplace, where employers can never predict what is just around the corner, the old-fashioned, stable, until-retirement-do-us-part employer-employee relationship just doesn't fit. The key to continued success for companies today is the ability to adapt rapidly to new circumstances—staffing may have to expand rapidly in one skill area, or contract rapidly in another—or do both at the same time. Staffing strategy must be geared to face this reality.

People in today's workforce want to know what you want from them today, tomorrow, next week, next month, and exactly what you have to offer them in return. Create a compelling recruiting message by answering the fundamental question people want answered: "What's the deal?" To be effective in today's labor market, you need to be communicating that message through an aggressive and year-round effort to a wide range of well-chosen candidate sources. Why? So that you attract an applicant pool that is sufficiently large that you can be very, very selective when it comes to the ultimate hiring. You must be prepared to implement a rigorous selection process that is all about collecting proof that potential hires have the skills they need to get up to speed and start contributing right away.

What you'll find in this book is a step-by-step process with detailed instructions for taking a logical, systematic approach to getting the right new-hire in the right place at the right time every time. We all owe Lou Adler our thanks for the second edition of this gem.

BRUCE TULGAN
Author of *Winning the Talent Wars*
(W.W. Norton, New York 2002) and
founder of RainmakerThinking, Inc.®

Preface

I became a line manager for a Fortune 100 company in my mid-twenties. Within days, I was sent on a corporate recruiting trip to a few of the top MBA B-schools in the country. The vice president of human resources called me before leaving and gave me some advice on how to interview. What he said still sticks in my mind today. It was wrong, but it was the only training I had, and it seemed reasonable at the time.

He said to consider only candidates that had at least three of the four A attributes of success—assertive, affable, attractive, and articulate. (Of course, if this was the guideline, I wondered why they hired me.) With this benchmark and a decent resume, I could determine competency in 15 minutes. Or, I at least thought I could. As I look back, this process was about 60 percent to 65 percent effective in predicting subsequent success. This was for the 30 to 40 people I hired to work for me personally, and for the 50 to 100 I recommended to work for others. I hired some duds, but enough great people that I got promoted very quickly. Within five years, I was a business unit manager for a decent-sized business. One thing I did learn was that hiring great talent is the key to a manager's career progression. I also found out that being a headhunter and helping other managers hire great people was a more lucrative career. It was also much less painful than working for someone who always told me what to do.

Despite the weak predictive value of the four A interview approach, I still used it with great success as a headhunter in my early days. Since I started out as a contingency recruiter (only getting paid when a candidate was hired), it wasn't too hard to find people who met the superficial four A criteria and who could last the short 90-day guarantee. At the time, most of our competitors offered only 60 days, so this gave me a competitive advantage. Everything changed when I became a retained recruiter and offered a one-year guarantee. Under this provision, the person also had to be competent. This was a strange new world. A decent resume and the four A criteria were no longer sufficient for judging talent. Finding a better criteria was how POWER Hiring was born. It took about five years to figure it out. Fifteen years later, I'm still working at it.

As I studied the recruiting and hiring process, I found out some interesting things. Foremost was the fact that the best candidate rarely got the job, the best interviewee did. The person who could present himself or herself most effectively generally got the offer. Here's some other interesting things I discovered along the way about top candidates:

➤ The best candidates aren't the best interviewees. So using interviewing skills was a terrible way to judge competency.

➤ The best people (the top 10% to 15%) don't use the same criteria to explore jobs as the rest. So typical advertising and screening methods were targeting the wrong pool of candidates—those that needed another job, or any job, and would do whatever they could to get it. Traditional sourcing did not target those that wanted a better job, or those that could choose among competing jobs. The best, while being more discriminating, also wouldn't jump through silly pre-employment tests.

➤ The best people use more decision variables before accepting an offer. They also take longer to decide, and they consult with more advisors. For the best, a new job is the beginning of a career. The needs of the best are normally not taken into account during the interviewing and recruiting process. Most hiring processes are geared around the needs of the average candidate, not the best. For the average candidate, a new job is considered the end of an ordeal. Salary, location, job content, and speed to hire dominate their decision. You can't use the same process to hire the best.

➤ The best candidates didn't typically have all of the skills, experiences, and education described in the job description. They are made up with traits that can't easily be filtered—potential, self-motivation, leadership, tenacity, vision. So if a company advertises and filters totally on skills, the best are often inadvertently excluded from consideration before starting.

➤ The best candidates get just as nervous in an interview as other candidates. Nervousness reveals itself in poor eye contact, weak communications, short or shallow answers, and less self-confidence. This is how many good candidates get excluded for superficial reasons.

If you don't address all of these issues in your hiring systems, you'll wind up seeing and hiring the wrong type of candidate. The best really are different from the rest, and hiring processes need to be designed around their unique needs.

Ignoring the needs of the best is only half of the problem. Here are some other things I discovered about hiring managers and those people on the interviewing and selection team:

➤ Most hiring managers and other members of the selection team aren't very good at interviewing, yet they all think they are. They think that everyone else involved in the selection process is pretty bad at assessing competency.

➤ Most members of the interviewing team don't know the real job, but they all have an equal vote. So candidates are not judged on how well they can do the job, or if they want to do it, but on first impressions, interviewing ability, and if they're prepared or not.

➤ The assessment process is in worse shape than the interviewing process. Most people don't know what to do with the answers to the questions, even if they ask the right questions in the first place. Without a common baseline, the most outspoken, or highest ranking person, most often decides who gets hired or not.

➤ More errors are made in the first 30 minutes of the interview than any other time. Emotions, biases, perceptions, stereotypes, and first impressions are powerful human forces that profoundly affect individual judgment.

➤ When anyone on the interviewing team finds a candidate they think is hot, they go into immediate sales mode. They also stop listening and stop evaluating competency in a transparent attempt to excite the hot prospect about the merits of the job. This not only cheapens the job and drives many top people away, but requires premium pricing. More times than not, the hot candidate is just an overpaid flash in the pan.

➤ Very few people know how to deal with the legal issues. Stupid things are said and done causing companies to pay outrageous defense and liability penalties that could have been avoided. Other companies overreact to the fear of these costs and establish policies and procedures that preclude them from hiring the best.

➤ Few people know how to negotiate salaries and make offers. Hiring the best requires a consultative process addressing a number of short- and long-term career management and personal issues. The best candidates must balance these against competing alternatives. You can't make hiring the best a transaction. You wouldn't think of sending out untrained salespeople to sell a complex process, yet that's what we do when we ask managers to close a deal. It's like selling a custom product through the Yellow Pages.

If you want to hire superior people, you need a system that is designed to hire superior people, not one that is designed to fill positions. It's hard enough to hire one great person. It's even harder to hire five or ten. But when we get to thinking about hiring tens or hundreds, we somehow lose sight of what it takes to hire just one great person. In this book, we'll show you how to hire one great person hundreds of times. For it to work, every one of the problems noted above needs to be addressed.

While I've observed all of these problems over the years, I've also observed a number of managers, human resource people, and recruiters who seem to get it right most of time. They've mastered the rules of the game. Most learned through trial and error. I've watched them in action, then tried their ideas out. I then refined these ideas, and tried them out again. I've also tracked candidates for years to see what were the best predictors of subsequent success. Eventually it became clear there were five fundamental principles at work that seemed to form the foundation for hiring top people every time. This became the POWER Hiring methodology described in this book.

Then came the Internet. Everything was supposed to change as a result. Hiring the best would be easy for all. Just post an ad, and be done with it. The best would then come flocking. The Internet overpromised, and underdelivered. Much did change. Some good ideas and new techniques survived, even if the overall promise was like a hot candidate without substance. Despite the turmoil, the five POWER Hiring principles remained unscathed. The execution did change as a result of the Internet, but by and large, hiring one great candidate isn't much different now than it was in the pre-Internet days. We'll describe how to take advantage of the Internet for hiring top talent in the book, but this represents a small change in tactics, not a change in philosophy.

The new buzz is human capital management, winning the talent wars, and creating a talent-driven culture. This is all critical stuff. Hiring top people is #1, after all. But in all of the hurly-burly looking for a silver bullet, we still have a tendency to lose sight of what it takes to hire one great candidate.

Here's what I'd like to propose as the primary goal of this book: Show every manager how to hire one great person. The second goal is to show how to do it again, and again, and again. Here's what's required to pull this off:

➤ Make the job description the real job. Most job descriptions list skills, required experience, academics, competencies, and personality traits, with a little about duties and responsibilities. This is more a people description than a job description. When the job description becomes the real job, everything about hiring changes. This is the P in POWER—**P**erformance Profiles.

➤ Give all interviewers some simple easy-to-learn questions that can be used to accurately assess candidate competency. This is the O in POWER—**O**bjective Evaluations.

➤ Understand what motivates the best to consider a job, and then build your sourcing and recruiting strategies around these needs. This is the W in POWER—**W**ide-Ranging Sourcing.

➤ Learn how to overcome the natural tendency to over rely on intuition and emotion to make hiring decisions. This is the E in POWER—**E**motional Control.

➤ Negotiate and close offers using a consultative approach to selling, not a transactional one. This is the R in POWER—**R**ecruiting Right.

➤ Hire people who are both competent and motivated to do the work. This is just about everything in POWER.

While these underlying POWER Hiring principles are presented throughout this book, this book is mostly about tactics. It clearly shows how to hire one great person again and again, every step of the way. Don't lose sight of this goal as you build systems to hire dozens, or hundreds, of great people. Each great person is unique. Treat them this way. This is the real principle of POWER Hiring.

LOU ADLER

Mission Viejo, California
March 2002
louadler@powerhiring.com

Acknowledgments

This book was not done alone. It started out by tracking hundreds and hundreds of candidates. Some did it right, some wrong, but valuable lessons were learned nonetheless. It continued with dozens and dozens of hiring managers, company executives, human resource leaders, and other recruiters. Some did it right, some wrong, but valuable lessons were learned nonetheless. Special thanks to Jack Lantz, Linda Duffy, Larry Cassidy, Eric Boden, Rich Shields, Bernie Suttle, Francine Meza, Larry Rutkowski, Monique Love, Dave Rader, Mike Noggle, Keith Swayne, Dave Kipp, Leigh Belden, Howard Oringer, Chris McGurk, Brad Remillard, Barry Deutsch, and Dennis Buster. Many of my original ideas were reworked, honed, and polished by Jim Schreier, Bryan Johanson, Carl Bradford, Keith Adler, Dani Mariano, Haroon Elsarrag, Elaine Orler, Eric Lane, Kevin Wheeler, Jerry Crispin, Barbara Spector, Jack Higgins, and Mary Berry.

Jeff Herman, my agent, deserves a special round of thanks. Without his trust and support, this project would never have gotten started or completed. Without Rosemary Ford, who made me rewrite every page of the first edition six times, this book would have been one run-on sentence. Rosemary, I finally took your advice completely in the second edition, and I thank you for your wisdom and persistence. Rob Bekken, a senior partner at the labor law firm of Fisher & Phillips, deserves credit and thanks for reviewing everything said here and making sure it's both legal and valuable. He's written a lengthy review of the importance of performance-based hiring, which is in the Afterword. Charles Handler, PhD, did much of the technical review to make sure what we advocate truly does a better job of predicting on-the-job performance. I thank him for a thorough and complete assessment. Matt Holt, my editor at Wiley, is due my full gratitude and thanks for instigating this whole affair. He was the one who decided to make a second, and better, edition of *Hire with Your Head* happen.

I'd also like to thank TEC in San Diego. We conducted over 200 three-hour workshops with this great group of CEOs who tried out much of what we suggested and allowed us to improve our process. I want to particularly thank those TEC company presidents who implemented POWER Hiring and contacted me personally with their feedback and suggestions.

Finally, I want to thank those who read the first edition and gave me your words of thanks and support. For those of you who read this second edition, please contact me after you've had a chance to try out some of these ideas. Remember, the best are different than the rest, and I especially want to thank them for going the extra mile. This book will help you find them, and then you can thank them for yourself.

Contents

Chapter 1

The POWER Hiring Approach to Hiring Top Talent

Hire smart, or manage tough.

Red Scott

■ A RUDE AWAKENING—WHAT IT REALLY TAKES TO GET AHEAD

I still remember this like it was yesterday. I got the call some-time in the morning on a mid-October day in 1972. It was my first management job, Financial Planning Manager at Rock-well's Automotive Group in Troy, Michigan. At the time, I was working on my first presentation to the Group President and Vice President of Finance, due the next day. It was going to be a very long night. I didn't mind, since my new wife hadn't made the move yet. My boss, Chuck Jacob, and the reason for my being in Detroit, was on the phone with a desperate plea. Chuck was a 29-year-old Harvard MBA whiz kid, just out of Ford Motor Company, trying to prove to everyone that he deserved his position as Controller for this $900 million truck-axle busi-ness. He was also my idol. I listened. He was at the University of Michigan interviewing MBA students for planning analyst positions to fill out our department. We needed these people urgently. The good news—too many had signed up for the interview, and Chuck needed me there to interview the overflow. We were going head-to-head with Ford, P&G, IBM, and every other top Fortune 500 company, who wanted the best candidates from this prestigious MBA program. He told me there were stars in this group that we needed on our team. The bad news—I didn't have a minute to spare. I protested, vehemently, pleading 14-hour days, a long night, and a critical presentation the next day. There was a momentary delay. Chuck's response still blasts in my ears today. *"There is nothing more important to your success than hiring great people! We'll somehow get the work done. Get your ____ over here now."* He then hung up.

I was there within the hour. Together we interviewed about 20 people, took eight of them to dinner that night in Ann Arbor, and hired three of the top MBA students within two weeks. I've lost track of Russ, Joe, and Vivek, but I want to thank them and Chuck (who passed away at too early an age) for an invaluable lesson: There is nothing more important to your personal and company's success than hiring great people. Nothing. Chuck and I got back to the office at 10 P.M. that night and worked together until about 3 A.M. to finish the report. The handwritten version was presented the next day to Bob Worsnop and Bill Panny. We apologized for the format and lack of preparation, but told them we were doing something more important. They agreed.

■ BENCHMARKING THE BEST

I learned 50 percent of what I needed to know about hiring that day. Since then, I've been trying to understand the rest. I'm not quite there yet, but close. For the past 25 years, I've been fortunate to be able to work with other people, like Chuck, who always seem to hire great people, year-in and year-out. Few have had any formal training. They learned through trial and error. Equally important, I've lived and worked with managers who've made every possible hiring mistake in the book. This is their book, too. It's the collective stories of the good and the bad. What to do and what not to do. You'll find some great techniques in this book, but none are more important than your belief that hiring great people is the single most important thing you can do to ensure your own success.

Many years later, I heard Red Scott's adage, *"Hire smart, or manage tough."* This said it all to me. I've never met anybody who could manage tough enough. No matter how hard you try, you can never atone for a weak hiring decision. A weak candidate rarely becomes a great employee, no matter how much you wish or how hard you work. Instead, hire smart. Use the same time and energy to do it right the first time. Brian Tracy of Nightingale-Conant fame said on one of his recent tape programs that effective hiring represents 95 percent of a manager's success. This seems a little high, but with what I've seen, 70 percent to 80 percent seems about right to me. This is still enough to keep hiring in the number one position.

Every manager says that hiring great people is his or her most important task; however, few walk the talk. Although important, it never seems urgent enough until it's too late. When it comes down to the actual hiring process, our words don't match our actions. Test yourself and see how you score as a hiring manager. Rank the performance of every member of your own team. Are most of them top-notch and exceeding expectations? If they are, consider yourself a strong manager. Unless you're hiring people like this 80 percent to 90 percent of the time, you need to throw out everything you've learned about hiring, and start with a fresh slate. If you're already in the elite 80 percent to 90 percent, this book reinforces how you got there, and gives you a few new techniques that will boost your performance even further.

You might try a similar exercise with your next candidate for a management position. This should become part of your standard interviewing practices. When you're hiring a manager, make sure he or she has a track record of hiring good people. Have the candidate draw an organization chart and rank each person's performance. Ask him or her to describe all hiring successes and failures. Do this for the last two or three management positions. You'll quickly discover if the person is a good manager or not.

Most managers find the hiring process frustrating and time consuming. With this built-in negative bias, it's not surprising we're easy prey to the energetic, attractive, affable, and articulate candidate. This is the one who eventually falls short of our lofty expectations once on the job. Knowing we're prone to this problem is the first step to overcoming it.

We have developed many of the techniques presented in this book by observing people who consistently hire top people. This is a process called *benchmarking,* and much of the book has been developed this way. Just do what the best interviewers do, and you'll get similar results. In fact, modeling good interviewers this way is similar to modeling good performers for any type of job. Just find out what the most successful people do that makes them successful, and find other people who can do the same things. This principle of benchmarking is a theme of the book and is at the heart of the POWER Hiring performance-based hiring system we present. You don't need to be a trained psychologist to hire good people. Psychologists look for the underlying traits of high performers. Why bother? Just look for high performers. They possess the necessary underlying traits.

One critical factor has been observed through our benchmarking: The best interviewers use two different critical thinking skills, one for the hiring decision and another for information gathering. They recognize that the hiring decision must be intuitive, since there's never enough information to match abilities, needs, and interests completely. Instead, they substitute a broader group of 8 to 10 generic and job-specific factors to assess competency. Despite this intuitive approach, they recognize that an analytical, fact-finding method is needed to collect as much appropriate data as possible about these traits before making the hiring decision. These great interviewers also have the ability to suspend their personal reaction to the candidate long enough to make an unbiased assessment.

From my observations, it appears that weaker interviewers, those who make many mistakes, fall within three broad categories. A large percentage of them are too emotional. These people make quick, simplistic judgments based largely on first impressions and personality. Not unexpectedly, their hiring results are random. The overly intuitive interviewer short-circuits the process, superficially assessing only a narrow group of important traits. Every now and then, they'll hire a star, but more often it's a person strong in only a few areas and not broad enough to handle the whole job. I call these the partially competent. The technical interviewers are at the other extreme. These people are good at the fact-finding part of the process, but weak at decision making, believing they never have enough information. As a substitute, they overemphasize the need for years of experience and an abundance of skills. The result is a solid, but often unspectacular staff, since they ignored hard-to-measure potential. The key to hiring both competent and high-potential people is to collect enough of the right facts. Trouble occurs when this delicate balance is broken.

■ HIRING IS TOO IMPORTANT TO LEAVE TO CHANCE

If you want to hire superior people, use a system designed to hire superior people, not one designed to fill jobs. The emphasis of too many hiring processes is to reduce costs and fill jobs as rapidly as possible. Somehow the idea of hiring the best is an afterthought. Hiring the best must dominate every aspect of a company's hiring process. This is the clear theme of the latest McKinsey Consulting research project, *The War for Talent*.[1] The authors surveyed over 200 major companies. The conclusions were obvious—hiring the best is an essential component of long-term success, requiring a comprehensive and well-executed plan. Talk by itself, no matter how eloquent, is not enough.

In the mid-1990s, everyone thought the Internet was going to be the new tool that allowed everyone to hire great people quickly and at low cost. What a terrible forecast. For 2001, surveys indicate that less than 10 percent of all hires were made as a result of job boards on the Internet.[2] And this was the best year ever! Trends indicate that this number won't grow much more. There's much more to hiring great people than posting an ad.

Hiring the best requires a system designed around the needs of hiring the best people. This is what POWER Hiring offers—five steps to hiring great talent every time. Part of the reason a formal

---

If you want to hire superior people, use a system designed to hire superior people, not one designed to fill jobs.

---

hiring process is so important is that the people involved in the hiring process are generally untrained and unsophisticated when it comes to hiring. Some of the biggest problems—the weakest links—are the people involved in the hiring process: candidates, recruiters, hiring managers, and interviewers.

Setting up a fancy hiring system with all the latest database, Internet job sites, and filtering and tracking software does not address the problems of hiring top talent. It hides them. Systems are about managing data and preparing reports, not hiring the best. These weakest links are the cause of our biggest problems, and, as a rule, we ignore them. If these problems aren't solved first, everything else is just wasted activity. Not understanding the needs of the people involved in the hiring process, what motivates them to act, how they make decisions, and their biases and prejudices makes all of us the weakest links in the hiring process. Hiring processes will not improve until these issues are understood and addressed.

Here's how these issues affect the hiring process:

- ➤ It's too hard for the best candidates to apply for your job openings.
- ➤ Recruiters and hiring managers are looking for different candidates.
- ➤ Emotions, biases, prejudices, and first impressions dominate the hiring decision.
- ➤ The best candidates have different needs that aren't addressed.

Without enough good candidates, nothing else matters. If you look closely at your hiring process, you'll see plenty of these weak links. Here are a few I found on some recent client engagements. It takes only one or two of these problems to negate everything else you're doing. Do any of these common problems sound familiar?

Classic Hiring Problems

1. *Can't find the ad.* One of our clients was hiring 20 sales reps. The 30-day-old ad was on the 37th of 40

pages of monster.com listings. The top 20 percent won't spend the time going through every ad. Listings must always be on the first one or two pages wherever they are posted.

2. *Boring ads.* When I finally found the ad, it was boring, exclusionary, and demeaning. Ads need to be compelling—fun to read and inspiring.

3. *Skills-based ads that turn off the best.* "Use your CPA to see the world," is much better than, "Must have a CPA and be willing to travel 70 percent, including international." Most ads ask for too many skills. It's better if you include just a few, with more attention devoted to the challenges.

4. *Skills-based filters.* The best candidates have 60 percent to 70 percent of the skills, lots of potential, and the motivation to grow. You filter out the best if you ask for 100 percent of the skills. They won't even apply if you insist on them in the ad.

5. *Web-based applications that are negative or exclusionary.* As a test, I applied for a customer service job the other day directly on my client's Web site. The questions were sophomoric. Would I take a drug test? Would I be willing to work overtime? Would I be willing to travel? Did I live within 50 miles of the facility? They never asked if I wanted a great job, if I would be willing to put in extra effort if the company offered a challenging career opportunity, or if I would be willing to relocate for the chance to work with a company creating Six Sigma customer service.

6. *Incompetent recruiters.* Passive or active, the best candidates always have more than one opportunity. Recruiters must be career consultants, not used car salespeople.

7. *Emotional assessments.* You'll never build a great, diverse team if assessments are filtered through first impressions, personality, stereotypes, and prejudices.

8. *A flawed voting system.* Hiring the best is challenging enough. It's impossible if one "no" vote based on a

superficial interview can outweigh three or four solid "yes" votes.

9. *Selling too soon.* In our haste, a great resume and a great first impression are often all it takes to begin the sales job on an apparently great candidate. A job has more value when it has to be earned. You'll drive away the best if you give your jobs away too soon.

10. *No one knows the real job.* The best candidates accept offers based on what they'll be doing, learning, accomplishing, and becoming—not on the use of their skills. Everyone on the interviewing team must agree to the deliverables upfront and not worry about degrees, years of experience, and industry. The best candidates can spot an unprofessional team during the first round of interviews. The clues: Everyone describes a different job, nobody asks challenging questions, everyone is selling, and no one's listening.

11. *It's not just about the money.* The best people are looking for careers, not just jobs. If your close is more about the money and the benefits, and less about the comparison of career growth opportunities among various job alternatives, you've lost. For the best, compensation is always third or fourth on the list. A great career opportunity is always more important than everything else.

If you can eliminate these problems, you need only a pretty good applicant tracking system, a pretty good Web site, and a pretty good interviewing system. But you'll still wind up with a great hiring system. The weakest link is people. Don't ignore these problems. They won't go away, even with the greatest technology money can buy.

It has been my experience with hundreds of different hiring situations that the performance profile—the P in POWER— is the common denominator of all effective hiring processes. Once you know what the real performance needs of the job are, hiring is relatively easy. When you don't know what's really required, you substitute your biases, perceptions, and stereotypes in assessing candidate competency, not the person's ability to do the work. This is why different people can all meet the same candidate for the same job and each come up with a different assessment.

For the past 12 years up through 2001, we have trained over 20,000 people in our POWER Hiring workshops. Some of these workshops have been in 90-minute online mini-sessions; most have been half-day classroom workshops. In these sessions, we always take a quick survey of hiring processes and attitudes. The following is a summary of the results. Not much has changed since 1990. How does your company compare?

**The POWER Hiring Survey of Hiring
Practices and Attitudes**

- ➤ Ninety-five percent of hiring managers said they've made bad hiring decisions.
- ➤ Ninety-five percent of hiring managers indicated that hiring is number one or number two in importance.
- ➤ Ninety-five percent of hiring managers don't like the hiring process.
- ➤ Less than 10 percent of the companies indicated that they have formal hiring processes used by all managers.
- ➤ Just about everybody felt that the interview process isn't very accurate. Few were surprised to learn that a study conducted by Professor John Hunter of Michigan State indicated that the typical employment interview is only 57 percent effective in predicting subsequent success, 7 percent better than flipping a coin.[3]
- ➤ There are as many different assessments of the same candidate in a one-hour interview as there are interviewers.
- ➤ It takes at least three weeks to three months after a candidate starts to determine true competence for most jobs.

Despite all of the books, articles, and the wealth of evidence supporting the importance of hiring the best, little has changed. Everyone is still looking for the magic fix. The Internet wasn't it. While hiring the best is not easy, it's no harder than setting up a worldwide distribution or accounting system, or designing a new disease-fighting medical product, or launching a new Web site, or starting a business. It's just a process that needs to be implemented, like any other process. Most important, it requires a commitment from the executive management of the company that hiring is important, and that the resources and time will be devoted to making it happen.

While the solution to hiring revolves around the performance profile, the primary problem revolves around the interview itself. This is a random process that doesn't work very well. It's one reason most managers find the whole process frustrating. Consider this: Hiring, the most important thing we do as managers, is based on a random process. When you think about it, there are no other processes in our organizations that are random, much less one of this importance. Companies will spend hundreds of thousands of dollars, even millions, to reengineer a flawed process that has a 5 percent to 10 percent error rate. One with a 20 percent failure rate would be considered out of control and shut down! Yet the one that is considered most important has a 40 percent to 50 percent error rate. This is unacceptable. Something can be done. To begin, shut down your current hiring process and start over.

➤ It Starts with Sourcing

The best candidates want careers, not jobs. Unfortunately, most companies are just offering jobs. If you want immediate proof, look at 10 random ads on any job board. Each describes a job in terms of skills, experience, and requirements. They don't describe career challenges or opportunities for growth. If you want to attract the best people, you need to attract them with the best jobs.

Even a top candidate who is looking for a job has multiple opportunities. In a slow economy, there are more top people looking, but you still need to offer something more than just another job if you want to attract their interest. In normal economic times, you'll want to attract top candidates who are not actively looking. They'll be willing to explore a better opportunity, but they won't even consider just another job. Companies lose out on hiring the best by not understanding what the best want—careers, not jobs. If you're not an employer of choice with top candidates knocking down your door, you'd better offer a job of choice. As you'll discover, this is the performance profile, the P in POWER. It describes a job in terms of challenges, major accomplishments, and team-building needs. Describing a great job is the first step in finding great candidates.

In this book, you'll discover some great ways to find great people. When you start seeing these top people, something else will become readily evident. Top candidates don't evaluate jobs the same way average candidates do. For the best, the job is the start of something—a great job, a new career opportunity. For the rest, a new job is the end of an ordeal. For these candidates, accepting a job is about the salary, the job itself, and the location. For the best, accepting the job is a more strategic decision. It involves outside advisors including friends and family. They take longer to decide and want more information. Recruiting these top candidates is more a career management counseling session than a transaction. This is the R in POWER, recruiting right. You can't oversell these candidates. You'll either lose them or wind up paying an unnecessary premium. Instead, you must demonstrate how your open opportunity compares favorably to all other jobs under consideration. Top candidates need a consultative sales and assessment process, not a transactional one. It's just like trying to sell a custom product through the Yellow Pages. It can't be done.

■ WHY YOU SHOULD THROW AWAY EVERYTHING YOU KNOW ABOUT HIRING

The common interview, the one used by most managers, is a flawed means to hire anyone. Emotions, biases, chemistry, and stereotypes play too big a role. The competency of the interviewer is questionable. True knowledge of the job is weak. Some candidates give misleading information because they're not asked appropriate questions. Others are nervous. Standards fall as desperation grows. Some of these problems can be eliminated just by knowing their causes.

The number one cause of hiring mistakes is over-reliance on the interaction between the candidate and the interviewer, and too little on the candidate's ability and motivation to do the job. See Figure 1.1 for a graphical presentation. Over the past 25 years, I've been personally involved in over 4,000 different

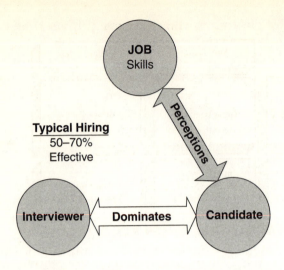

Figure 1.1 Why hiring accuracy is low.

interviewing situations. Most of the hiring decision is influenced by the interpersonal relationship developed early in the interview between the applicant and the hiring manager. Sometimes this can be in just a few minutes. This has to do with chemistry, first impressions, emotions, biases, stereotypes, the halo effect (globalizing a few strengths), and the tendency to hire in your own image.

In most cases, real job needs are poorly understood, and even if they are well understood, they're filtered through these interpersonal relationships and biases. This is how randomness enters the hiring process. If you like a candidate, you tend to go into chat mode, ask easier questions, and look for information to confirm your initial impression. If you don't like someone, you put up a defense shield, ask tougher questions, and try to end the interview quickly. You go out of your way to find information to prove your initial impression that the candidate is incompetent.

In both cases, the hiring assessment is inaccurate because the wrong things are being assessed. The candidate's ability to get the job is what's really being measured, not the candidate's ability to do the job. Presentation is more important than substance. Getting the job includes things like personality, first impression, handshake, affability, social confidence,

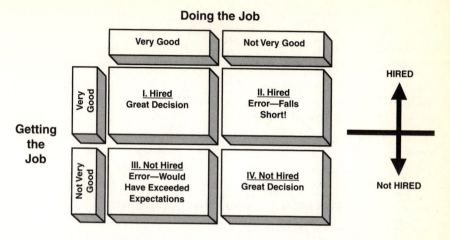

Figure 1.2 The impact of doing versus getting the job.

assertiveness, appearance, extroversion, and verbal communications. Doing the job includes initiative, team skills, achieving objectives, technical competence, management and organizational skills, intellect, and leadership, to name a few. We all overemphasize the "getting the job" part when assessing a candidate. The impact of this is shown in Figure 1.2.

➤ What Happens When Getting the Job Is More Important Than Doing the Job

When the hiring decision is based more on a candidate's ability to get the job rather than do the job, two bad things happen. One, we frequently hire people who fall short of expectations (situation II). These are the people who are good interviewers, but weak performers. We also don't hire people who are strong candidates, but weaker interviewers (III). Two good things can happen, but they're inadvertent. We hire people who are good at both the getting and the doing (I), and we don't hire those weak at both (IV). You don't even need to read this book or take a single training course to get these two parts right. It's all luck. As my former partner once said, "Even a blind squirrel finds a nut every now and then." It's how you handle the other 50 percent that will improve your hiring effectiveness.

When the hiring decision is based primarily on the candidate's ability to do the work, everything changes. You still hire those good at both (I), and don't hire those bad at both (IV). More importantly, you also eliminate the other two major hiring errors. You stop hiring those that always fall short of expectations (II), and you start hiring those that are really great but might be a little weak on the interviewing side (III). You need to hire people who are very good at doing the job, not those just very good at getting the job. Making this shift is what POWER Hiring is all about.

➤ Substitute the Job as the Dominant Selection Criteria

Moving the decision-making process from "getting" to "doing" is hard work and mentally challenging. It's especially difficult when we need to counteract the natural tendency to judge people based on first impression, personality, and a few select traits. If you can overcome this problem, you'll quickly eliminate 50 percent of all common hiring errors. The lack of real job knowledge represents much of the balance. The majority of hiring errors can be eliminated when both issues are addressed together. Over the past 25 years, I've had an opportunity to work with more than 1,000 different hiring managers on a variety of different search and hiring training assignments. Most, including me, fall prey to the personality bias just noted. A few don't. This select group of managers have the ability to suspend their emotional reaction to the candidate until they've determined competency. They also know what real competency looks like. Once they find out if the person can do the work, they then find out if they can work with the candidate. Figure 1.3 shows this fundamental principal, which is a more effective decision-making process.

➤ Get Candidates to Give Good Answers

One other issue needs to be addressed to improve hiring effectiveness. It took me about 10 years before I figured out that the best candidates aren't the best interviewers. In over 1,000

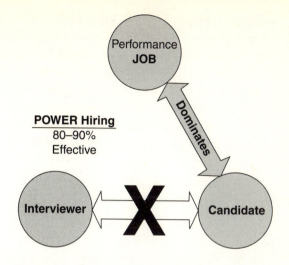

Figure 1.3 How to increase hiring accuracy.

interviews, I have found no correlation between interviewing skills and job competency. The best candidates aren't generally the best interviewers, and the best interviewers aren't generally the best candidates. Most interviewing methods measure interviewing skills, not job competency. This is a huge problem and can be minimized by controlling our biases and the impact of first impressions. This is only a partial solution. Interviewers need to proactively take responsibility for obtaining complete information about job competency from each candidate. Interviewers need to train candidates to give complete information. If you leave it up to candidates to provide this information on their own, you're measuring interviewing ability, not job competency. We show you how to do it right in this book.

Interviewers need to proactively take responsibility for obtaining complete information about job competency from each candidate.

■ KEY STEPS TO EFFECTIVE HIRING

Here's the short list of what's needed to get hiring right:

1. Target the best. Create careers, not jobs. Hiring the best is a solution, not a transaction.
2. Be proactive. Hiring requires forward-looking planning. This gives you the time to use all available sourcing options.
3. Clearly understand the performance needs of the job. Define success, not skills.
4. Control the impact of first impressions. Emotional biases are the number one source of hiring errors.
5. Measure job competency, not interviewing skills.

This requires new sourcing and advertising programs, new ways of thinking, changes in writing job descriptions, emotional control, and different interviewing and recruiting techniques. At CJA Executive Search, we've made over 1,500 placements using these techniques in a variety of positions, from staff accountant to division president. It's been our collective experience that when using POWER Hiring, our overall hiring effectiveness has been greater than 95 percent. This is based on fall-outs, or people being terminated during the first year. When mistakes were made, they could always be traced back to someone having short-circuited one of the basic principles of effective hiring. At POWER Hiring, we've trained over 200 different companies since 1990. Those that use the process report similar findings. The conclusion: Good hiring is a system, not an event. To consistently find and hire top people, a company must make the hiring process a core business process, planned and designed around its strategic initiatives.

■ FIVE STEPS TO GETTING HIRING RIGHT—AN INTRODUCTION TO POWER HIRING

Five basic themes are always present when a company or manager consistently hires top people. These become the five basic principles of the POWER Hiring methodology.

Performance Profiles
> *. . . if you want to hire superior people, first define superior performance*

Objective Evaluations
> *. . . past performance is a best predictor of future performance*

Wide-Ranging Sourcing
> *. . . sourcing is marketing, not advertising*

Emotional Control
> *. . . measure personality and performance, but measure performance first*

Recruiting Right
> *. . . recruiting is career counseling, not selling. Candidates then sell you.*

The P in POWER stands for **P**erformance Profiles. This is the most important of all of the principles, since it impacts all of the others. I've read over 2,500 different job descriptions. Most of them were no more than lists of skills, duties, responsibilities, and required experiences. At best, they defined basic competency. At worst, they defined the person, not the job. Yet in these same 25 years and over one thousand assignments, no client has ever asked us to find them anything other than a superior candidate. If you want to hire superior people, you first must define superior performance. Traditional job descriptions are not effective for finding, assessing, or hiring top people. Define success instead. This will represent a major step in improving your hiring decisions. Once superior performance is defined, it's much easier to find superior people. If you don't clearly define superior performance, everyone will substitute his or her own perceptions and stereotypes. This is how the hiring process begins to fall apart. Unfortunately, the way most job descriptions are now written precludes you from ever hiring the best.

The O in POWER stands for **O**bjective Evaluation. Once performance expectations are defined, the interviewer must use an objective, performance-based approach to determine if the candidate is both competent and motivated to do the work. This needs to run the gamut from the one-on-one interview to reference checks, testing, panel interviews, and take-home tests. The interview is only one part of a multistep evaluation process. Despite the need for a comprehensive assessment, we'll show how you can distill the one-on-one interview to four essential questions. With these alone, you'll have 75 percent to 80 percent of what you need to get it right every time.

The W in POWER stands for **W**ide-Ranging Sourcing. The quality of the hiring decision first depends on the quality of the sourcing program. If you're seeing only the bottom third of all possible candidates, that's whom you'll hire, even if you're great at using all the other techniques. On the other hand, if you're seeing only the top 10 percent, you'll eventually hire one of these great people, even if you're the worst interviewer in the company. For most organizations, sourcing falls somewhere between these extremes. As a manager, don't assume that your current sourcing programs are adequate. Be proactive. Stay on top of what's going on. A good multi-tiered sourcing program is a critical component of an effective hiring program, including compelling advertising that offers careers, not just jobs, and a strong employee referral program. Sourcing also must be proactive. Most hiring is needs driven. If you start looking only when you need someone, you've just lost the advantage of time. Desperation is the second most significant cause of hiring mistakes because standards fall. To prevent this you need to start sourcing at least 90 to 120 days before you need the candidate.

The E in POWER represents **E**motional Control. While desperation is the second basic cause of hiring mistakes, it directly impacts the primary cause of hiring errors—the lack of emotional control. More hiring mistakes are made based on emotional reactions and gut feelings. First impressions and affability are unfortunately more important than competency in deciding to bring a candidate back for a second interview. The emotional link between the interviewer and the candidate must be broken to remain objective. We're programmed to make major decisions based on first impressions. If positive, we tend to be less discriminating. If negative, we hold the applicant to a higher standard, or ignore their responses entirely. This double standard is the primary source of most bad hiring decisions.

The R in POWER stands for **R**ecruiting Right. Eventually, you'll meet a candidate you want to hire. Good recruiting skills then become essential. Recruiting is the process of persuading a candidate to take the job and then closing all of the details. Most managers believe recruiting is the ability to sell or charm a candidate about the merits and terms of the position. This is the least effective form of recruiting. Emotional control is a critical need at this point. Once we meet a great candidate, there is a tendency to start selling. If you oversell, you cheapen the job. That's why good recruiting is more counseling than selling. By creating a compelling career opportunity, the candidate is more likely to sell you, rather than the other way around. Recruiting is an essential aspect of a well-developed hiring program. It's the final piece toward building a great team.

It took 20 years for POWER Hiring to emerge. It started with the desire to find out what it took to make one great hiring decision, then another, and then another. During this time, I've sat between hundreds of hiring managers and a few thousand candidates, listening and observing. Sometimes it took a few months or a few years to learn about a mistake that could have been prevented much sooner. After a while, patterns emerged from all of these hundreds of small mistakes repeated over and over. By modeling the successes and avoiding the failures, we discovered a realistic process that could be documented, learned, applied, and repeated. As you'll discover in these pages, POWER Hiring is practical, natural, and based on common sense. You'll also discover how to hire one great person, over and over again.

■ PUTTING THE PIECES TOGETHER—A ROAD MAP TO THE ORGANIZATION OF THIS BOOK

A little about the organization of this book is in order. POWER Hiring involves five separate stages, many conducted concurrently. Some of the processes, like sourcing, take place earlier than others, but you need to know something about the later stages before you can be effective at it. The book is organized with this learning and implementing process in mind, as shown in Figure 1.4.

The hiring process starts by first defining superior performance, which allows you to measure substance, not style. Controlling emotions and understanding the performance needs

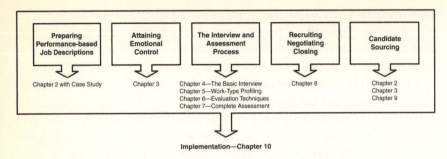

Figure 1.4 The POWER hiring system overview.

of the job are prerequisites to hiring with your head. Chapters 2 and 3 are devoted to these critical subjects and form the foundation of this book. The balance of the book is geared toward implementing POWER Hiring.

The complete interviewing and assessment process is presented in Chapters 4 through 7. The basic performance-based interview is introduced in Chapter 4. This powerful interview is built around four core questions. Once you try them, you'll see your accuracy soar.

The candidate assessment starts in Chapter 5 with the introduction of a new concept, work-type profiling. This categorizes work into its four basic components—technical, managerial, entrepreneurial, and strategic. With it, you can easily compare job needs to a candidate's abilities. This will improve job fit and prevent some of the classic mismatches. Additional evaluation techniques including reference checking, testing, and panel interviews are described in Chapter 6. Collectively, these techniques broaden the effectiveness of the performance-based interview. The candidate assessment is pulled together in Chapter 7, which includes checklists covering all-important points.

Chapters 8 and 9 deal with good recruiting and sourcing. Getting the candidate to join the team is critical. We describe how to negotiate and close an offer, and what to do when things go wrong. By the time you get to the sourcing chapter, you'll discover that you've already eliminated 50 percent of your sourcing problems. You'll be able to broaden the candidate pool by defining the performance needs of the job (Chapter 2) and eliminating your own personal biases (Chapter 3). The sourcing chapter presents a literal grab bag of tips, techniques, and methods you can quickly use to find the top 10 percent.

The last chapter shows how implementing POWER Hiring can create a talent-driven culture. This is based on a 20-step program covering all critical aspects of hiring. The basic program can be implemented in days with a little effort and training.

With the introduction of POWER Hiring, every manager now has a chance to hire great people using the same techniques as the most seasoned hiring pros. POWER Hiring is as much about good management as it is about good hiring. The two are inseparable. You become a better manager in the process of hiring better people. Hiring better people, in turn, makes you a better manager. Creating a performance profile is the first step in hiring great people.

To *Hire with Your Head,* you need to combine emotional control with good fact-finding skills and intuitive decision making. This whole-brain thinking provides the critical balance to match job needs, the interviewer's personality, and the candidate's abilities and interests. This needs to be combined with sourcing. Without enough good candidates, everything else is futile. Once you start meeting strong candidates, good recruiting skills become essential. Recruiting starts at the beginning, not the end. It must be part of an integrated interviewing and assessment process to work effectively. This is the strength of POWER Hiring. It brings all of the critical hiring processes together. While each step is easy to use separately, its effectiveness lies in the integration. Overlook any aspect and the whole process collapses. Do them all and you'll get consistent great hiring results.

POWER HIRING HOT TIPS: MAKING HIRING #1

✔ There is nothing more important to a manager's personal success than hiring great people. Nothing.

✔ Management is easy as long as you clearly know the performance needs of the job and hire great people to do it.

(continued)

(Continued)

✔   Hiring is too important to leave to chance.

✔   Hiring is the only major process in a company that's random. Any other process that's this unreliable would have been redesigned long ago.

✔   The key to better hiring decisions—"Break the emotional link between the candidate and interviewer and substitute the job as the dominant selection criteria."

✔   Hiring is a whole-brain activity. Collect enough unbiased facts to make an intuitive decision.

✔   Measure a candidate's ability to do the job, not get the job. Determine if you like or dislike the candidate after you've determined his or her competence. Substance is more important than style, but it's sometimes hard to tell the difference.

✔   Great hiring requires more than just good interviewing skills. POWER Hiring brings everything together into an integrated, systematic core business process.

✔   *"Hire Smart, or manage tough."*—Red Scott

Chapter 2

Performance Profiles— Define Success, Not Skills

Begin with the end in mind.

Steve Covey

■ IF YOU WANT TO HIRE SUPERIOR PEOPLE, FIRST DEFINE SUPERIOR PERFORMANCE

Everyone wants to hire superior people. Yet the criteria most people use to define work, write ads, filter resumes, and interview candidates is based on a misleading job description. This chapter establishes the foundation for POWER Hiring by demonstrating that traditional job descriptions listing skills, experience, academics, and competencies are misleading, can often preclude you from hiring top people, and should largely be ignored in the hiring process. In their place, profiles describing superior performance will be used. This is a prioritized list of deliverables and accomplishments that everyone involved in the hiring process has agreed defines success.

In addition to better understanding the real work involved in job success, these performance profiles may be used to source and filter candidates, conduct comprehensive interviews, and negotiate and close offers. By clarifying expectations for success up front, the performance profile also serves as the foundation for (1) the new employee's transition program; (2) how you'll manage, motivate, and conduct regular follow-up; and (3) how you'll review, reward, and promote the new employee. Hiring top people starts by defining superior performance. This sets the foundation for better hiring decisions. It is the performance management concept underlying POWER Hiring.

The following example establishes the differences between traditional job descriptions and performance profiles. Compare the two job descriptions for a product manager. In the one on the left, the more traditional skills and experiences are described. The one on the right lists the required results, or deliverables. Given only one choice, who would you rather hire, the person with all of the skills and experiences or the one who can deliver the desired results?

Experience and Skills	Desired Results, Deliverables
BS degree, MBA a plus	**Evaluate** the product marketing function and upgrade the team and capability.
5 years consumer products	**Establish** strong focus group and research programs to identify key buying needs.
Strong market research	**Prepare** a market research report in the first month.
Strong PC skills, statistics	**Upgrade** the internal product management status reports and lead program reviews.
Good team skills	**Coordinate** the product launch plan with engineering and operations.

Over the past five years, I've asked 5,000 people this question. More than 98 percent want to hire someone who can deliver the results. If this was your answer, start by throwing away traditional job descriptions for hiring purposes, and define the results instead. In this chapter, we'll show you how doing this will provide the foundation for increasing the quality of the people you hire, improving productivity, reducing turnover, and minimizing errors due to bad hiring decisions.

■ USE THE SAME CRITERIA FOR EXTERNAL HIRING AS YOU DO FOR INTERNAL MOVES

When performance is the basis for making hiring decisions, successful decisions increase dramatically. Most companies already use this type of performance-based assessment approach for internal moves with great success. We suggest using a similar approach for outside hiring. Here's a quick demonstration. Whose performance is more predictable—an internal person transferred or promoted, or someone hired from the outside? Obviously, the internal candidate. For an internal person the predictability of subsequent performance is very high, about 80 percent to 90 percent, even for a promotion. For the external hire, predictability is only around 55 percent to 65 percent accurate. The reasons for this disparity are obvious. The internal move is more accurate because we know the person's past performance, attitude, work habits, intelligence, leadership and team skills, ability to learn, management style, potential, and commitment. All of these are educated guesses for the unknown outsider. A person we don't know is assessed differently. The assessment is usually based on experience, skills, academics, and personality as measured in the interview. All are poor predictors of success. This comparison is:

Comparison of Outside Hire to Internal Transfer/Promotion

Outside Hiring Factors	Internal Move or Promotion
Degrees, certifications	Ability to deliver results
Excessive experience	Balance of strengths and weaknesses
Strong base of skills	Potential and capacity to learn new skills
First impressions	Team skills, attitude, character, values
Interviewing personality	True personality, commitment, motivation

The decision-making process between outside and inside hiring is fundamentally different. Personality and experience dominate the selection for outside hiring. Past performance, potential, and teamwork are the criteria for the internal candidate. A performance profile provides a simple means to make past comparable performance the basis of the external hiring decision, not experience and personality.

➤ Focus on the DOING, Not the HAVING

The internal decision is more accurate since it is based on *DOING* activities. The employee's actual past performance dominates the decision. The external decision is too *HAVING* oriented, based largely on a candidate's experience, level of skills, and academic background. This can't substitute for the work that needs to get done. The misguided hope is that enough experience, skills, academics, and personality will be sufficient to meet the performance requirements of the job. This is flawed logic. A candidate can HAVE all of this and not be able to DO the job. Conversely, there are many people who can do the job without having all of these skills, especially if they're highly motivated. Just consider all of the people who've been success-fully promoted or laterally transferred. It's what a person does with his or her skills, experiences, and abilities that determines success, not the absolute level. By changing the focus to DOING rather than HAVING, the basic approach to hiring can be al-tered and accuracy dramatically improved.

■ IDENTIFY THE CRITICAL PERFORMANCE OBJECTIVES OF EVERY JOB

Job descriptions must be redefined to reflect what needs to get done rather than what a candidate needs to have. The outcomes are more important than the inputs. When you do this, the ex-ternal hiring decision more closely parallels an internal move. Performance profiles define what needs to get done, not the skills and experiences the candidate needs to have. It's been shown that the ability to achieve measurable objectives is a bet-ter predictor of future performance than the candidate's level of skills and experiences. Comparable past performance is a leading indicator of future performance. We want to be able to use this basic concept when hiring candidates from the outside.

Many companies are now moving away from skills and expe-rience-based job descriptions, recognizing their inadequacies.

Jack Welch, in *Jack: Straight from the Gut* describes how GE has changed its applicant selection criteria. They consider performance and potential over experience and skills. In Tracey and Weirsema's book *The Discipline of Market Leaders,* Intel's approach to hiring is described. David House, at the time a senior vice president with Intel, mentions that job descriptions include the expected deliverables the candidate must provide in the first 12 months. Intel believes this is a better indicator of subsequent performance than skills and experiences. EDS and Cypress Semiconductor are long-time users of performance-based hiring systems. In *First Break All the Rules* (Simon & Schuster, 1999), Buckingham and Coffman echo a similar theme. Based on extensive interviews with thousands of people, they describe the best managers as those who first clearly define performance expectations for every job. These positions are then filled with people who have both the ability and the motivation to do the work required. General Electric measures talent by those who can execute and deliver results. In *Good to Great* (HarperCollins, 2001), Jim Collins examines how great companies emerged from the average. His dominant conclusion is that each had a leader who built teams of great people who could define and deliver the results. Hiring great people is about defining the desired results, and then finding people with the ability and desire to deliver those results.

After preparing a thousand different performance profiles or so, and tracking subsequent performance, I've concluded that every job has six to eight critical performance objectives that ultimately determine success. This is true for the entry-level position or the CEO of a Fortune 500 company. While these performance objectives are different for every job, they fall within similar categories, including effectively dealing with people, achieving objectives, organizing teams, solving problems, using technology, and making changes. Creating these performance objectives starts by asking what the person taking the job needs to do to be successful, not what the person needs to have. Following is a good example for a sales representative position. You can prepare something similar for any position. Just develop performance objectives for each of the categories noted, and then put the top six to eight into priority order.

Performance Objectives for a Sales Representative

Category	Desired Result
Major objectives, projects, and key deliverables	Achieve quota within 60 days after training. Add six new accounts per quarter.
Subobjectives	Improve the close rate by 20 percent using the new solution selling system. Learn the complete product line within 30 days. Meet with the top 10 accounts the first month.
Management and organization issues	Maintain complete status of each open account, new accounts, and progress of open orders.
Changes and improvements needed	Upgrade the new contact report to reflect order size and timing.
Problems to solve	Insure 100 percent customer satisfaction despite potential delivery delays.
Technical objectives	Learn to use PC sales management and order-entry software to insure 100 percent accurate order processing.
Team, people issues	Develop quick-response program for order delays with shipping department.
Long-range, creative, or strategic issues	Develop new territory management techniques to improve identification of major new accounts.

➤ Clarify Understanding — Create SMARTe Objective

To build a performance profile from scratch, develop two or three performance objectives for each of the categories shown in the sample. This ensures that all aspects of the job are considered. The preliminary list could consist of a dozen or more performance objectives. For ease of use, this list should be narrowed down to the top six to eight objectives, prioritized by order of importance. This prioritized list of deliverables is the key to clarifying expectations and job understanding. Everyone on the interviewing committee needs to know and agree to this performance profile before interviewing candidates. Use of a performance profile solves one of the biggest source of hiring errors—lack of understanding about real job needs.

To ensure complete understanding about job needs, we want to make these performance objectives as SMARTe as possible. By SMARTe we mean:

Create SMARTe Performance Objectives

Specific: Include the details of what needs to be done, so that others understand it.

Measurable: It's best if the objective is easy to measure by including amounts or percent changes.

Action oriented: Action verbs are essential like build, improve, change.

Results defined: This complements the measurable piece by clearly indicating what needs to happen.

Time based: Include how long it will take to start and complete.

environment described: Describe the company culture, pace, pressure, resources available, and politics.

Here's an example SMARTe objective for a budget analyst:

Even with the timing tight, complete the upgrade of the performance reporting system by June. This needs to tie into the main JDE accounting system with weekly reports available to department heads on the company's intranet.

Creating an objective this way greatly improves understanding by all who are involved in the selection team. When performance objectives are too general, they're subject to many different interpretations. Sometimes objectives are too broad, covering too many issues. This is why being specific is so important. If you can't quantify the objective the employee never knows when it has been achieved. When you clarify expectations this way, the performance profile becomes a statement of work for hiring a person, and later it becomes a tool to manage performance.

■ HOW TO WRITE SMARTe OBJECTIVES

This approach works for all types of jobs. It's great if you can prepare and prioritize these SMARTe performance objectives with the interviewing team. When everyone who has an input knows the real needs of the job, their assessments will be more accurate. Getting everyone on the same page this way has value beyond the interview. They'll all have a vested stake in the candidate's subsequent success. They then take the whole interviewing process more seriously. Ask the hiring manager, or team, to describe what the person taking the job must do to be successful in each of the major performance categories. Depending on the job, some tasks will be more important than others. The action verb is the critical part of the SMARTe objective. Actions verbs like *create, build, change, improve, establish, develop, design, analyze, identify, prepare, conduct,* and *lead* are good choices. They're much better in describing the work that needs to get done than passive verbs like *have* and *be responsible for* that are found in most job descriptions. Begin each SMARTe objective with one of these action verbs. It will help you focus on the required result.

Following are some examples of SMARTe performance objectives for each category for a product marketing manager in a software company:

1. *Major objectives*—This includes all the major requirements of the job. It would include things like setting up a new department, developing new products, or increasing sales. For the software product manager position it could be: "Develop and launch the new Internet buying program within 15 months with limited resources."

2. *Supporting or sub-objectives*—Include some of the key steps needed to meet the major objectives. Often these are more important than the primary objective itself since they describe the critical milestones and processes used to achieve the primary objective. Here's a supporting objective relating to the product manager's primary task of launching the new product line: "During the first quarter, identify the size and buying patterns of the user community." Here's another: "Despite the challenge

with engineering and the limited research available, prepare the marketing requirements specification for review within 120 days." This objective also addresses the underlying environment. Insight like this impacts the type of person selected.

3. *Management and organization issues*—Consider all of the team and management requirements needed to be successful in the job. Often these are minimized or ignored. You want to consider the size, scope, and complexity of the management challenge. "Identify key resource requirements including team members and budget needs and prepare a detailed plan of action within 45 days of starting," is a good example.

4. *Changes and improvements*—What do you want changed, upgraded, or improved? Take everything into account, like systems, methods, processes, and people. Consider anything that could be done better and include it on the job specification. Here's one for the product manager: "Improve the project tracking system to better identify critical constraints and bottlenecks."

5. *Problems*—Include any existing problems or those likely to be encountered. Minor ones don't matter, but the major ones do. Lack of time, resources, or special situations fall within this category. One problem the product manager needed to consider: "During the first quarter, develop some alternate PR plans to penetrate the direct mail channel, since our current agency has missed some critical dates."

6. *Technical issues*—Focus more on the application, expected outcome, or use of these technical skills rather than on an absolute level. Instead of asking for five years of hardware design plus a BSEE, it's better to request that a new engineer "Lead the design effort on a new optical switching system." One technical issue for the product manager could be: "Complete the database interface requirements to ensure efficient online ordering by June." This is much better than stating that the product manager needs to have at least five years of experience writing marketing requirements for software products.

7. *Team and people issues*—Some of this might have been covered in the management category, but also include any special interpersonal needs or problems, or cross-functional team issues. Dealing with another department or dealing with customers is an important component of many jobs that is often ignored. Here's one for a cost accountant: "Develop a new team approach with manufacturing to upgrade the cost and productivity reporting system." The previous product manager had problems with an egocentric development manager. The objective became: "Develop a new communications approach to deal with a very dominant, yet talented, software manager." This was better than saying, "Have good interpersonal skills and a balanced ego." This is an ineffective requirement found on many traditional job descriptions.

8. *Long-range, creative, or strategic needs*—Think about the creative and strategic needs of the job, addressing long-range planning issues or developing new approaches or concepts. For the product manager, a creative project was: "Lead the effort for a multimedia ad campaign using Internet, radio, television, and print in an intense Super Bowl-like, product launch." A strategic objective was "Develop a long-term marketing plan based on competitive analysis and technical trends."

Sometimes you won't have all the information necessary to complete each performance objective. In that case, make sure you have at least the action verb and the specific task identified. This is a good start. Complete SMARTe performance objectives are the best, since they clarify it all—a specific and measurable task, the expected result, the action verb, a time limit, and a description of the environment. Performance objectives written like this are the best way to clarify real job needs and improve communications. This will be critical when the candidate starts, since it will help guide the transition and track subsequent performance. In some cases, you won't know the time frames or specific needs. In other instances, you'll want to negotiate these with the candidate or let her determine them after starting.

While you should strive for a complete SMARTe objective, keep in mind the need to be flexible based on these circumstances. The primary and mandatory shift needs to be from having to doing; that's why the action verb is critical. You'll obtain a still higher level of insight by including the measurable result and the time factor. This improvement in understanding is shown in Table 2.1. Columns one and two represent the transition

Table 2.1   Use SMARTe Objectives to
Transition from HAVING to DOING

The HAVING	The DOING	
Classic Having Requirements	Partial SMARTe Objective Action Verb and Specific Task	Complete SMARTe Objective
Responsible for financial reporting.	*Upgrade* the monthly financial reporting package.	Within 120 days *upgrade* the monthly financial reporting package to include product line profitability analysis, and obtain approval from reluctant department heads.
Have 3 to 5 years' manufacturing experience controlling expenses.	*Reduce* operating overhead by $30,000 per month.	*Reduce* operating overhead by $30,000 per month within six months.
Have 10 years telemarketing industry experience.	*Improve* the performance of all telemarketing sales personnel.	During the first quarter, *improve* the performance of all telemarketing sales personnel by 6 percent through new training and tracking tools.
Have a BS Engineering and 5 to 8 years in the plastic molding industry.	*Lead* the design effort on a new high-volume injection molding line.	Immediately *hire* three new designers and *lead* and complete the design effort on a new high-volume injection molding line within a very tight six-month schedule.

from having to doing. Columns two to three represent the change from a partial SMARTe objective to complete understanding.

Complete and agreed on SMARTe performance objectives enable everyone on the selection team to determine candidate competency and better understand real job needs. This will be critical during the interview and evaluation process. It's important to recognize that these SMARTe performance objectives are more than just a list of—Management by Objectives (MBOs). MBOs are not deep enough. They just cover the broad top-level outcomes. For hiring purposes, SMARTe performance objectives need to consider each of the eight performance criteria categories noted earlier. When these are narrowed down and put in priority order, everyone involved knows what the job entails. It's been our experience that the ability to consistently hire great people is predicated on understanding these real performance issues.

Dennis Buster, vice president of Human Resources at Everett Charles Technology, a division of the Dover Corporation, has been using performance profiles like this for a number of years. He considers getting understanding and agreement up-front the key difference in hiring outstanding people. Before, reaching consensus on a candidate was always a compromise, based on too much subjectivity and personal biases. The results speak for themselves. With performance profiles, getting agreement whether to proceed or exclude a candidate from consideration was far easier, and the quality of people hired was much improved. Linda Duffy, the director of Human Resources at Lantronix, a high-tech company based in Southern California, had similar experiences. In the few cases when someone was hired without using the performance profile, his performance always fell short of expectations. When a performance profile was used as the basis of the hiring decisions, the quality of the candidates seen was better, and the performance of the person ultimately hired was superior. Jack Lantz, the CEO of Unitek-Miyachi, an international capital equipment manufacturer, has been using performance profiles since the early 1990s. He told me that more than 90 percent of the 30 to 40 people he has personally hired in this time have been outstanding people. Most of them are still with him. Before using performance profiles his results were not nearly as good.

■ DEFINE THE JOB, NOT THE PERSON

Look on monster.com or any company's Web site for proof that most job descriptions just list skills, duties, responsibilities, and describe required experiences. There are plenty of good examples here of bad job descriptions. This approach excludes strong candidates with related, but not identical experience. It also overvalues factors that have been shown to be misleading predictors of success. You want to motivate top performers to apply for these jobs, but skills and competencies establish artificial hurdles two ways: (1) the best do not look for work based on what skills they possess, they look for work based on what they'll be doing and learning; and (2) the best want to be stretched. If the job is exactly the same as what they're currently doing, there's no incentive for them to check it out. Job descriptions built around performance-based SMARTe objectives minimize these problems.

Define the job, not the person. Define the results, not the skills. When you define the job, rather than the person, you fundamentally change the way you find candidates and assess their competency. It's better to understand the expected outcomes of a job, rather than the inputs. This is the fundamental difference between performance and experience-based job descriptions. If the candidate can achieve the performance objectives, she obviously has enough experience and skills. She couldn't achieve it, or something similar, otherwise. Reversing the logic, just because someone possesses this arbitrary list of required skills and experiences, it doesn't mean she can deliver the results. We've all seen different people with a different set of skills and experiences deliver the same results. Therefore, it's better to spend the time in the interview determining what the candidate achieved that was most comparable, and how she went about it, rather than examining the amount of education and experience she has.

■ THREE DIFFERENT WAYS TO PREPARE SMARTe OBJECTIVES

There are three different ways to develop these SMARTe performance objectives. Depending on the type of job, you might

Method	Description	Example
Macro or The Big Picture Approach Ask: *"What will the person hired need to do to be successful?"*	Get measurable objectives for each major factor in the job. Cover technical needs, management issues, team issues, projects, needed changes, and problems.	➤ Launch three new products within the next 12 months. ➤ In the next 90 days, upgrade the planning system for manufacturing.
Micro Approach Convert skills into actions.	Determine what needs to be done with each skill or experience. Develop a measurable objective that demonstrates competency.	➤ Use PCs to develop a new project tracking system. ➤ Have enough experience to design three new products per year.
Benchmark the Best!	Compare the best people already in the job and select traits that best predict success. Avoid the traits of the underperformers.	➤ Prepare complex spreadsheets for long periods looking at pricing and cost issues. ➤ Use initiative in dealing with customer return problems and making quick decisions.

need just one, or all three, of the approaches to define outstanding performance.

The SMARTe Objective worksheet in Figure 2.1 is a good template to use to help guide you through each of the steps involved in preparing performance profiles.

➤ 1. The Macro Approach

Jobs with lots of projects, like the software project manager discussed earlier, are generally the easiest to prepare. Use the macro approach in this case. Put aside the traditional job description and ask what the candidate must do to be successful in the job. Consider each of the performance categories. This is the technique we use in preparing most management or project-type performance profiles. A time line can help clarify

POWERhiring SMARTe Objectives
Best Practices for Hiring Top Talent

Define the Job, not the Person — Create SMARTe Performance Objectives

Position:	Department:	Hiring Manger:	Date:

Instructions for Creating the Performance Criteria for Any Position

- Every job has six to eight major things that need to get done (performance objectives) for the new employee to be successful.
- Make all objectives **SMART** - **S**pecific, **M**easurable, **A**ction Oriented, **R**esult-based, **T**ime Bound, describe **e**nvironment.
- Ignore job spec. Use macro approach to develop performance objective for each major area of job. Follow template below.
- Use micro approach (over) to convert traditional experience/skill spec to performance. Find out what's done with each criterion.
- Use benchmark approach (over) by finding traits and capability of people now in the job known to be competent.
- Prioritize the top 6-8 performance objectives and include on performance-based job description.
- ANCHOR and VISUALIZE each SMART objective to determine competency (over and Fact-Finding Worksheet).

Determine Performance Objectives using the Macro Approach

Job Factor	Example of HAVING vs. DOING	Comments and Descriptions	SMARTe Objectives
Major Functional Objectives	Misleading: Have 10 years OEM sales experience. BETTER: Increase OEM sales by 15% in year 1 and build new team.	Objectives need action verb (e.g., increase, change, improve) and measurable objective (e.g., 10% in 90 days).	
Subordinate Objectives	Misleading: Have good planning skills. BETTER: In 90 days submit plan and hire 3 people.	Include the sub-steps necessary to achieve key objectives. Ask for examples.	
Management & Organizational Issues	Misleading: Have good management skills. BETTER: Assess and rebuild the team within 120 days.	Provide measurable objectives to determine quality of management skills needed.	
Changes and Improvements Necessary	Misleading: Be an agent of change. Better: Upgrade the client contact tracking system before the next promo.	Be specific regarding the needed changes and upgrades. It's easier to compare applicant's accomplishments this way.	
Problems to Be Solved	Misleading: Be a problem solver. BETTER: Work with IS to eliminate customer service bottleneck before May.	Describe actual problems needing work and then ask applicants how they would solve them.	
Technical Skills in Actual Situation	Misleading: Have good PC skills. BETTER: Develop PC-based tracking system by June.	Provide specific example of how technical skills will be used. It's better to have open discussion of real work	
Team Skills in Actual Situation	Misleading: Have good team skills. BETTER: Jointly develop inventory reduction plan with sales and manufacturing.	Describe situations that demonstrate good interpersonal/team skills and get similar examples from the applicant.	
Long Range, Planning, Strategic, & Creative	Misleading: Have good strategic thinking and planning skills. BETTER: Develop a long range product plan.	Cover anything that hasn't been addressed above. Also describe actual examples of creative and strategic projects.	

Figure 2.1 The performance profile template.

(continued)

POWERhiring® SMARTe Objectives Part II
Best Practices for Hiring Top Talent

Creating SMARTe Performance Objectives

Create Performance Objectives with the Micro Approach		Benchmark the Best
Traditional Job Spec Skills and Experiences	**Performance Criteria** What's the outcome of each skill?	**What do the best people do who have held this position?** Create performance objectives by comparing to the "best in class."
		Advice: This is a great technique for process oriented jobs. Think about what the best people in this job do that makes them best. Seek these traits. Reverse this and avoid those traits of the weaker people. Some examples, "handle angry customers," "accurately input data for 6 hours per day."
Advice: Convert each skill, experience, responsibility or trait into a measurable objective. Ask "What will the person do with this that determines competency?" For example, for strong PC skills, indicate what they'll do with the PC skills, e.g., "Set up detailed project tracking system."		

Prioritize the Objectives
Use this Checklist to Prioritize the Top 6-8 Objectives and Transfer to the Performance Profile
Check those objectives that must get done.

- ❑ Rank the impact on the company on ABC scale.
- ❑ Are there any alternatives? If so you might want to eliminate an objective or lower its priority.
- ❑ Don't duplicate. Be broad. Make sure final list covers all important job criteria.
- ❑ Get appropriate balance between management and individual contributor.
- ❑ Are technical objectives properly placed?
- ❑ Have interpersonal and culture issues been covered in the objectives?
- ❑ Make sure there's a balance on the technical, tactical and conceptual (strategic) level.
- ❑ Include thinking and intellectual skills in one of the objectives.

The Preliminary List - Top 6-8 Performance (SMARTe) Objectives
Summarize Major Objectives from Macro, Micro and Benchmark Approach Here

Objective (Summarized)	Check if a Must Have	ABC Ranking of Importance	Eliminate Duplicates	Management or Individual	Balanced Thinking	Priority Ranking

Figure 2.1 *(Continued)*

this process. Consider the job needs over a one- to two-year time horizon, starting with the first 30 days. Break the job into appropriate time segments and determine what the candidate must do or achieve at each point. First get the two to three top projects or deliverables and make them SMARTe performance objectives. Then determine what interim steps need to occur along the way. Determine what's the first problem, challenge, or issue the person will face. It could be something like, "break the bottleneck in order processing," or "determine the status of a major project."

Next move out to the 90-day and then to the six-month mark. Figure out what the person must achieve during this time frame. It could relate to staff assessment or rebuilding, or closing a few major deals. After a year, ask what other major things need to be accomplished. Develop many SMARTe performance objectives. Get everyone involved. After they're all developed, review each one, eliminate the less important ones, and put the rest into priority order. The top six to eight are all you really need to define the performance requirements of the job. Each of these SMARTe performance objectives should cover a different aspect of the position. You want to address a broad diversity of ability covering each critical game-breaker issue.

Figure 2.2 is an example of this macro approach combined with a time line. The overriding SMARTe objective is to set up

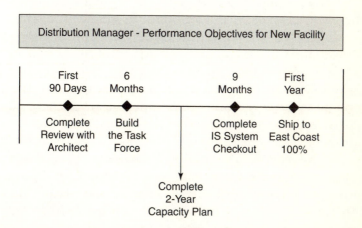

Distribution Manager - Performance Objectives for New Facility

First 90 Days	6 Months		9 Months	First Year
Complete Review with Architect	Build the Task Force		Complete IS System Checkout	Ship to East Coast 100%

Complete
2-Year
Capacity Plan

Figure 2.2   Use a timeline to better understand performance.

a new distribution facility over the next year, a few interim objectives are to coordinate with the design group to complete the physical layout of the site by a certain deadline, and negotiate a contract with the software vendor to meet critical system needs. Understanding these sub-objectives is often the difference between success and failure on the job. By identifying them early, you'll eliminate major hiring and performance problems later on.

In addition to the time line, it's important to directly consider some of the tactical and managerial needs of the position. Tactical has to do with obtaining short-term results, either individually, as a team member, or as a manager. Here's an example of an individual tactical objective for a salesperson, "Improve the ratio of closes/calls 15 percent by developing improved selling techniques." This gets at specific behaviors and traits much better than the classic, "have good sales and closing skills coupled with five years experience selling office products."

It's always better to describe the management objective, rather than the level of experience. For most management positions, the classic job description just lists the years of management experience required. It's better to describe what the manager needs to do to build, develop, or manage the team. For instance, "During the first 60 days, establish an employee development program to support a 20 percent increase in order processing," is a clear tactical management task. During the interview, ask the candidate to give real examples of comparable accomplishments. Generalities regarding these types of tactical tasks can get you into trouble if you assume managerial competency based on years of experience.

Many jobs require strategic or creative skills. You can get at these by describing the outcomes expected from these conceptual skills, long-range or creative skills. Some examples include: "Design a new system protocol," "Create a new technology to support high-speed data switching," "Develop a long-range planning system," "Create a new marketing promotional program," and "Prepare a five-year global manufacturing plan." The verbs used in the SMARTe performance objectives need to describe the creative or strategic nature of the work. When you prioritize all of the SMARTe performance objectives, the importance of these conceptual skills will stand out.

What to Do When You Don't Know What You Want the Person to Do

Every now and then you'll want to hire someone that you know you need, but have little idea of what the person is supposed to do. In this case, make the creation of these little understood or unknown requirements the primary performance objective. Suppose you need someone to take your existing product line into a new distribution channel, one you have little experience in. An appropriate SMARTe objective in this case would be "During the first month, prepare and implement a plan of action identifying all of the key requirements for a direct marketing channel for the xyz product line." Let the candidate tell you what the needs of the job are, the appropriate resource requirements, and the time line. During the interview, the candidate needs to describe comparable accomplishments and discuss how he would implement the program if he were to get the job.

One of my clients had a product that could potentially be used in the managed health care industry. He wanted to hire a vice president to head the new program. The primary SMARTe objective for the position was to "prepare a five-year business plan within six months." The second one was to "build the team needed to launch the business." The CEO, while aware of some of the issues, needed a leader to take charge of this new opportunity and define what needed to get done. In fact, during the first interview, the president and the candidate who ultimately got the job spent two hours together developing a detailed operational plan for this new business. This was after reviewing some of the candidate's accomplishments in setting up similar ventures. So even before starting the job, the candidate and the CEO were doing real work together. The CEO later told me that the candidate exhibited the same insight, organizational skills, and approach to problem solving on the job that he did in the two-hour session.

You can't be expected to know everything about every job. By delegating this "need to know" to a subordinate, it becomes the performance objective. Higher level jobs often have these kinds of needs. Setting up a new business, developing a new system, or creating a new product fall within this category. If a job now has little structure you need to find people who are real leaders—those that can build the teams and create the structure.

The macro approach starts by asking, "What does a person taking this job need to do to be successful?" Then covers everything in-between. This is the critical step in understanding the real nature of work. Not only will it help you hire better eople, but once they're hired, it will make you a better manager. You'll minimize two of the most common management problems—poor communications and not clarifying expectations—by creating a performance profile this way.

➤ 2. The Micro Approach

The micro approach can be used for all job types. It converts each job requirement or skill described on the traditional job description into an outcome by asking what's done with the skill. For instance, rather than saying the candidate must have strong PC skills, it's better to state that the candidate must be able to upgrade the performance reporting package using personal computers. This gets at the use of the skill in accomplishing the task, rather than the skill itself. The use or application of the skill is easier to measure than the absolute level of the skill. Our goal is to covert each "having"-based skill into a "doing" activity.

This is a great approach to use for technical positions. Rather than state that a job requires three years of tax accounting, it's better to say, "Upgrade the state sales and use tax reporting system by June." This gets at the application of the skill in a real situation and more accurately defines the work that needs to be performed. For a technical design position, something like "Develop two new electromechanical devices to handle the measurement of fluid flow in high speed oil lines" is better than "Have three years' experience in fluid flow controls and product design." During the interview, you'll get examples of real comparable designs to determine competency.

Behaviors and personality traits can be treated the same way. Everyone wants good interpersonal skills, but this is job and culture dependent. It's better to convert the behavior into an outcome. For example, rather than saying "work well with engineering," you'll gain more insight with "develop a means to deal with a very technically oriented engineering manager in developing product launch plans." Asking the candidate to describe comparable situations will get directly at this issue during the interview. Another behavior classic is to "have good team skills." It's better to describe the actual team situation and then ask the candidate for comparable examples of team accomplishments and the role played in persuading and leading others. "Lead the process improvement team for order entry to reduce cycle time by two days by August," is a good SMARTe team objective.

Sometimes preparing SMARTe performance objectives changes the very nature of the job or eliminates a criteria altogether. In Table 2.2 two original skills-based objectives for a director of sales and marketing have been converted to their performance equivalents. In each case, we asked the hiring manager what the person will do with each skill. The results were startling.

The skills-based criteria were not representative of the actual work that was required. This client had been looking for months to fill this position, yet no one could agree on what was required. It's not surprising. When you convert skills and experiences to outcomes, you clarify the real needs.

Most job descriptions fall short because they rely on an underlying absolute level of skills, years of experiences, academics, and required behaviors. This short-cut approach ignores the real need and gives the hiring manager a false sense of security.

Table 2.2 Comparing Skills Converted to Performance Objectives

Original Skill-Based Criteria	Skill Converted to Performance Objective	Comments
Strong one-on-one selling skills.	Set-up training program for new sales staff to penetrate national accounts.	The person needed to be a great sales manager and trainer, not an individual sales person.
Very creative at the product level.	Take the lead on coordinating the introduction of three new products per year.	The person didn't have to be creative at all. He just had to coordinate the activities of creative people.

Also specifying an arbitrary level of skills and experience can inadvertently exclude a strong candidate. By converting skills and experiences to outcomes, the problem is easily eliminated. After you've done this, just combine the SMARTe performance objectives created using this micro approach into your master list. You might not use them all, but you won't eliminate something important this way.

➤ 3. The Benchmarking Approach

Building a performance profile is relatively easy for a task or project-oriented job. It's a bit more challenging for a process, transaction-oriented, administrative, or entry-level position. In these cases, the benchmarking approach works best. Examine the best performers in the job to determine what makes them effective. This criteria then becomes the basis of the assessment. Just determine what the best people do that makes them best, and look for these same traits, skills, and behaviors in the people you hire. Also study the worst people, discover what they do that makes them poor performers, and avoid these traits, skills, and behaviors in the people you consider.

Some examples will help you understand this approach. We had a client in the jewelry business that had too much turnover in their polishing department. It turned out that the best employees had a great eye for detail work, they could quickly determine which pieces were good and bad, and they tended to stay in each previous job for more than two years. Turnover was dramatically reduced using these selection criteria. For an entry-level accountant, the ability to learn new processes quickly and produce 100 percent accurate reports became the dominant selection criteria. The ability to handle rejection, make lots of calls, and the ability to persuade others were the performance issues for a telemarketer. The key in all of these situations was to find out what made others successful in the job, and look for these same traits in the candidates hired.

When to Use the Benchmarking Approach

You can use this benchmarking technique for all kinds of positions, but it works best for jobs that follow a routine or a standard process. For REI Corp, one of our retail clients, we determined that the ability to engage customers quickly and constantly presenting the merits of various outdoor products was essential to success. At Southwest Airlines, the ability to proactively engage with groups of customers was a critical performance trait. Marriott uses a similar approach to assess service personnel. We're working with a fast-food restaurant chain to develop a standard for their entry-level positions. Good candidates for this position need to have perfect attendance, possess mechanical dexterity, proactively work with customers, have an internal motivating need for the job, and be able to achieve team objectives. Once the performance criteria were established, we created a customized interview that store managers could use to easily assess these abilities.

When you prepare your list of SMARTe performance objectives using the macro, micro, and benchmarking methods, it's possible you might have more objectives than you need. Some might be redundant or unimportant. Pare the list down to the most important six to eight. Then put them in order of importance. These SMARTe performance objectives have two purposes. One is as a guideline to select candidates. Later, you can use this same profile to transition and manage the new employee after starting the job.

■ THE LEGAL AND DIVERSITY ASPECTS OF PERFORMANCE-BASED HIRING

Rob Bekken, a senior partner at Fisher & Phillips, one of the largest labor law firms in the country, estimates that the average cost of a wrongful discharge lawsuit is $600,000. This is for someone who should not have been hired in the first place. The firm has prepared a white paper describing the legal benefits and importance of implementing POWER Hiring. This is included in the appendix to this book. Bekken concludes that "*Hire with Your Head* and POWER Hiring represents an important breakthrough from both a practical and legal standpoint. By utilizing this approach, employers are now equipped with the tools to hire the right employee and to legally defend their decision."

The preparation of performance-based objectives is also a practical way to implement a diversity hiring program. We're now working with Hattie Hill and Hazel Wood-Lockett at Hattie Hill Enterprises, a leading diversity training company. Many of their clients have started diversity initiatives, but haven't seen a great deal of success. While many companies have good intentions, without practical tools to eliminate biases and prejudices, they go nowhere. This is where a performance profile can help. Diversity needs to be considered from two perspectives: (1) Giving equal consideration to all potential candidates, both male and female, regardless of their racial, religious, ethnic backgrounds, or physical challenges. (2) Diversity should address the increasing need to effectively work with these same people in the workplace, both as customers and coworkers. Both of these issues can be directly addressed using this performance-based hiring approach.

The first diversity issue is eliminated by making the dominant selection criteria the candidate's ability to meet the performance needs of the position. Under these circumstances, achieving the SMARTe performance objectives drives the selection process. This is the most fair, legal, and appropriate way to overcome the typical diversity problems. If a candidate can meet the performance needs of the job, he or she deserves the opportunity, regardless of background, religion, or any physical challenges. Conversely, if a candidate can't meet these requirements, background, gender, or physical condition should be immaterial in the selection.

In the case of physical challenges, the United States has passed the Americans with Disabilities Act (ADA) to address possible inequities. Under these circumstances, some workplace modifications might be necessary to assist the candidate in meeting the required performance objectives. The key to fairness is that all of the performance objectives be required. As long as all candidates are measured against the same SMARTe performance objectives, performance profiles are the most fair and legal means to determine job competency.

With workforces and customers becoming more diverse, it's also important to directly consider these issues in the preparation of the SMARTe performance objectives. This addresses the second important diversity issue. For example, for marketing or sales positions, this might mean directly mentioning the need to effectively deal with a variety of ethnic backgrounds in the performance objective. Rather than just say *"Increase market share by five points,"* it's better to expand this to say, *"Increase market share by five points, half coming from the Hispanic community."* Manufacturing positions often require management of multiethnic labor groups. The SMARTe objective should include this important need. For instance, *"Install a total quality management program addressing all the needs of a diverse labor team."* This sets up the requirement for applicants to be sensitive to the cultural differences and needs of these important work groups. If you want to create a diverse workforce, a performance objective might be, *"Over the next two years establish a multiethnic workforce and training program that gives every employee an opportunity to grow."* By incorporating these requirements directly into the SMARTe performance objectives, companies can begin considering these important diversity issues directly in the interviewing and evaluation process.

■ THE BOTTOM LINE BENEFITS OF A SMARTe APPROACH TO DEFINING PERFORMANCE

1. Use performance profiles to write ads and screen candidates. When you write ads based on the having, rather than the doing, they come across as boring, and you can exclude great candidates. Screen resumes on comparable accomplishments, not skills, experience, academics, and industry. You'll interview better candidates this way. One of our clients, a restaurant chain in Southern California, started looking outside of the restaurant industry for managers and serving staff, as a result of focusing on doing rather than having. Within six months, they were fully staffed with outstanding people, a first in seven years. Many of their new crop of stars came from a retail background, where service and support are essential to success. A major portion of your sourcing issues will disappear when you eliminate the artificial barriers to entry. Compromise on experience, not performance.

2. It helps in recruiting. Candidates will exclude themselves if the job is too much of challenge or not big

enough. Instead, you'll attract those that see the job as an important career move. They will understand the importance of the job using SMARTe performance objectives as the expected standard of performance. Asking for examples of comparable accomplishments during the interview allows the candidate to clearly understand the job and the opportunities. Top people get turned-off when the interviewer focuses more on past experience, than past performance.

3. The performance profile can be used as a natural transition program for the new employee. Since you've established the objectives during the interview, the new employee has a clear sense of job expectations. Expect to reprioritize and renegotiate the performance objectives after the candidate starts. This establishes buy-in and ownership. The process helps clarify expectations between you and your new employee from the beginning. Lack of clear expectations is one of the biggest causes of employee turnover and poor performance. This is what Ferdinand Fournies describes in his classic book, *Coaching for Improved Work Performance* (McGraw Hill, 1978), as the biggest problem with management. A performance profile is a great way to eliminate a serious potential problem and become a better manager in the process.

4. The SMARTe performance objectives form the basis of a complete performance management system. With these as a baseline, you'll be able to use them to monitor performance and conduct more meaningful reviews.

■ PERFORMANCE PROFILES ARE A UNIVERSAL SOLUTION FOR BETTER UNDERSTANDING SUCCESS IN ANY JOB

Performance profiles are applicable for any position, in any type of company, and for any level. Whether a contract temp position or CEO, understanding the process of success will help you find and more accurately hire top talent. The macro and micro approaches are great for staff and management positions. Benchmark and micro approaches are perfect for technical, administrative, or process-oriented positions.

A similar process can be used for consultants or outside contractors. Create the list of prioritized SMARTe performance objectives the same way, even if the time frame is less than a year. Expectations are rarely defined up-front, so much unnecessary time is wasted. Clarifying the SMARTe performance objectives should be the topic of the first meeting. When work is quantified in detail, it eliminates much of the confusion typically associated with working with people who aren't familiar with your company's jargon and ways of doing business.

■ SMARTe OBJECTIVES SAVE TIME

"It takes too much time." This is the biggest complaint we hear when first describing the SMARTe objective process. Not true; it saves time. The list of performance objectives is essentially what you'd discuss with the new employee on her start date. Why wait? Discuss it three weeks sooner during the interview process. The preparation of these objectives is a basic part of the management process. If a manager chooses not to do it, he's abdicating an essential aspect of the job. Since you need to do it anyway, our suggestion is to just do it sooner.

You'll save time by clarifying expectations during the interview, eliminating unqualified candidates sooner, and reducing the likelihood of hiring a weak candidate. The time involved in managing an underperformer is far greater than the time it takes to prepare one of these performance profiles. The cost and time involved in eventually dismissing a person you should never have hired in the first place would justify any time added to the evaluation process.

During a recent workshop I asked a facilities manager who complained loudly about the time element, to list the five biggest problems he wanted his new plant engineer to address once he came on board. He put the list together in less than 10 minutes! We waste time not knowing what we want our people to do. If you want to save time, preparing performance-based SMARTe objectives is an obvious alternative.

■ WORKING WITH PERFORMANCE PROFILES

In this section, we'll examine three different performance profiles. This will provide some real insight into how these are used and prepared.

These three performance profiles are suggested formats. Use any form that fits best within your company needs. Nonetheless, the SMARTe performance objectives and the organization chart should represent 80 percent to 90 percent of the profile. Alternatively, you can attach these to your existing job descriptions.

➤ Organization Chart

Draw or describe the organization or work team chart for the position. Include the traditional superior and subordinate relationships and describe the internal and external team members typically interacting with the person in this job. This includes other departments, outside suppliers, and customers. During the interview, you'll ask candidates to draw a comparable work team chart. This will help determine the comparability of previous team and management experience. We often overvalue individual contributor traits at the expense of team and management skills. Knowing the organizational and team needs ensures that this critical area is not overlooked. As part of the SMARTe performance objectives, you should also include any organizational changes that are required. This could include rebuilding or upgrading the team, training, supporting growth, addressing new responsibilities, or downsizing.

➤ SMARTe Performance Objectives

This is the list of prioritized objectives developed using the macro, micro, and benchmarking approaches. It's best to develop this list with all members of the hiring team. Include human resources, staffing, and other managers interviewing the candidate to gain agreement and understanding. Also make sure that any subordinates interviewing the candidate are completely aware of these performance objectives. Judge candidate competency against these standards of performance by getting examples of comparable performance. Using this as the benchmark minimizes the impact of first impressions, personality, built-in biases, and prejudices from dominating the selection decision. When you don't know what you want the person to do once on the job, each interviewer will use his or her own criterion. Often this is misguided, sometimes it's wrong, and rarely does each member of the team agree to the standard. Use of these SMARTe performance objectives eliminates each of these potential problems.

➤ Americans with Disabilities Act (ADA) Requirements

From the SMARTe objectives list identify all of the physical requirements of the job. Include lifting, traveling, use of equipment, and mobility. If they're not required, don't include them. For example, lifting anything other than a briefcase is not required for most office jobs. According to ADA, you don't have to compromise your performance standards as long as they're essential. You do have to provide a reasonable level of accommodation (ramps, access devices, larger screens) for those who can otherwise meet the performance objectives. If physically challenged candidates can meet these performance objectives with some reasonable level of accommodation, they deserve the job. Conversely, if a person can't meet these requirements, or you found someone who is better at meeting them, this SMARTe performance objectives approach will allow you to justify your decision. Make sure your decision is documented and get specific legal advice if you have any questions. This area is constantly being evaluated in the courts, so it's important to have the latest advice.

➤ Basic Experience

This section is part of the classic job description. It includes education, level of experience, and specific technical requirements. This is the people description, or the "having" part of the traditional job description. List the absolute minimum

PERFORMANCE PROFILE ONE

Product Manager Consumer Products

Position Summary

A Product Manager for consumer products is involved in working with product development and engineering in developing the product, coordinating with purchasing and production in building the product, and coordinating with marketing communications, advertising, and public relations in launching the product.

Organization Structure and Interfaces

The position reports to the director of marketing. There are three other product managers in this group. Reporting directly to the product manager is a marketing analyst and an administrative assistant. The product manager will also coordinate the activities of the marketing communications, advertising, and public relations team. From a product management standpoint, the product manager will coordinate the efforts of engineering, manufacturing, purchasing, and logistics in meeting all product development and launch schedules.

SMARTe Performance Objectives

1. *Conduct a comprehensive review of all new product programs:* During the first 30 days, prepare an analysis of all new product programs. Include status of product development effort, budget versus forecast comparison, status of launch efforts, and major challenges and problems.
2. *Coordinate the development and launch of all new products for the current season:* Work with engineering, manufacturing, and marketing to determine status of all products to be launched this season. Identify hurdles and constraints and develop work-arounds as necessary to meet plan dates.
3. *Lead the development of the two-year product plan:* Take the lead on preparing the two-year product program due within 120 days, coordinating with product development and engineering. This needs to consist of competitive analysis, assessment of technology trends, and market and consumer research.

PERFORMANCE PROFILE ONE *(continued)*

4. *Work with production in developing realistic build programs to support the nationwide launch of the ____ product line:* The launch of the _____ product line require adequate inventory levels at dealers to support major promotional program. Determine status of production and refocus efforts as necessary.

5. *Prepare a competitive feature comparison analysis:* As part of the repricing efforts, complete a feature comparison against the top competitors for the ___ line. This should be available with ____ days.

6. *Problems: coordinate with purchasing to ensure availability of products from Asian suppliers, and develop alternative sources:* Take the lead on assessing the status of the new procurement program. Address logistics and scheduling problems. Also, coordinate with engineering on quality issues and design changes.

7. *Prepare the product requirements document for the _____ project:* Within ___ days, work with product development and engineering to complete the products requirement document for this new line.

Basic Requirements—Essentials Only

A product manager for a consumer products company needs to have at least ___ to ____ years background in a few of the various phases of marketing and product management. This includes market research, competitive analysis, pricing, distribution and channel programs, product development, and/or project management. Experience in consumer products sold through clubs, or mass merchandisers would be helpful. Solid knowledge of marketing communications and demand creation is very important. This includes advertising and promotional, point-of-sale display advertising, development of channel strategies, and Internet marketing.

PERFORMANCE PROFILE TWO

Customer Service Director

Position Summary

The Director, Customer Service will be responsible for rebuilding the customer service department, organizing the group to handle the anticipated growth, and leading many of the efforts toward upgrading the customer service activity. The key to success in this position is to ensure a companywide focus on improving all aspects of customer service. This includes direct support, new systems, and better handling of complaints. The person selected will be responsible for customer service, order processing and tracking, returned goods, warranty sales, and technical support. The company's future growth depends on establishing new procedures in all aspects of customer service especially online ordering and tracking.

Organization Chart

The position supervises 24 people through three supervisors.

Titles of Direct Reports	Subordinate Staff	Key Duties— Major Responsibilities
Customer Service Manager	12	Handles telesales and customer rep group—clerical/admin
Warranty and Returns Supv	7	Physical responsibility for spares, warranty and returns—warehouse
Technical Support/Applications uct	5	Tracking, updating prod- usage and approved applications. Technical product focus

SMARTe Objectives

1. Improve customer service from 93 percent to 99 percent and reduce customer complaints by 75 percent within 12 months.
2. Rebuild the customer service department to support a 25 percent per year growth rate. This includes upgrading supervisors, a reduction in turnover, and a complete process reengineering of the group.

PERFORMANCE PROFILE TWO *(continued)*

3. Take a management lead on organizing a multifunction task force in developing companywide customer service improvements. This will support the 18-month IS conversion program now underway incorporating new technologies like EDI, bar-coding, and Internet catalog and ordering.
4. By June, conduct a complete process review of all aspects of the department identifying key staff issues, system problems, customer complaints, and bottlenecks. Coordinate with major customers addressing their needs and begin a corrective action plan immediately.
5. Develop a series of interim solutions to reduce backorders, improve returned material replacements, and improving communications with the field support team. Present action plan within 90 days.

ADA Requirements

The key physical requirements for this position include the ability to travel to the company's five warehouse locations around the country, use of standard office equipment including PCs, and movement within a standard office and distribution warehouse.

Basic Experience

The candidate selected for this position needs to have 5 to 10 years in a high volume distribution operation with a track record of implementing process-based changes. Experience must include a strong systems background, especially in the area of automated order systems, including bar-coding and EDI. This should include knowledge of alternative system configurations and approaches. The ability to build and develop strong teams of at least 15 to 20 people is essential. The person needs to be able to handle the demands of a fast-growing company and provide direction to other functional departments in the area of improving customer service.

PERFORMANCE PROFILE THREE
Staffing Manager

Position Overview

A Human Resource Staffing Manager is involved with recruiting and staffing for the organization, usually supervising a small team of contract or in-house recruiters. The focus is on hiring the best people into the company in an efficient manner.

Organization Chart

The position reports the vice president of Human Resources. Reporting to this position include six senior recruiters, two researchers, an Internet analyst, and a date-entry person.

SMARTe Performance Objectives—Deliverables

1. *Improve the Recruiting Process and the Quality of Candidates Hired:* The primary objective during the first year is to completely upgrade the existing hiring processes at the company. This requires the installation of new hiring practices, improved sourcing, better assessment tools, and an ability to quickly react to short and long term hiring needs.
2. *Conduct a Hiring Needs Analysis:* During the first ___weeks, meet with all hiring managers and determine the status of all open requisitions, and identify all hiring requirements for the next six months. Put this in priority order, and implement a staffing plan-of-action during the first month.
3. *Develop Short-Term Staffing Alternatives:* Given critical needs and time frames, develop alternative staffing approaches to eliminate existing open requisitions within ___ days. This plan needs to be completed within ___ weeks.
4. *Conduct a Process Review:* During the first ___ days, conduct a detailed review of all hiring practices and processes. Identify key constraints and problems and develop a plan to overhaul the process by within ___ months.
5. *Train and Rebuild the Team:* During the first week, meet all staff members and assess capabilities against departmental objectives. Implement necessary training and during the first ___days, rebuild the team as necessary to meet company hiring requirements.

6. *Reduce the Time to Hire:* Over the next ___ months, reduce the time to hire typical positions from an average of ____ days to ____ days.

7. *Improve the Assessment Process:* Within ___ days, establish the staffing department as the benchmark for identifying and assessing competency. Provide tools and guidance to line managers throughout the company to upgrade the quality of all candidate assessments.

8. *Upgrade Internet Recruiting Efforts:* Within ___ days, ensure that the staffing department is on the leading-edge of Internet recruiting.

ADA Requirements

The person selected for this position needs to lead meetings using conferencing and presentation equipment. The person selected needs to have the ability to travel domestically frequently. No lifting is required. The ability to use PCs and telephone equipment is essential.

Basic Requirements—Essentials Only

A staffing manager needs to have at least ____ years total experience in recruiting and management. A BS degree is preferred. The person should have basic knowledge of compensation and staffing issues. Responsibility for manpower planning and recruiting for a firm that has experienced significant growth is important. A combination of hands-on ability combined with solid and management experience over small teams is also important.

requirements. Let the performance objectives dictate how much of any one skill is really needed. If the time to complete an objective is short, more experience is necessary. But some people are quick learners. Others are highly motivated to succeed despite the challenges. To attract these people, you'll want to minimize the requirements for screening purposes. Offset this with a track record of growth with good companies. This way you'll be seeing strong people, even if they're not a 100 percent hit on the experience side. One of the biggest hiring errors made when focusing on skills and experiences is hiring a person who's competent, but not motivated. Motivation makes up for many voids. Make sure you don't eliminate it by over-specifying skills.

Even with limited interviewing experience, anyone using these performance profiles as guidelines will do a better job of assessing competency. By clarifying expectations this way, everyone on the assessment team is better prepared. We suggest that every interviewer summarize their assessments about a candidate against the SMARTe performance objectives. The key to good interviewing is to get a comparable example of a past accomplishment for each SMARTe objective. This will dramatically improve accuracy. While this type of job description has a great many benefits, this is the most important.

■ PERFORMANCE-BASED HIRING—IT STARTS WITH THE "P" IN POWER

If you want to hire superior people, first define superior performance. This sets the foundation for a shift from an experience-based selection process to performance-based. When you create SMARTe performance objectives based on what a person needs to DO, rather than HAVE, interviewing accuracy increases dramatically. Advertisements including the deliverables are more compelling and meaningful, and it becomes easier to screen and filter candidates. Unqualified candidates are eliminated early, and strong candidates, previously excluded for the wrong reasons, now have a chance. Well-qualified candidates often are excluded from consideration because their backgrounds aren't identical matches to the misstated skills and experience requirements. There is now a better alternative.

Past-performance is the best predictor of future performance. Every aspect of hiring is improved when superior performance becomes the selection standard, not an arbitrary level of skills and experience. When performance isn't the benchmark, the candidate's personality and interviewing skills becomes a poor substitute. A clear understanding of superior performance is the first step in hiring superior people.

POWER HIRING HOT TIPS: PERFORMANCE PROFILES

✔ If you want to hire superior people, first define superior performance.

✔ A performance profile describes the required results, the process used to achieve the results, and the environment in which this all happens.

✔ Define the job, not the person. Define success, not the skills. It's best to separate the job from the person. This allows for a more objective appraisal of true competency.

✔ Focus on the *DOING*, not the *HAVING*, to improve hiring accuracy. It's what people do with their skills that determines success, not the skills alone.

✔ Experience and personality are poor predictors of subsequent performance. It's better to define and use the real performance needs of the job to screen and interview candidates.

✔ Every job has six to eight performance objectives that define real on-the-job success. Once developed, they form the basis of the recruiting and selection decision. These range from dealing with people, meeting technical and business objectives, organizing teams, solving problems, and making changes.

✔ Create six to eight prioritized SMARTe performance objectives (**S**pecific, **M**easurable, **A**ction Oriented, **R**esult, and **T**ime-based, **e**nvironment described) to clarify expectations.

✔ Use the *macro* approach to create SMARTe performance objectives. Ask the hiring manager what the person taking the job needs to do throughout the first year to be successful in the job.

✔ Use the *micro* approach to create additional SMARTe performance objectives. Convert each required skill or experience into an active task by asking what the person needs to accomplish or do with each skill.

(continued)

(continued)

✔ For entry-level or process-oriented positions, benchmark the best (and worst people) already doing the job. Use this to create performance objectives for any type of position.

✔ The performance profile establishes the framework for better hiring and better management by clarifying the expectations for the job. This helps in selection and subsequent management. Everyone involved is on the same page.

Chapter 3

Emotional Control

It ain't so much the things you don't know that get you in trouble. It's the things you know that just ain't so.

Artimus Ward 1834–1867

■ TO GET IT RIGHT, DON'T MAKE IT TOO SOON—DELAY THE HIRING DECISION 30 MINUTES

A few years ago, the CEO of a fast-growing marketing company cornered me before I was to speak at his trade group breakfast seminar. He had an interview with a vice president candidate the next day and wanted a few quick tips on hiring. In response, I gave him the most important secret of hiring success. I told him not to make a hiring decision in the first 30 minutes of the interview. More hiring mistakes are made in the first half hour of an interview than at any other time, and if he could just delay his decision, favorable or unfavorable, by 30 minutes, he'd eliminate 50 percent of his hiring mistakes.

First impressions based on emotions, biases, chemistry, personality, and stereotyping cause more hiring errors than

---

The Shortest Course in Interviewing

Wait 30 minutes before making any decision about a candidate's ability to do the work.

---

any other single factor. In this pivotal chapter, we show you how to get past the deceptive impressions we all use to make hiring decisions. Using our head means that first we have to understand why our head is often not used at all.

Once we accept or reject a candidate, the evaluation essentially stops. For many, this happens in 5 to 10 minutes. New information, even if it conflicts, has less value than the original. We go through the motions of asking more questions, but it's largely self-serving. The new facts surfaced are either used to support our initial assessment or ignored if they don't. It's difficult to change an opinion like this once it's formed. An article in the *Wall Street Journal's National Business Employment Weekly* (March 12, 1992) stated that 70 percent of the hiring decision is made based on these initial impressions.

When we don't particularly care for a candidate, we ask tougher questions and minimize or ignore positive information. If we like someone, we look for a few additional facts; then we start selling them on the merits of the job and stop evaluating. Staying objective and getting lots of information to make a well-informed hiring decision is hard work. Why bother, when we can apparently get 50 percent of the answer in less than five minutes? It's much easier to take these intuitive and emotional shortcuts. Only much later do we discover we're on the wrong path.

One of our clients, the president of a small retail store chain, recently told me a revealing story. He and all of his managers had attended one of our workshops and wanted to implement the ideas in their company. When we spoke, the implementation was just beginning. After only a few months of use, they had experienced a significant improvement in hiring accuracy and a reduction in turnover.

More important to the president was the deeply personal impact the program had on him. He said that before he understood how his emotions affected his judgment, he always made quick hiring decisions based on personal biases and stereotypes. Most of these had to do with physical appearance, ethnic background, affability, and intelligence. He would exclude anyone who fell outside of this narrow range of acceptability, and he felt that he could confidently make this important decision in less than five minutes. After implementing our program, the president has found that many of the candidates he would have previously discounted are actually outstanding performers. We recently conducted another workshop for this company, approximately five years after our first meeting. Their management team was as diverse and competent as any I've seen. Today this company is far larger and stronger.

This is powerful and revealing testimony. It took courage for the president to admit this to me and even more for him to be honest with himself. But this understanding has changed his whole outlook on the hiring process. Most of us are guilty of the same offense. It's the biggest obstacle we need to overcome if we want to make better hiring decisions.

■ HOW EMOTIONAL TRIGGERS AFFECT YOUR JUDGMENT

The key to effective hiring is to move beyond this type of emotional reaction to the candidate and use the performance profile as the dominant selection criteria. We're programmed to make instantaneous judgments about people based on first impressions. It's part of the fight versus flight response. If you like someone, you relax; if you don't, you get uptight. Within 5 to 10 minutes, this response is neutralized. Unfortunately, by this time, many of us have already made the yes or no hiring decision. We're now poisoned. We then spend the rest of the interview collecting enough facts to support our initial flawed impressions, good or bad.

Positive or negative, it's important to bring this emotional reaction to the conscious level. If you buy in too soon, you tend to ignore negative data, globalize strengths, begin selling, and stop listening. Lack of skills will be dismissed as unimportant or something easily learned. You'll start selling, trying to convince the candidate why this is such a great job. You won't ask tough questions covering real job needs. You'll assume that the candidate can do them all because he or she possesses a few, apparently important, characteristics. In fact, you'll go out of your way to find easier questions to ask, and you'll even unknowingly give your favorite candidate the answers. This approach not only gives the strong candidate the upper hand, but also you waste time considering candidates like this, who are more fluff than substance. We've discovered that about a third to half of the candidates you meet who make strong first impressions are really just average performers. You'll discover this only by using the performance-based interviewing and fact-finding approach introduced in the previous chapter.

Conversely, if you don't like the candidate, you immediately feel uptight or disappointed. You grit your teeth and begin thinking of how you can end the interview as soon as possible. Sometimes boredom sets in. If you listen at all, you'll ignore all positive data as being a fluke or unrepresentative. Weaknesses will be magnified. Different approaches are instantly judged as worthless or ill conceived. If candidates have been highly referred or seem pushy, you'll undersell the job as something beneath them, hoping they'll exclude themselves. We've discovered that about 30 percent to 50 percent of the candidates you meet who make a bad first impression turn out to be much stronger once you get to know their accomplishments.

It's easy to be seduced. I've been interviewing candidates daily for over 20 years, and I still have to fight these first impression biases. If we like someone, we don't question him or her hard enough. Seemingly good candidates are hard to come by and we don't want them to fail. Unfortunately, they often do fail once they get on the job, if they were hired based solely on a good first impression. Even in *Straight from the Gut,* Jack Welch admits that he didn't start making good hiring decisions until he overcame the tendency to overvalue first impressions.

➤ Candidate Nervousness Increases Error Rates

Most interviewers make biased decisions based on first impressions. To make matters worse, many candidates get nervous and make weak first impressions. These two effects are the cause of more hiring errors than any other reason. In our recent poll of over 500 candidates, 75 percent indicated that they get nervous in an interview. This is why interviewing is fundamentally flawed.

The emotional reaction for a candidate is equivalent to making a public speech, asking someone for a date, asking for a raise, firing someone, or engaging in some unusual, new activity. You've probably experienced this type of semi-panic situation at some time. When the ego is on the line, this type of nervousness leads to dry mouth, constricted voice patterns, shallow answers, forgetfulness, and an increased level of perspiration. Even smooth salespeople can fall prey to these unkind effects. If it's a temporary condition, these physical affects will dissipate in about 10 to 20 minutes. While generally unimportant, here's how typical interviewers judge these temporary nervous conditions.

Incorrectly Interpreting Temporary Candidate Nervousness

Nervous Trait	Likely Interpretation
Shallow responses, dull, slow-witted	Not very intelligent, no sense of humor, lack of judgment
Sweaty palms and/or brow	Weak, too soft, nerdy, couldn't make a presentation to a customer or executive
Twitching	Too nervous, uncomfortable with people, not a team player
Too chatty	Dumb and superficial
Lack of confidence	Not aggressive enough
No eye contact	Untrustworthy
Say stupid things without thinking of consequences	A real jerk, weak team player, insensitive to others
Lack of warmth	Arrogant
Superficial questions	Wrong priorities, no character
Dry throat, strained voice, coughing	Lacks confidence, not a lot of insight, unprepared

These conclusions are totally wrong. Yet, once they're drawn, it's easy to find facts to support them. This is the real concern. If you can get past these superficial and temporary conditions, you'll find some great candidates sitting across the desk from you. Of the candidates I interview, 90 percent become very natural in 10 to 20 minutes using the fact-finding and performance-based questioning process we advocate. A 30-minute cooling-off period is a great way to get candidates to relax and for interviewers to regain their objectivity.

Unfortunately, for both the candidate and the interviewer, it's hard to recover from these very negative first impressions. Interviewers need to work with candidates to get them to relax and open up. Recognizing the physiological reactions will help. If these conditions still persist for more than 30 minutes, it could be something other than nervousness. Then it's best to move on to other candidates. We don't want to minimize the importance of interpersonal skills. Personality and cultural fit are critical to job success. We just want to delay their measurement until both the candidate and interviewer are past the emotionally charged first 30 minutes of the interview.

■ UNDERSTANDING YOUR INTERVIEWING STYLE IS THE FIRST STEP TO REPROGRAMMING

We all have a tendency to hire in our own image. In his landmark book *Up the Organization,* Robert Townsend said, "hire complementors, not reflectors." This is great advice. Preparing a performance profile is the first step. This then becomes the benchmark to assess competency, not first impressions and biases.

The "hiring image" we use to judge candidates is reflected by our emotional triggers. These are the traits that quickly engage the initial positive/negative response. Here's a quick way to gain a sense of this for yourself. Complete the table on page 67. In the *Yes* column, write those attributes that get you excited about a candidate, and in the *No* column, list traits that bother you. Write down how long it takes to react to these. Then compare your answers to the Yes and No criteria in the table on page 68.

The table categorizes these emotional triggers into three different interviewing styles. Review the table to determine your interviewing style and see what you need to do to minimize the adverse impact.

Unfortunately, most of us are a combination of the emotional plus either the intuitive or the technical interviewing style. A combination of the intuitive and the technical styles will dramatically reduce hiring errors. Here's why.

Emotional Triggers and Hiring Hot Buttons Worksheet

"Yes" Criteria w/Time Example: Friendly -3 minutes	"No" Criteria w/Time Example: Too Quiet—5 minutes

List positive and negative traits and attributes and the time it takes in the interview to observe.

The hiring decision is primarily intuitive, because you rarely have enough information to make a 100 percent accurate assessment. You just can't gather enough information in a few hours to make a foolproof decision about performance. Intuitive thinking, therefore, needs to be used to compare aspects of the candidate's abilities and interests to job needs. But to do this right requires more detailed information than the typical intuitive interviewer wants to get into. Most intuitive interviewers want to make the judgment in 10 to 15 minutes. To offset this natural bias, it's important to incorporate the fact-finding skills of the technical interviewer.

The technical interviewer is conservative and skeptical and naturally does a good job of data collection. While this time-intensive, fact-finding approach is important in data gathering, it's usually not the right data being collected, and it's not the right way to make the decision. It's too conservative, overemphasizing skills and experience. That's why the best of the intuitive and technical style should be combined, while at the same time holding emotions and biases in check. This allows true ability and potential to emerge as the dominant selection criteria.

Review the following tips to determine what you need to do to overcome your dominant style. You need to bring your biases to the conscious level at each interview. Then you have a

Recognizing Your Hiring Criteria and Interviewing Style

Interviewing Style	Description	"Yes" Criteria	"No" Criteria
Emotional	Makes decision based largely on first impressions, personality, appearance, emotional reactions, and feelings about the candidate. Other factors might include academics, personal biases, stereotypes, and racial or gender issues.	Time: less than 5 minutes ➤ Poise and social confidence ➤ Affable ➤ Articulate ➤ Positive appearance ➤ Extroverted ➤ Good chemistry	Time: less than 5 minutes ➤ Poor eye contact ➤ Weak handshake ➤ Poor appearance ➤ Nervous—distant ➤ Short answers ➤ Introverted ➤ Bad chemistry
Intuitive	Decision based on gut feelings and having a few critical traits. Decision is then globalized—with them the candidate can do everything and without them, nothing. More general factors include character, religion, values, appropriate style, and location where raised.	Time: 5 to 15 minutes ➤ Intelligence ➤ 1 or 2 great talents/skills ➤ Verbal communications ➤ Assertive ➤ Initiative	Time: 5 to 15 minutes ➤ Not enough intelligence/talent ➤ Not enough confidence ➤ Shallow answers ➤ Lack of energy
Technical	Decision based on possession of strong skills, experiences, and methodologies. The yes is long, but the no is quick.	Time: over one hour ➤ Lots of relevant experience ➤ Similar process thinking ➤ Strong skills ➤ Great technical capability	Time: 5 to 15 minutes ➤ Not enough experience ➤ Not enough education ➤ Not enough skills ➤ Difference in approach

fighting chance to get to the 30-minute mark before making any decision.

➤ The Emotional Style

If you're EMOTIONAL, you tend to globalize competency, or the lack or it, based on just a few superficial traits. You make judgments within a few minutes based on first impressions, personality, and appearance. Emotional interviewers have the most random results and make more hiring mistakes than any other style. To overcome this problem, you need to work hard to delay any instant judgment. Change your frame of reference. Be tougher on those you like. Obtain lots of examples, facts, and details to validate your initial first impression. If you don't like a candidate, give him or her the benefit of the doubt. This will make you a more technical fact finder. Become analytical. Keep written notes. Because no two jobs are exactly alike, you need to compare real job needs to the candidate's comparable accomplishments. This is tough enough, but if you're making a purely emotional decision, you are short-circuiting the rational decision-making process. It's a fundamental problem that affects most of us at some time.

➤ The Intuitive Style

If you're INTUITIVE, you tend to globalize strengths and weaknesses based on only a few, normally important, traits. This takes about 5 to 15 minutes. Not surprisingly, sometimes these traits are very similar to those that have made you personally successful. This is where the "hire in your own image" problem comes into play. While these traits may be important, you still need a more balanced and complete perspective. Intuitive interviewers often hire some stars, but they just as frequently hire those who can't meet all the needs of the job. We call these "the partially competent." They usually can talk a good game, but often can't execute. The key is not to overvalue a few traits such as intelligence or assertiveness at the expense of others. Neutralize your biases and conduct a complete assessment. You need to be more analytical in collecting relevant data. Using a technical fact-finding approach might find some weaknesses not initially considered or some offsetting strengths. In fact, you might find some of these missing traits when you look again in more depth. Candidates don't need to be just like you to be successful. In the long run, it's probably better if they're not.

➤ The Technical Style

If you're a TECHNICAL interviewer, you're too conservative and check too many boxes. It takes you at least one to two hours to come to a favorable decision. You tend to overvalue years of specific experience, degrees held, specific areas of technical competence, and thinking skills. Technical interviewers have the ability to build solid, if unspectacular, teams, with few mistakes. Unfortunately, this approach often excludes from consideration the high-potential candidates who don't yet have the "required" level of experience. They also exclude themselves because they don't want to do the same work over again. While this analytical style is good for data collection, it's not good for hiring top performers, because the wrong data are being collected. The hiring decision should be based on traits that better predict performance, not on an absolute level of skills, education, and experience. It's better to determine competency by finding out if the candidate has ever delivered comparable results. Don't immediately dismiss a candidate who lacks some of the prerequisites. Find out what he or she accomplished without much experience to determine motivation and ability to learn. You'll discover that this is a much better predictor of success than identical experience.

■ USE THE POWER HIRING FORMULA TO MAKE MORE OBJECTIVE HIRING DECISIONS

Over the years, I've discovered that for an accurate assessment, candidate competency needs to be measured across three broad measures—performance, character, and personality—not first impressions. In this definition, *performance* means the ability and desire to do the work, *character* represents the person's underlying value system and how it affects work, and *personality* relates to emotional intelligence and interpersonal fit. All three are essential to job success, and each needs to be evaluated objectively before ever hiring someone. This is the POWER Hiring formula for hiring success. In Chapter 2, we presented just the performance piece. While a great candidate needs to meet the four performance requirements of the job as described in Chapter 2, the person must also have the character needed to deal with the challenge of the job and the personality to work effectively with the team.

The POWER Hiring Formula

A Great Hire = **Performance** plus **Character** plus **Personality**

Consider some of your most effective people. The best—the high potential, high performers—tend to be strong in all three of these trait categories. If they're strong in one or two, but weak in another, overall performance suffers in some way. That's why it's important to consider all three traits when hiring.

However, while performance, character, and personality are all essential to an accurate assessment, they're not all equally easy to measure during the course of the interview. This is the biggest problem with interviewing. Personality is easier to measure during the course of the interview than competency and character. Unfortunately, personality as measured in the interview is a weak predictor of on-the-job performance. In fact, it's not even a good predictor of true personality. Most people can fake being nice during the interview; others are temporarily nervous. To account for this, we've modified the POWER Hiring formula:

The Modified POWER Hiring Formula for Interviewing Success

While performance, character, and personality are all critical to an accurate assessment, measure performance first.

True personality is critical to job success, but interviewing personality is just a façade. It's a poor predictor of subsequent performance. You can have personality, charm, and style in the interview and be a dud on the job. Conversely, you can be a 30-minute dud in the first interview and be great on the job. Deciding too soon based on interviewing personality is the number one cause of hiring errors. A few years ago, a "60 Minutes" segment applauded a three-week program that taught minority candidates how to be upbeat, confident, articulate, and assertive in an interview. This bothered me because it elevated the value of the superficial over the substantive. In most situations, this is usually all it takes to impress interviewers. Combine a great opening with a polished resume, solid academics, and some reasonable experience, and the interview can be over in a few minutes. If the company's need factor is great, even those of lesser acclaim can pass this hurdle with a great first impression.

You might want to try this exercise to get a sense of how interviewing personality is different from true personality. In a recent seminar, I asked the 75 attendees to count everyone they've ever worked with for more than a few years that they truly didn't like, or couldn't work with. Most came up with only a handful. I then asked what percent of candidates they didn't think they could work with when they first met them in the interview based on first impressions. This ranged from 30 to 40 percent on the low side to 80 percent on the high side. This is shocking. Consider the implications—once we get to know people through their work, we tend to like them. How many great people have you excluded because you didn't like them for some superficial reason in the first 5 to 10 minutes of the interview? Don't measure candidates based on their ability to be great friends or on some artificial standard of appearance, affability, and enthusiasm. Hold them to a more reasonable standard—coworkers. This is an important distinction. Don't be too quick to include or exclude anyone on the basis of interviewing personality.

Character, while also important, is not a great predictor of job success. Having strong character doesn't imply great performance (remember Jimmy Carter). And not having strong character doesn't mean the lack of good results (consider more recent politicians). True character is harder to measure than personality; but for most, it doesn't have the same emotional tug as personality, so we don't have to worry too much about it affecting our judgment in the interview. Like personality and cultural fit, character, while important for on-the-job success, is a poor predictor of subsequent performance.

However, past performance is a great predictor of future performance. The POWER Hiring interview and assessment approach is designed around this important theme. Determine future performance through the performance profile, and measure past performance using the first three questions of the four-question interview. When the assessment is first made on the candidate's ability to meet the performance needs of the job, the evaluation is more accurate. The key is to first determine if the candidate can do the work, then determine if you like the person. Wait 30 minutes, and measure first impression and personality through the person's accomplishments.

Listen to the comments you and other interviewers make about candidates right after the interview. They will reveal a performance or personality bias. Here are some typical negative comments from an interviewing team. Each is a clue that personality was more prized than performance.

➤ "Too arrogant. Not a leader."

➤ "Too stuck in his ways. Probably won't listen."

➤ "A little too quiet. I would have difficulty working with him."

➤ "I'm not sure he's a team player."

➤ "I don't think I could learn anything from him."

➤ "His experience is all with big companies. We're a small company. I don't think there's a fit."

➤ "He's smart, but kind of distant."

These were all real comments about one of my candidates for a Director of Sales and Marketing spot for a medical device manufacturing company. When you hire on personality and presentation, the assessments are superficial and the results random. When we measure the ability to get the job, rather than do the job, different interviewers have a diversity of opinions about the same candidate.

The following comments are also real; and even though they're positive, they're also superficial.

> ➤ "I like her. I think she can do the job."
> ➤ "A real go-getter—confident, affable, and really positive."
> ➤ "Great personality. A real team player. Just what we need."
> ➤ "Really fits with the company culture."
> ➤ "Smart and assertive. That's what we need around here."

When everyone likes the candidate for personality reasons, raise the caution flag. This is another reliable indicator of a bad interview. It means the assessment of performance was compromised.

It's appropriate to eliminate a candidate who can't do the work, but make sure that the decision to exclude is based on lack of performance. You'll know you and your team have reached emotional maturity if the yes/no comments are based on ability to do the work, rather than personality traits.

In the case of the candidate for the Director of Sales and Marketing at the medical device manufacturer, the president intervened before the candidate was eliminated. He did not believe the negative assessments were warranted. I was there in the meeting and I can still hear his comments:

> *This young man is one of the finest people I've ever had a chance to meet. His accomplishments in every job he has held have been spectacular. I'd like you to meet with him again. We can't afford to lose a star because he's a little quiet in the interview.*

The candidate was reinterviewed and hired. Within six months, he was the general manager. After 60 days on the job, the comments from his peers and subordinates on the interviewing team were effusive. They all agreed that this quiet young man was a superstar. They would have observed the same thing if they had judged his performance rather than his interviewing personality.

A potential mistake in this case was averted. To minimize these types of hiring errors, listen for comments like the following. Notice that they're longer and each comment is based on facts, not opinions or feelings.

➤ "She anticipates problems, understands customer needs, and is very detail oriented."

➤ "A strong team player. He provided numerous examples of going out of his way to support others to ensure that the team's projects were completed on time and within budget."

➤ "This person has made an impact in every job. She has built solid teams, set up development programs for each staff member, and can weed out the weaker players."

➤ "This candidate is technically top-notch. We worked a couple of problems together and I could tell that he knew the issues involved, was logical, understood the impact on the other systems, and was very inquisitive."

➤ "What a great salesperson! We discussed specific major accounts, and I could tell that this candidate knew how to prospect, cold call, present our complex product, negotiate, and close big orders."

When the assessment is based on the ability to do the work, it is always more uniform and more accurate. Fight the tendency to judge competency in the first few minutes based on personality. Measure performance first.

■ DIVERSITY HIRING REQUIRES A DEEPER UNDERSTANDING OF EMOTIONAL CONTROL

Controlling emotions is no easy matter. Remaining objective throughout an interview is hard to do when first impressions are weak, the candidate is nervous, or the person doesn't meet your image of a top performer. For some, this problem is magnified when dealing with diverse candidates. The issues of race, age, religion, gender, and physical challenges impact each interviewer at a powerful emotional level. Aside from moral and legal issues, these biases and prejudices must be held in check to build a talented and diverse workforce. Yet, they all come to the surface to disturb our objectivity at the moment we meet a candidate for the first time. It's easy to come up with some rationale to eliminate a candidate that doesn't fit your comfort zone. It's hard to do it right.

"Measure performance first" is easy to say, but sometimes hard to do, especially in the case of diverse candidates. In this case, you need to know your prejudices as well as your emotional triggers. Write them down. However uncomfortable, bring them to the conscious level every time you interview a diverse candidate. Then change your frame of reference. Do the opposite of what your initial reaction suggests. Go out of your way to disprove your stereotypes. Look for patterns of success and excellent performance before you judge cultural fit. The interviewing tools described in Chapter 2 will allow you to accurately measure true competency. First, you need to overcome your own biases and prejudices. Giving every candidate a fair chance is part of what I refer to as character in the POWER Hiring formula. Character is what it takes to build a diverse team of outstanding performers.

■ REPROGRAM YOURSELF TO OVERCOME BIASES, EMOTIONS, AND PREJUDICES

Ten tactics that will help increase objectivity during the interview follow. Each one will help you get to the 30-minute mark before measuring competency.

➤ 1. Recognize Your Emotional State

Keep track of your initial emotional response to the candidate. In your notes, describe the candidate's impression and your reaction to it—measure the impact of the candidate's first impression on you. As soon as you feel uncomfortable or bored, or relaxed and casual, write down when and why this occurred. A quick note like "++/5min/energy" is your clue that within five minutes you felt good about the candidate because of his or her enthusiasm; "–/2min/nervous" means a negative response due to applicant nervousness. These notes help you recognize your interviewing style and biases. If you do this five or six times, you'll soon be able to catch yourself and delay the yes/no decision for at least 30 minutes. I've been interviewing candidates for 25 years, and even today, I have to fight the tendency to make a decision within 10 minutes. It's a constant battle, but worth it. About 50 percent of the time, the conclusions I draw about a candidate are completely different after 30 minutes than after 10 minutes. It takes that much time to get below the surface and understand a candidate's true abilities.

➤ 2. Conduct a 20-Minute Performance-Based Phone Interview

A few years ago, I read that a major European orchestra started conducting black curtain auditions. The performer was unseen by the audition team during his or her performance. Before the black curtain approach, the competency of the women was always judged inferior to the men. Afterward, competency of men and women was judged equivalently.

A preliminary phone interview is the interviewer's black curtain. It helps minimize the initial first impression emotional reaction. The phone interview creates instant objectivity. You'll be less influenced by a weak or strong first impression. Candidates will also feel better. They'll be less nervous knowing that they've already passed muster on some critical aspects of the job. A preplanned phone interview is a key component of any effective hiring system. Try it out a few times and compare the quality of your assessment with and without a phone interview.

I was a guest speaker at a real estate seminar a few years ago. The group's president had heard me speak at one of her company functions the year before. Her introduction illustrated the importance of the phone interview. She told the group that while she used all aspects of the POWER Hiring program, the most important to her was the phone interview. With this screening tool alone, she was able to reduce the number of personal interviews by over 50 percent. In addition, she said that about 80 percent of those she did personally interview were extremely competent. Knowing the candidate through the phone interview helped establish a bond that minimized the emotional aspect of the first impression. Now she never meets a candidate without first conducting a phone interview.

➤ 3. Delay the Start of the Interview

Delay the interview to reduce nerves on both sides of the desk. Do something different. A few of my clients give facility tours. During this tour, they make it a point to visit areas that are related to the job. This could be a factory problem, a server glitch, the CAD design room, or the product demo room. Reviewing financial results or discussing a relevant newspaper article can have the same impact.

Solicit questions during this delaying phase. Their quality reveals both insight and inquisitiveness. By putting the candidate at ease, you go a long way toward minimizing the impact of first impressions and your own personal biases. The objective of this normalizing session is to establish open, nonjudgmental, two-way communication. Don't use it to give a 15-minute spiel about your great company. By delaying the inevitable, you will often increase candidate nervousness.

➤ 4. Use a Preplanned Structured Interview

If you consistently ask the questions in our structured interviews, you'll naturally overcome the impact of the first impression, good or bad. We suggest that you ask the same questions whether you like or dislike the candidate. In fact, you should ask the same questions for all candidates so that you can compare answers. Getting to 30 minutes is easy with a preplanned interview. You'll discover many of those candidates that initially seemed great often lose their glow, and those without one often shine brightly. Observe these changes. You'll learn as much about yourself as you do about the candidate.

➤ 5. Measure First Impressions Again After 30 Minutes

Measure first impression traits again after 30 minutes when you're no longer affected by them. Do this whether you like the candidate or not. Then ask yourself why you initially liked or disliked the candidate. Compare your initial impression to the second more objective delayed assessment of first impression. They'll usually be different. Determine why. Was it you or the candidate? If first impressions get worse, raise the caution flag. Ask some tough questions. Revisit some of the questions asked earlier in the interview. If the candidate's first impression has improved or has become less important, you might have a top person who doesn't do well early in the interview. Consider starting the interview over if you've inadvertently dismissed this candidate. We often meet great people who don't interview well. These are the pleasant surprises, but you'll also discover that many great first impressions often hide weak performance.

➤ 6. Change Your Frame of Reference

Do the exact opposite of what you feel like doing. This will counteract your initial emotional response to the candidate. Get tougher with those you like. Give the benefit of the doubt to those you don't like. This is another critical step in your reprogramming. The moment that you feel yourself sliding into a yes or no decision, take action. Changing your frame of reference is the first step. For those you like, make a mental assumption that they can't do the work and begin asking tougher questions. Something like, *"Can you describe in detail the steps you used to implement the change and the critical challenges you had to overcome?"* works for most situations. This approach will offset the positive emotional bias and provide more balance to the assessment.

I'm reprogrammed now. Whenever I see an affable, articulate, assertive, and attractive candidate, I raise my guard. I assume I'm going to be conned. I become the cynic and assume he or she can't do the work. A smooth talking, highly educated marketing manager comes to mind. This person was a good consultant type with great business insight and strong persuasive skills. The position required a line manager, though; and while he could talk a good game, I didn't think he was the best candidate. I made him give me specific details of how he would implement his programs, rather than discussing their strategic impact. These answers were shorter and more shallow, clearly indicative of a person out of his element. This was a very strong and competent guy, but not for this role. We tend to ignore this factor when we meet people we really like.

The same approach can be used for those you don't like. As soon as a negative starts to form, whatever the reason, take some opposing action. Go out of your way to prove that the candidate can do the work. Listen more, become less judgmental, and get the candidate to be more open. Lean forward and say something like *"That's really interesting. Can you explain the steps you had to go through to achieve that result?"* Be friendly and sincere. By getting the candidate to open up and talk more, temporary nervousness declines. Then get specific examples of accomplishments to judge ability. There are some great candidates sitting across the desk from you who might not have great interviewing skills. It takes work to find them, but it's well worth the effort.

➤ 7. Listen Four Times More Than You Talk

When we like someone, we have a tendency to overtalk and underlisten. An accurate interview requires fact finding, not social conversation. I met a candidate recently for a senior level marketing position in the automotive aftermarket. I had worked in this industry in an earlier life and we had many common acquaintances. I realized after 30 minutes that I hadn't learned anything about this person's ability to achieve results. While I liked him personally, it was time for a shift. I told him I needed to know specific details about what he accomplished at each past job. At that moment, the interview changed from casual cocktail conversation to a serious interview. He wasn't nearly as competent on this basis.

If you can't fill out a page of notes to validate each of the candidate's accomplishments, you haven't done enough fact finding. Whether you write them down or not, this takes about 10 to 15 minutes each. At the beginning of the interview, don't spend more than two or three minutes describing the company. Start asking questions right away. Don't feel compelled to editorialize or comment about your reactions or feelings. These are unnecessary. Listen four times more than you talk. Don't judge the candidate's answers during the response. Stay objective and don't interrupt. The fact-finding approach we recommend prevents the need to think of something clever to say next. Just follow the thread, or get an example for clarification. Listen to the responses and write your notes.

➤ 8. Treat the Candidate as a Consultant

The interviewer normally has the power position. If you change this balance of power, you can create more open discussion. Treating the candidate as a consultant is a great way to accomplish this. We tend to listen more and become less judgmental with those we consider to be superior to us in some way. This is why we're more deferential toward experts, customers, and supervisors than suppliers and subordinates. We do this all the time when we take advice from lawyers, doctors, consultants, and customers. It works equally as well with candidates. Treat candidates as knowledge experts. Suspend your judgment on how work should be accomplished. Take an active interest in what the candidate has to say. Candidates will quickly relax using this approach, and their answers will be longer and more insightful.

Ask follow-up questions that demonstrate your active listening. Ask for advice on real job-related problems. Provide positive feedback to the candidate. Something like "I like that idea" is appropriate. These affirmations will spark the candidate to tell more without much prompting. (This is not a bad strategy for managing subordinates either.) You'll be amazed at how well this simple technique can open the floodgates to communications and valuable information.

➤ 9. Talk About Real Work

Accuracy will soar if you can make the interview a give-and-take discussion about a real problem. Treat the interview more like a problem-solving session than an inquisition. Work through a relevant problem during the interview. Ask the candidate to describe how he or she would handle a typical issue that's likely to come up on the job. These could be specific problems, business objectives, people or management problems, or a technical matter. Go on a tour of the facility. When you come to a problem or important issue, ask the candidate for advice on how to address it. Feel free to use the white board. Allow questions. This type of give-and-take discussion is more like "real talk" than Q&A interview talk. Not only does it provide great insight into an applicant's ability to visualize an objective, but it naturally reveals style and personality during the response because the candidate is more relaxed.

Here are a few typical problems that can be turned into good interviewing discussions:

- ➤ Sales—difficulty closing an important account.
- ➤ Accounting—tracking down a reconciling item.
- ➤ Manufacturing—eliminating a bottleneck.
- ➤ Customer service—dealing with an irate customer.
- ➤ Systems—designing a new interface.
- ➤ Engineering—overcoming a technical challenge that has everyone stumped.
- ➤ Marketing—getting some quick competitive analysis completed.

Talk is sometimes cheap, so there is a caveat. Ask the candidate to describe some comparable past accomplishments. This adds a foundation of reality to the candidate's responses. Many people can describe how they would accomplish a task, but can't actually do it. Conversely, many people can't adapt their experiences to different environments. This approach will uncover the few that can do both.

➤ 10. Use the Panel Interview

The panel interview technique is not only one of the best interviewing approaches ever advocated, but also it has the double benefit of minimizing emotions. It's not generally appropriate for the first interview because it's too intimidating for the candidate. For the second round or later the same day, though, it's a great way to minimize the personality-based interviews common to people who have less stake in the candidate's success. A panel interview with three or four people is also a good way to save time and involve more people in the assessment process. It will increase objectivity by allowing the panel members more time to evaluate the answers without having to continually think of what to ask next.

Ten Great Reprogramming Techniques

Reprogramming Technique	Comments and Description
1. Recognize your emotional state.	If you're uptight or relaxed you'll look for facts to support this feeling. Fight it. Stay neutral. Ask every candidate the same questions. This way all information has equal value.
2. Conduct a 20-minute phone interview.	When you talk to someone on the phone first, you automatically minimize the impact of personality and first impressions.
3. Don't start the interview right away.	Go on a tour, see a demo, but get in to a give-and-take discussion. This will help minimize emotions and set up the framework for a good dialogue.
4. Use preplanned structured questions.	Write down a few performance-oriented questions to ask right away, whether you like the candidate or not.
5. Measure first impressions again after 30 minutes.	After 30 minutes, revisit first impressions. Compare to the original and evaluate your reaction. This will help restore balance.
6. Change your frame of reference.	If you like the candidate, be skeptical and ask tougher questions. Be more interested in, and more open with, those you don't particularly like.
7. Listen 4 times more than you talk.	The interview is not casual conversation. It needs to be a fact-finding expedition. Keep notes for each accomplishment.
8. Treat the candidate as a consultant.	We always listen more to those who are experts or have a superior position. Treat candidates the same way to elicit more open responses.
9. Talk about real work.	Discuss problems and related business issues. Accuracy will increase if the interview is more like a problem-solving session rather than an inquisition.
10. Use panel interviews.	You'll save time and minimize emotional reactions, since there's less of a one-on-one relationship.

The panel interview can be an even more powerful tool if you give the one or two finalists a take-home problem to present to a panel. Because this takes some extra time, give the candidate a few days to make sure he or she is sincerely interested in the job. The problem or mini-case should represent a real issue and should take at most a few hours to study and summarize. Have the candidate present a 5- to 15-minute overview of his or her findings and then move to a Q&A session. A panel interview by itself, if well-organized, minimizes emotions because emotions are held in check by the other interviewers. With the addition of a take-home problem, you also test true competency and interest. Some ideas for take-home cases include real business problems, a review of the financials, a marketing issue, a technical or design problem, or some operating plan review.

Try this technique if you want to reduce the emotions in your company's hiring decisions. The response we've had from candidates and clients alike has been very positive. One of the few problems we've observed has been lack of organization. Someone does need to orchestrate the process or anarchy prevails. Assign this to the hiring manager and generally allow other interviewers only to ask follow-up questions.

■ PULLING IT ALL TOGETHER—A REAL-LIFE EXAMPLE

It has been many years now, but I remember this situation as if it were only yesterday. A very big guy came into my office for a sales manager position. My reaction to his size was very negative. This was aggravated by the fact that I had been working on this assignment for six weeks and had no other candidates for the position. To make matters worse, the day before, I had talked to my client about the many strengths of the person who now sat across from me. I had even gone out on a limb by setting up a client interview based solely on a phone interview. For added emphasis, I had strongly suggested to my client that he'd probably hire this person.

Luckily, our emotional responses are short-lived once we recognize these fears as unfounded. It took about five minutes for me to regain some control. I then remembered the phone interview. During that 20-minute conversation, I had asked this candidate to describe his most significant accomplishments at his prior two jobs. We also talked about his management style and team building skills. Remembering these positive impressions relaxed me even further, and I conducted the next 30 minutes of the interview asking probing questions about management, team leadership, and initiative. I even had my candidate draw a point-of-sale display and walk me through the four-month selling process for a multimillion dollar order. He turned out to be a great candidate—extremely competent, with strong interpersonal skills. He was also affable, bright, and energetic.

After about 30 minutes, I measured his first impression again. Talk about shock. Except for my initial five-minute blowup, for the last 30 minutes I had been in detailed, animated discussion with this candidate and completely ignored his physical appearance. On reevaluation, I discovered this candidate was neither as large as I first imagined, nor as unpresentable. In fact, he had shrunk about four inches in height and lost 40 pounds in this short time span. He was still big, a football lineman type, but not *that* big. When I first saw him, my negative emotions exaggerated his size. If I hadn't used a 30-minute delay, a great candidate would have gotten away. There are some great candidates out there who don't fit our personality or physical templates so well. If you can suspend your emotional reaction for 30 minutes, you'll find some stars hidden behind your own emotional blinders. By the way, he did get the job and did very well, although I cautioned my client that he was meeting a football player.

In most companies, a $25,000 to $50,000 investment decision takes a formal justification requiring at least a few hours. A $100,000 investment requires some level of sophisticated financial analysis taking at least 10 to 20 hours, if not more. Yet, the decision to hire a $50,000 employee, the equivalent of a $250,000 investment,[1] can often be completed in a few hours! Hiring requires and deserves the same kind of sophisticated analysis as any important investment. It starts by breaking the emotional link between yourself and the candidate, and substituting the job as the dominant selection criteria. Measure performance first, then determine if the candidate's personality helps or hurts his or her performance. Just switching the order in which the three trait groups are measured works wonders.

In this chapter, some practical techniques were provided to break the powerful emotional response to personality and first impression. We all have our own examples of how our emotions got the better of us. The more obvious are those candidates we've hired who fell short of expectations. If they're still with you, you're reminded every day of your own hiring tendencies and failure modes. Study these real examples. They provide some good lessons. Unfortunately, you know nothing about most of your failures. These are the good ones who got away. To minimize mistakes in the future, examine those people you've hired in the past. Determine if the hiring errors were because of superficial emotional decisions or a weak understanding of the real job needs as described in the performance profile. Do your successes reveal a different approach, or were they just random luck? Maybe you didn't cover all the critical job needs, assuming competence, but not validating it. Often fatal flaws are ignored. Start developing a personal profile of your hiring decision criteria.

From these clues and what we've presented here, you'll be able to tailor a hiring program that works for you. Our goal is to use job competency, not interviewing skills, as the selection criteria. Getting your emotions under control is the first step. This is what hiring with your head is all about.

POWER HIRING HOT TIPS—CONTROL YOUR EMOTIONS TO INCREASE HIRING ACCURACY

✔ Wait 30 minutes before you make any hiring decision.

✔ Most hiring errors are made because we look for facts to justify an emotional decision.

✔ Break the emotional link between you and the candidate and substitute the job as the dominant selection criteria.

✔ Recognition is the key to controlling emotions. Take some countermeasures whenever you feel too good, or too bad, too early.

(continued)

✔ Fight with yourself to focus on the candidate's ability to do the job, not get the job.

✔ Use the POWER Hiring *Performance First!* Formula. First measure performance, then determine if you like the person.

✔ At the end of the interview, write down your evaluation. If your assessment had more to do with personality than competency, redo the interview.

✔ Image isn't everything. In fact, it's nothing when it comes to hiring. Know your biases and seek diversity.

✔ Combine the intuitive hiring decision with enough fact-finding to minimize errors.

✔ Conduct a 20-minute phone interview before you see the candidate. This minimizes the impact of first impressions when you first meet the candidate.

✔ Delay the buying decision until the end of the interview to give all data equal relevance.

✔ Delay the start of the interview. Take a tour. An informal dialogue about relevant business issues can counteract the impact of any initial emotional response to the candidate.

✔ Measure first impression again after 30 minutes, when you are more objective.

✔ Change your frame of reference. Be easier on those you don't like and tougher on those you do.

✔ Listen four times more than you talk and don't judge the answers during the answer.

✔ Treat the candidate as an expert. Assume she knows more than you, and you'll automatically listen more.

✔ Talk about real work in a give-and-take manner.

✔ Use take-home mini-cases, letting candidates present their summaries at a subsequent interview.

✔ Use panel interviews. Emotions are minimized and you have a better chance to assess responses since you don't always have to think of what to ask next.

Chapter 4

The Basic
Four-Question Interview

Q: When you choose men and women to promote, to be a leader of the company, what qualities do you look for?

A: *You clearly want somebody who can articulate a vision. They have to have enormous energy and the incredible ability to energize others. If you can't energize others, you can't be a leader.*

Jack Welch, CEO, General Electric, *Business Week,* May 29, 1995

■ THE FOUR CORE TRAITS OF UNIVERSAL SUCCESS

In *Jack: Straight from the Gut* (Warner, 2001), Jack Welch discusses the importance of building outstanding teams, considering this his core legacy. He also describes the four Es that General Electric leadership used to assess competency: the ability to energize yourself, the ability to energize others, the edge to make tough decisions, and the ability to execute.

As a headhunter since 1978, I've had an opportunity to work with some great talent. I've tracked many of these top people over the course of their careers for 5, 10, some even as long as 15 to 20 years. It was clear to me that the best had four common characteristics that were observable in the initial interview:

1. They were self-motivated—everyone who achieved any level of success worked hard.
2. They showed an ability to motivate others, inspiring peers, superiors, and their own team to work hard.
3. They achieved results comparable to what needed to be achieved.
4. They solved realistic problems in real time.

While not identical to General Electric's four, they're certainly close. Collectively, our four became the POWER Hiring formula for predicting performance in a new job.

The POWER Hiring
Formula for Predicting Performance

$$\text{Future Performance} = \text{Talent} \times \text{Energy}^2 + \text{Team Leadership}$$
$$+ \text{Comparable Past Performance}$$
$$+ \text{Job-Specific Problem Solving}$$

In our formula, energy^2, is by far the most important component. Energy is self-motivation and identical to the first of the four General Electric Es. It's squared because it has this kind of impact. We've all met people with great talent, but little energy. Sadly, they never live up to their expectations. Others of average talent, but with enormous energy, often achieve success beyond all expectations. That's why self-motivation is so important. In over 25 years of dealing with some of the best people in the country, I've come to an obvious conclusion—the best work harder than everyone else. They make an impact (Talent × Energy^2 = Impact). They make things happen. They do more than required. They consistently deliver more results than expected, and they do it on time, all the time. This, to me, separates the best from everyone else.

They consistently deliver more results than expected, and they do it on-time, all the time. This to me, separates the best from everyone else.

Some call this quality initiative, self-motivation, work ethic, drive, ambition, commitment, or anything else related to going the extra mile. Without it, even the most talented fail. With it, people with only average talent can become extraordinarily successful. These people consistently exceed expectations. They do more than they're required to do, year in and year out. Look for this pattern early in the interview. Measuring self-motivation is the objective of the first question in our four-question interview. A word of caution: Don't be seduced by affability and assertiveness. Assertive or socially confident people are not necessarily highly motivated, although many interviews falsely assume they are. This is a common error. Another common error is to eliminate quiet people for lack of energy. Being quiet or outgoing does not predict personal energy, initiative, or work ethic. You can observe this only through examples of accomplishments.

The second component of the POWER Hiring formula is team leadership. The ability to persuade and motivate others to achieve results is an essential component of long-term success. It allows a person to tap into the personal energy of others—a boss, a subordinate, a peer, or an outside advisor. Even the ability to cooperate is a component of what I call team leadership. As Jack Welch said, *"If you can't energize others, you can't be a leader."* This is his second E—the ability to energize others—and ours as well.

We all want good team leadership skills. Surprisingly, we rarely ask about these skills during the interview. The focus is all too often on individual contributor skills. Lack of team leadership skills is a common weakness of those who don't work out. This is the classic fatal flaw often ignored during the interview. Focusing on team skills is the second of our four core questions.

The combination of high initiative and strong team skills is a winning combination. You won't find many successful people without them both. It doesn't matter if they're in accounting or sales, in a creative or technical position, the president or a clerk. It also isn't important if the person has 20 years of experience or is just starting out. Those who continually succeed have the core traits of personal energy and team leadership the foundation of performance and potential. I've minimized my failures and maximized my successes by setting my performance standards for all jobs to include these core traits. I also start measuring them right away, in the beginning of the interview.

The third predictable trait of success in the POWER Hiring formula is past comparable performance. To increase the likelihood of success in a new job, the candidate needs to have a track record of accomplishments that are similar to the required performance objectives of the job. In Chapter 2, we created performance profiles describing the critical job deliverables. The third question is nothing more than getting detailed examples of the candidate's accomplishments that are most similar to these job needs.

The fourth trait of success I've observed is job-specific problem solving. The best performers in any job, from entry-level accountant to company president, have the ability to solve problems related to the job. For the accountant, it might be how to reconcile an account. For the president, it might be to determine the cause of poor financial performance, or to develop a new product strategy. So I just ask them to solve these problems during the interview. This is the fourth question.

■ THE MOST IMPORTANT INTERVIEW QUESTION OF ALL TIME

Please think of your most significant accomplishment in your career. Now could you tell me all about it?

This is it. With this question alone, you can learn 65 percent to 75 percent of everything you need to make a hiring decision. Let me show you how with a real example. In fact, let me interview you right now. Write in the space below the accomplishment question, what you'd like to talk about. Just write the headline. If you can't think of an accomplishment, think about a project or an assignment you worked on that you're very proud of.

My most significant accomplishment is . . .

Now imagine you're sitting across the desk from me, and I ask you to tell me about this accomplishment. Over the next 8 to 12 minutes, maybe even for 15 minutes, I prompt you further and obtain this information.

HOW FACT-FINDING CAN HELP YOU BETTER UNDERSTAND THE ACCOMPLISHMENT

☐ An overview of the accomplishment and the actual results obtained.

☐ Your actual title, your organization chart, your supervisor's title.

☐ Details about your team, their names and titles. Rank each team member's performance, including yours, and the role you played building and developing this team and the people involved. Do this even if you're not a manager.

☐ The bottom-line or business impact of the accomplishment.

☐ Whether the objective was met, completed on time, and if this was difficult, and how you performed against the plan or budget.

☐ When it took place—the year and duration in years and months, even the actual date.

☐ The major steps and deliverables involved in accomplishing the task.

☐ A detailed description of your actual role.

☐ Examples of where you took the initiative and did things not required.

☐ What processes you improved or changed.

☐ What you did from a leadership standpoint, getting resources, or obtaining approval.

☐ Some of the biggest challenges you faced, or most difficult aspects of the task.

☐ Determined what constraints you overcame, and what resources you had.

☐ What the pace was like and how decisions were made.

☐ Determined why you considered this a significant accomplishment.

☐ Some of the biggest people challenges, with specific examples, and how you overcame them.

☐ Examples of when you had to change the opinion of others and how you dealt with conflict.

HOW FACT-FINDING CAN HELP YOU BETTER UNDERSTAND THE ACCOMPLISHMENT *(continued)*

☐ How you personally grew or changed as a result of this effort.

☐ What technical skills you needed to accomplish the task and what skills you learned.

☐ Determine why you were chosen for this role.

☐ How you would rank the overall success of the task and why.

☐ What others (supervisors, peers, subordinates) would say about the candidate's performance in this task.

☐ The aspects of the accomplishment the candidate enjoyed or disliked and why.

☐ How you would rank your overall performance on this project on a scale of 0 to 10, and what the most important thing you would do differently if you could to move it up one point.

Imagine that I could obtain most of this information from you during the course of a 10- to 15-minute session. Do you think I would know much about you? You bet I would. Now, do you think you would give me all of this information without any prompting on my part? No way. Yet, this is the information you need to make an informed decision about any candidate's competency. If I left it up to you, or if you leave it up to your candidates, then we're measuring interviewing competency, not job competency. The interviewer needs to take responsibility to obtain this information from the candidate. It is not the candidate's responsibility to provide it to you. This is one of the basic rules of interviewing. Interviewers need to train candidates to provide this type of information. You do it through fact-finding. This is what the checklist is all about. Accurate interviewing is more about getting detailed answers about accomplishments, not about asking a bunch of clever questions.

Accurate interviewing is about getting detailed answers about accomplishments, not about asking a bunch of clever questions.

Now imagine I ask this same question again for at least two more major accomplishments. Do you think I'd have even more information about your competency, especially if I put these accomplishments in time order? Your complete work history is clearly revealed with this type of questioning. During the rest of the interview, I'll make sure I ask about two to three team accomplishments, and two to three individual accomplishments to see the trend of these two important measures. These are the first two of our predictors of job success in the POWER Hiring interviewing formula, self-motivation and team leadership.

To round things out, I'm going to ask you about some accomplishments directly related to the SMARTe performance objectives on the performance profile. I'll spend another 10 minutes making sure I understand the accomplishment, the process used to achieve the accomplishment, and the environment in which the accomplishment took place. With this information, I can build a trend line of performance for the first three core traits of success—Talent × Energy^2, team leadership, and comparable past performance. This is the first of the three core questions—one question used three different ways. The first reveals a trend line of individual accomplishments. The second reveals the trend of team accomplishments. The third compares a candidate's accomplishments to the specific SMARTe objectives in the performance profile. This is shown graphically in Figure 4.1.

We'll get into the assessment aspect in great detail in Chapter 7. For now, recognize that the trend lines and anchor points are revealing. For the trend lines, an upward slope indicates that a candidate is still growing. A plateau or flattening out is not bad if the candidate is still highly motivated and continues to produce outstanding work. A decline or a roller-coaster trend is of concern. In each case, the interviewer needs to compare the candidate's accomplishments against the real needs of the job. This is where the anchors help. All of this can be accomplished with "the most significant accomplishment" question combined with fact-finding. Interviewing is less about

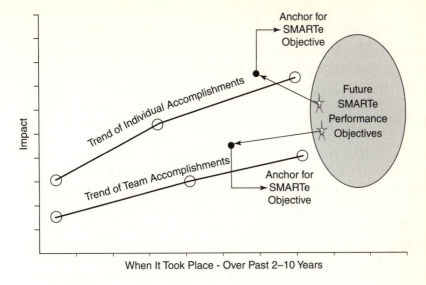

Figure 4.1 Use a trend of performance to predict success.

asking many questions, and more about getting the right answers to the most significant accomplishment question.

■ THE SECOND MOST IMPORTANT QUESTION—VISUALIZATION

You'll be able to determine the fourth core trait of success, job-specific problem solving, with this question. I call it the visualization question.

If you were to get this job, how would you go about solving this typical problem (describe the problem)?

Turn off the spotlights, and talk about real work. This type of question allows for a give-and-take discussion of real job needs. It's been my experience that every top performer has the ability to discuss what's needed to solve typical problems. Even if the person can't provide the answer right away, he or she knows what questions to ask and how to plan the task. The person can visualize the answer or anticipate what to do next. A problem for a maintenance worker might be how to go about fixing a problem with a piece of equipment; for a director of marketing, it might be how to prepare a comprehensive competitive analysis. With this fourth question, plus the trends of past performance observed with the most significant accomplishment questions, you'll have all you need to make a hiring decision.

■ THE FOUR-QUESTION INTERVIEW

The POWER Hiring Four-Question Interview Template in Figure 4.2 combines the four questions. It includes the fact-finding table and space to write down your answers. You can also download this template as a PDF from powerhiring.com.

➤ A More Thorough Look at the Impact and Team Leadership Questioning Pattern

The first two questions get at the first two core traits of success, Impact = Talent × Energy^2, and team leadership the ability to cooperate, persuade, and motivate others. Ask about these early in the interview. Both questions involve asking about significant accomplishments coupled with fact-finding. While the question about each accomplishment is important by itself, it becomes extremely powerful when the trend of these accomplishments is viewed over time.

Impact Question

Give me a quick overview of your current (prior) position and describe the biggest impact (or change) you made.

You can judge the scope, scale, and impact of the candidate's past performance by getting detailed information about the candidate's most important work over an extended period of time. The fact-finding is key. Don't accept generalities like "created a new market," "turned the department around," and "developed a new procedure." Also, don't feel stupid about asking for clarifying information. You'll feel a lot more stupid after you've hired a candidate who snowed or intimidated you in the interview. Many interviewers are afraid to ask follow-up questions because they don't want the candidate to think they're confused. This is where good fact-finding comes into

POWERhiring®
Best Practices for Hiring Top Talent

The 4-Question Interview

Develop a Trend Line of Accomplishments Over Time			
Candidate:	Position:	Interviewer:	Date:

Part 1 - Ask About Team and Individual Accomplishments for Each Past Job		Fact-finding Checklist
#1: Overview and Impact - Give me a quick overview of your job, the company, and describe your most significant accomplishment. (You can also ask for examples of initiative or accomplishment you're proud of.)	**#2: Organization Chart and Team Project** - Have candidate draw an org chart and describe a team or management project and specific role. (If a manager find out how candidate built and developed the team.)	Get this info for each accomplishment to validate it. Follow-up each previous answer with a related question to peel the onion. Spend 8-10 minutes on each accomplishment. ❑ Overview of the accomplishment. ❑ Describe complete team - titles, names
Title Most Recent: _____ Dates: ___	Titles of Direct Reports or Team Members:	❑ What was bottom line, business impact? ❑ When: dates, how long? ❑ Why: what was the problem? ❑ What was your actual role? ❑ How did you develop the plan? ❑ Why were you chosen for this role? ❑ What were the biggest challenges? ❑ What do you consider the most significant work you did in this job? ❑ What were the major deliverables involved in accomplishing the task? ❑ Get details of implementation steps ❑ Get three examples of initiative ❑ What did you change or improve?
Title Prior #1: _____ Dates: ___	Titles of Direct Reports or Team Members:	❑ How did you grow or change as a result of this effort? ❑ Was it completed on time, on budget? ❑ Find out how the candidate ranks the overall success of the task and why. ❑ What aspects did you enjoy (dislike) the most and why? ❑ How would others describe you? ❑ What would you do differently? **Team Issues** ❑ Get details about the team - names and titles. Find out the reporting relationships. Who was in-charge? ❑ Rank each team member's ability.
Title Prior #2: _____ Dates: ___	Titles of Direct Reports or Team Members:	❑ How did you build the team? ❑ Was team as strong as it could be? ❑ Describe how group decisions were made and get examples. ❑ Ask "Describe the people challenges and give me some examples." ❑ Get examples of persuading others. ❑ Get examples of handling conflict. ❑ Get examples of developing people. ❑ How did you change as team leader? ❑ How could you have improved your team accomplishment?

Figure 4.2 The four-question interview template.

(continued)

POWERhiring
Best Practices for Hiring Top Talent

The 4-Question Interview

Benchmark Performance - Determining Ability to Meet SMARTe Objectives

ANCHOR	VISUALIZE	SMARTe Objectives
State the performance (SMART) objective and ask the candidate to describe their most comparable accomplishment. Use the Fact-finding Checklist to validate each accomplishment.	Ask the candidate how they would achieve the objective if they had the job. First ask the candidate what information they would need. Then how they would organize and implement the task.	Prioritize the top 5-6 deliverables or performance objectives for the position. Make them SMARTe. For example, "Within 6 months improve factory performance by 3%."

SMARTe Objective 1:

- Specific
- Measurable
- Action Oriented
- Result-based
- Time Bound
- environment

Consider all the job factors as you prepare these performance objectives - major objectives, interim objectives, team and management issues, problems, technical issues, changes needed, and interpersonal problems.

SMARTe Objective 2:

ANCHOR

It's important to get a comparable past accomplishment to determine a candidate's ability to achieve the SMART objective. Use the fact-finding techniques on the front. Keep notes on this page under the specific objective.

SMARTe Objective 3:

VISUALIZE

All good candidates can anticipate the needs of the job before starting. Get into a give-and-take discussion with the candidate by asking how they would implement the task. You only need to do this for two or three SMART objectives. Here's some additional questions to ask.

- ❏ What are the critical issues involved?
- ❏ Is the time schedule realistic?
- ❏ What other resources would be needed?
- ❏ What other information would you need to obtain before beginning?
- ❏ What would you do in the first week or two?
- ❏ What types of people would you need to complete the task on time?
- ❏ What's the critical success factor?

SMART Objective 4:

Look for these important clues:
- the quality of the questions
- the depth of insight
- organizational skills
- alone or with a team
- ability to identify critical issues

SMART Objective 5:

The ability to ANCHOR and VISUALIZE is a strong predictor of success. Be careful of good ANCHORS only. These people are too structured. Good VISUALIZERS only are good consultants, but have never done it.

Figure 4.2 *(Continued)*

the picture. Probe deeply until you completely understand the true nature of the accomplishment and the applicant's role.

Use these questions to get more insight if the candidate is reluctant to open up:

1. I'm a little unsure of what you've accomplished. Could you give me another example?

2. What you describe does not seem that significant. I must have missed something. Could you explain it with more details, or give an example to demonstrate what you mean?

3. I'm unclear on the challenges you faced in this job. What were they and why do you feel these were significant?

There is a natural tendency for candidates to generalize and give short one-minute answers. It's important to get details; that's why getting examples is so important. Once you get candidates to speak freely, you'll discover that they tend to give more information on subsequent questions.

One of my clients told me she uses this technique when she hires computer software developers. She has them clearly define their contribution made on each of their last few major projects. She wants to know what their impact has been and the specific role they played. She looks for a continuing and larger contribution in each successive position.

In the second question about team projects, leadership and management skills are revealed. Here are two alternate formats:

Team Leadership Question—If the Person Isn't Directly Supervising Others

Please draw an organization chart and tell me about a team project you were involved in, and describe your role.

Team Leadership Question—If the Person Is a Manager

Please draw an organization chart and tell me how you built and developed this team, and describe the group's biggest accomplishment.

Again, ask this question for the previous few jobs. This will help you observe a pattern of change and growth over an extended time frame. You don't have to be in a management position to exhibit team or leadership traits. We've discovered that people who aren't yet managers, but will be soon, evidence strong team skills. The ability to motivate, work with, and persuade others is an important and recognizable talent. If the person is not a manager, or if you go back to a previous job when the candidate wasn't a manager, use the nonmanager version of this question. Ask for examples of team projects and be sure to explore the specific role the candidate played. Get specific. Look for a pattern of implementing change, doing more than required, motivating and persuading others, and helping to define team objectives.

Get names and specific results, determine key obstacles, and find out how the candidate handled conflict and differences. This fact-finding helps paint a word picture of actual past performance. Don't stop until you're satisfied. Fact-finding is hard work and you won't want to do it if you really like the candidate. In this case, you'll be trying to find reasons to hire the candidate, not exclude him. For candidates you don't like, you won't want to spend the time, but you still must. This is tough work, but this is how good hiring decisions really happen. They're not random events.

➤ Have the Candidate Draw a Team Chart for the Past Few Positions

Ask each candidate to draw a work or team chart, even if the person isn't a manager. A team chart shows all the people the person is involved with on the job—peers, subordinates, boss, people in other departments, outside suppliers, and customers. Knowing the team the person is involved with helps clarify his or her accomplishments. If the candidate is a manager, use the second version of this question. Have these candidates draw an expanded team chart that includes all of their direct reports. Ask how the person developed this group. Get names, dates, and specific changes that have been made. Have the candidate rank the quality of the staff and describe how he or she developed the team and improved the team's performance. Find out who they hired, fired, and why.

Do this for the past few jobs. If the candidate has developed a pattern of building only average teams, he or she is only an average manager.

Drawing the organization chart is important to gain a visual sense of the reporting relationships, and it helps clarify communications. Big-sounding jobs often look less significant when shown on paper with only a few direct reports. A director of accounting and planning job can be equivalent to a vice president of finance and look very big when it covers responsibility for five countries, seven direct reports, and a staff of 100. Be tenacious. Combine the impact and leadership questioning pattern with thorough fact-finding and good probing.

An East Coast distributor used this technique to hire an international manufacturing manager a few days after attending one of our seminars. The head of operations told me he truly understood the significance of the candidate's management skills when she described in detail how she developed an individual improvement program for each of her staff members. She was animated and involved during the exchange, presenting herself as she really was. She described strengths and weaknesses of each person and told how each one changed as a result of the program. The hiring manager felt this interviewing approach allows the candidate to move away from the staged presentation of most interviews into a relaxed, more natural style of communicating.

➤ Develop a Trend Line to Measure Long-Term Impact

The trend line is also important. By going back 5 to 10 years, you'll be able to observe the trend of these important traits over an extended period of time. This approach works for managers and nonmanagers alike, and entry-level or seasoned personnel. Students can demonstrate these traits early on, even in nonwork-related situations. You just have to look for them. Here's a simplified version of the track record of a woman I worked with on a vice president marketing search a few years ago. She had left the workforce about five years earlier to work in her home community. Not surprisingly, even there she left her mark. She was working with her local state government in establishing special tax opportunities for local industry. In each position she held, she made an increasingly bigger impact. The trend line approach summarizes it graphically as shown in Figure 4.3.

The trend line isn't always this obvious, but getting major objectives this way will help determine if the candidate's performance is on an upward trend, has flattened out, or is declining. One of my business associates recently asked me to interview a few candidates for his warehouse manager position. All of the candidates were strong and held similar positions, but only one was on an upward growth path. I recommended him, even though he was a little quieter. The other two had significant success early in their careers, but for the past ten years had settled into comfortable situations. While both of them could do the current job and professed a desire to grow, neither had taken any action to invest in themselves. The other candidate was taking night classes, learning and using personal computers, and was developing his staff. No matter what a candidate tells you, look for these signs of upward growth, even if they're not obvious in the candidate's titles.

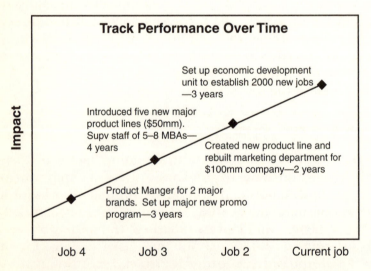

Figure 4.3 Plot candidate performance over time.

The best candidates don't mind this inquisitive approach. These people like to talk about their accomplishments. They also feel more positive about managers requesting this information. It tells the candidate that the manager has high standards, is thorough, and has probably built a team of other strong people. Good people want to work for these kinds of managers. They also feel very positive about the situation and the person conducting the interview. If every interviewer is this thorough, the inquisitive approach demonstrates the professionalism of the whole company. Weaker candidates get put off and squirmy with this style. Because they have less to show for their efforts, their answers are usually shorter, shallower, and more general. Don't settle for anything less than high energy, good team skills, and a good dose of talent, or the ability to learn. This is the stuff stars are made from, but you sometimes have to look deep to find the sparkle, or to determine its real source.

■ NEXT, FIND OUT IF THE CANDIDATE CAN DO THE WORK—DETERMINE JOB COMPETENCY

Use the first half hour of the first interview to assess the candidate's two core success traits—energy and team leadership—with the team and individual and team accomplishment questioning pattern. Getting three or four accomplishments will be enough to determine if you're meeting a strong candidate or not. Use the remainder of the interview to determine if the person can handle the specific accomplishments of the job as described in the performance profile.

➤ Anchor and Visualize Each SMARTe Objective

Asking the candidate to give you an example of an accomplishment most comparable to a SMARTe objective is called an *anchor.* When combined with fact-finding, you'll be able to determine if the candidate meets the third criteria for success— past comparable performance. Then asking how they'd go about achieving the task or solving the problem is called *visualization.* This gets at the fourth core trait of success—job-specific problem solving. Together, they'll give you great insight into a candidate's ability to both do and plan the work that needs to get done. This anchor-and-visualize questioning pattern is used to validate job-specific competency.

Anchor Every SMARTe Objective

One of our key objectives for the person selected for this position is (describe objective). Can you please tell me about something similar you've accomplished?

Use the anchor question to obtain an example of a relevant past achievement. Combine this with the fact-finding techniques discussed earlier to paint a word picture of what the applicant actually accomplished. During the course of a complete interview, you need to anchor all of the SMARTe objectives. Look for comparable accomplishments. The process used to achieve the results and the environment in which they were achieved are more indicative of fit than identical accomplishments. Get details like staff size, comparable scope and complexity of the assignment, and similar company environments.

Comparability of accomplishments minimizes the need for industry fit and years of related experience. For example, in our search practice, we place many salespeople from reps to senior executives. We've discovered that the process used to achieve sales success is more important than a specific product or customer. People who have track records of selling complex technology to extremely discriminating customers can do this whether it's telecommunications gear, computers, or capital equipment used in manufacturing. The track record of sales success is most important. Next is comparability of the process including dollar volume, length of time, type and sophistication of the buyers, and the support services provided.

The performance profile listed different types of accomplishments. By anchoring every objective, you'll get a better picture of the candidate's ability to handle every critical facet of the job. This is also true for candidates who seem initially weak. Often other skills discovered later in the interview can more than compensate for an apparent weakness. If you exclude too soon, you could inadvertently miss a great candidate.

The apparent weakness might not even be a real weakness. It could just be the result of an incomplete response.

I recently interviewed a financial manager who had tremendous technical skills. He was personable, smart, and well educated. One of the major performance objectives of the position, but not number one, was to work with other functions in setting up companywide performance reporting systems. He struggled with this anchor. His answers were more general and shorter—two classic signs of lack of experience or interest. Even fact-finding didn't help. His best examples were superficial. The candidate's greatest successes were all individual projects. While a likable person, it wasn't clear he could work with manufacturing and operations people to meet the company's needs. We moved on to another candidate for the job.

The visualization question reinforces the anchor. It's especially useful in assessing a candidate's ability to handle significantly different accomplishments.

Visualize the Two to Three Most Important SMARTe Objectives

As we've discussed, (objective) is an important aspect of this position. If you were to get the job, what additional information would you need to know, and how would you go about accomplishing this objective?

The visualization process is less like an interview and more like a real working session. This is how and what you would talk about after the candidate starts. Sometime during the first week, you'll sit down with the new employee to discuss the objectives of the position. You'll normally get into a discussion on how these tasks would be handled. You'll outline strategies and tactics, talk about schedules and resources, allocate staff, and reprioritize. This is also your first chance to understand the candidate's planning ability and insight. Why wait? You can do the same thing with the visualization question before the candidate ever starts. This is a great way to transition the new employee into the job. Candidates know what's expected of them before they start, and you have a better sense of how they'll function in the new environment.

It's been my experience that the best candidates for any position and any level have the ability to mentally organize the work before starting it. This is what good managers and leaders do on the job in planning new tasks. They work with others in brainstorming, anticipating the needs and challenges of the job before beginning. The visualization question during the interview is a way to test this ability. In the past 25 years, I haven't met one top-notch person who couldn't do this.

The questioning can take a variety of forms. One way is to allow the candidate to ask for more information. Another is to ask how the person would begin or organize an assignment. Good people know how to go from point A to point B and are not afraid to discuss how they'd do it, or to ask for more information. Some won't even take on an assignment until they're sure the resources are available or the company is committed to success. Allow this type of open discussion to take place. You'll see a lot of the thinking and planning skills emerge. You don't need to visualize all of the SMARTe performance objectives; just using the top two to three will provide you with the insight you need.

Chapter 2 was introduced with one of Steve Covey's "Seven Habits" from his all-time business bestseller, *Seven Habits of Highly Effective People:* "Begin with the end in mind." It stresses the need to understand the performance, or SMARTe, objectives of the job before interviewing candidates. Understanding the performance objectives of the job is an equally important trait for a candidate to possess. You directly test for it during the interview with the visualization question.

Here are some of the skills and traits you'll observe in a good visualization session:

➤ Job-specific problem solving.
➤ Verbal communications.
➤ Reasoning and thinking skills.
➤ Adaptability and flexibility.
➤ Self-confidence.
➤ Insight and job knowledge.
➤ Creativity.
➤ Organization and planning skills.
➤ Logic and intellect.

One of my clients used the visualization technique with great success to hire someone to head up a new business unit. My client told me they spent the whole second half of the first interview laying out the plan on a flip chart. He and the candidate developed the strategies, tactics, and an organization chart; they even prepared a preliminary budget. Both the candidate and my client believed this was one of the most revealing and insightful interview sessions either had ever had. A few months later, my client called to tell me how happy he was with the new employee. He indicated that the approach to problem solving and understanding shown during the interview was the same used by the candidate now on the job. You don't have to go to this extreme to get similar results for yourself. Discuss a problem that has just come up or an issue that needs to be resolved after the person comes on board. As long as the problem or issue is job-related, the subsequent discussion is a great way to assess planning and thinking skills.

➤ The DO–DO–DO–THINK Interview Pattern— the Key to Interviewing Accuracy

Some caveats are appropriate as you begin using the four-question interview approach. It's the combination of the significant accomplishments and visualization questions that make them so powerful. There are some great communicators who can visualize, but who have never actually done anything comparable. Consultants or staff people fall into this category. They're often bright, persuasive, and self-confident. This is a great combo, but an incomplete mix. They can tell you how to do it, but they have never done it before.

We placed a very bright MBA who had just finished a two-year tour with one of the top consulting firms in an industry job. His caseload had been impressive, and he had conducted high-level cost studies for two Fortune 100 manufacturing companies. He struggled in this new position, though. In his new role as a planning manager, he had to do many detailed, gritty analyses, wading through accounting detail. While important work, the lack of much conceptual planning, combined with the monthly routine, did him in. He was great at talking about and studying the problem, but not as effective at getting out with the functional departments and doing the real work. By combining the anchor and visualize questions, you'll be able to overcome this classic hiring problem.

Some behavioral interviewing experts don't like the situational nature of the visualization question. They contend that past behavior is the only accurate predictor of future behavior. In their minds, hypothetical questions are not valid. I agree with their concern when visualization questions are unrelated to the job. Job-related situational questions, however, are a great means to assess the required thinking skills used on the job. This type of situational question must be combined with a valid anchor to test complete competency.

The situational question minimizes the possibility of hiring someone who is not flexible, even though he or she has had some similar success in the past. I have met many apparently strong candidates who can effectively anchor performance objectives, but still sometimes fall short once on the job. No two jobs are identical. Some people don't have the ability to adapt their skills and experiences to new situations. They're more structured in their thinking, less adaptable, and often too analytical or rigid. By demonstrating an ability to apply knowledge in solving realistic job-specific problems, the visualization question minimizes this potential problem.

Some people are concerned that the anchor and visualize questioning pattern might give away company secrets. If this is the case, then just disguise the performance objectives with something ambiguous. For example, rather than describing your new e-commerce strategy in detail, be vague. One of our software clients watered down a specific game strategy to describe a broad, all-inclusive "edu-tainment" project. Just make sure the projects require the same kinds of personal attributes for success.

People sometimes express concern that they are telegraphing the answers to the candidate by openly describing the required performance objectives. I have not had this problem. While we're describing desired outcomes, we're not describing the desired process, nor the environment. The candidate needs to do this by describing comparable accomplishments. We also demand proof of competency. The anchor, visualizing, and fact-finding process we use validates the candidate's ability to do the work.

This approach works for all levels and different types of positions. If you are looking for a technical skill, some kind of test to demonstrate competency would be equivalent to an anchor. In a jewelry manufacturing company we've worked with, candidates are given pieces of jewelry to examine and asked to describe their quality level to test the candidate's eye for detail.

One of our engineering candidates for a consumer products company was asked to examine a detailed design drawing for adequacy. He was then asked how he would change the design to function better. This was a combination of the anchor and visualize approach. At a retail pet supply store, entry-level sales personnel, generally recent high school graduates, are asked how they would handle some typical customer complaints. Then they're asked to describe real examples of handling similar interpersonal conflicts. With this dual approach, the anchor and visualize pattern can be used to increase hiring accuracy for any type of position.

If there are many objectives, you'll never be able to complete all of your questioning during the first interview. I suggest you anchor the top two or three SMARTe performance objectives and conduct one visualization exercise. Leave the remaining for a subsequent interview or another interviewer. You can assign the assessment of specific SMARTe objectives to the person most impacted by it. For example, have the manufacturing manager interview a cost manager candidate, who would be required to improve the factory reporting system. Make sure that the interviewer knows he has to provide a written assessment of the candidate's ability or inability to do this work. Knowing that the write-up is a requirement helps minimize the initial emotional reaction of the interviewer to the applicant. This is important because these other interviewers won't have conducted a phone interview.

■ THE COMPLETE EIGHT-QUESTION INTERVIEW

While the four-question interview will give you a good understanding of candidate competency, there are a few additional questions I'd recommend to complete the assessment. The following POWER Hiring Eight-Question Interview (Figure 4.4) combines the four core questions with a formal opening and

POWERhiring®
Best Practices for Hiring Top Talent

The Basic 8-Question Interview

A Complete Performance-based Interview

Candidate:	Position:	Interviewer:	Date:

Use This Interview When the SMARTe Performance Objectives Are Known

The Deliverables - SMARTe Performance Objectives	Hot Tips and Fact-Finding Checklist
List SMART Objectives (Specific, Measurable, Action verb, Result, Time-bound) Example: *Improve product margins by 5% within 6 months.* 1. .... 2. .... 3. .... 4. .... Work-Type: ___ Technical ___ Organizer ___ Entrepreneur ____ Strategist/Creative Assign SMARTe Objectives to Work-Type and Indicate Dominant (1) and Secondary (2)	1. Be inquisitive. Get examples to turn generalities into specific responses. 2. Get trend of personal growth, energy, and team/management skills over time. 3. Listen 4X More Than Talk! Get this info for each accomplishment to validate it. - Get overview of the accomplishment. - Get actual title, size of team, titles of supervisor and subordinates, dates and duration of task. - Ask for bottom line, business impact. - Ask the candidate what his/her leadership role was - how did he/she develop program and implement it. - Find out the biggest challenges or most difficult aspects of the task. Ask "What constraints needed to be overcome?" - Ask "Why do you consider this a significant accomplishment?" - "What were the key steps and major deliverables involved in accomplishing the task?" - Ask "Describe the people challenges and give me some examples." - Get names and titles of staff and rank their performance. Get examples of how people were developed. - Get some examples when the candidate had to change the opinion of others and in dealing with conflict. - Ask "Was the task completed on time, and was this difficult?" - Ask "Why were you chosen for this role?" - "How would others (peers, subordinates, supervisors) describe you and your style?" - "How would you rank the overall success of the task and why?" - Ask "What was your real contribution or value-added to this project?" - "If you had a chance to do it over, what would you change?" - Ask "How did you grow or change as a result of this effort?"

Opening Question (Recruiting and Setting Performance Tone of Interview)

(First provide 1-2 minute overview of company and importance of job, and then ask...) *Please give me a quick overview of how your background and experience has prepared you for this type of leadership position.*

Benchmark Experience Question Pattern (ask these two questions for the past 2-3

Please give me a quick overview of your (current/prior) position and describe the biggest impact (change) you made (or when you took the initiative).	Describe your organization (draw org chart) and tell me how you developed, and managed your team (or tell me about some team project and describe your role).
Current/Most Recent Position - Title: Yrs:	
Prior Position #1 - Title: Yrs:	
Prior Position #2 - Title: Yrs:	

Figure 4.4 The eight-question interview template.

The Basic 8-Question Interview

Best Practices for Hiring Top Talent

A Complete Performance-based Interview

| Candidate: | Position: | Interviewer: | Date: |

Benchmark Performance (ask these two questions for each SMARTe objective)		Hot Tips - Assessing the Answers
ANCHOR: (State objective) *Describe your most similar past accomplishment.* Objective 1:	**VISUALIZE**: *How would you accomplish this task?* (O.K. for just top two objectives) Objective 1:	**Key:** Use fact-finding to learn everything about top 4-6 accomplishments and then use these tips to evaluate answers.
Objective 2:		**Work-Types**: Assign responses to these categories and compare to job needs:
	Objective 2:	- **Creative/Strategist**: long range, visionary, new ideas, concepts, strategy. - **Entrepreneur/Builder**: risk taker, fast-pace, persuasive, energetic. - **Improver/Organizer**: manager, upgrades, improves people and process. - **Technical/Producer**: analytical, detailed, quality, executes process.
Objective 3:		
Objective 4:		**Team and Management - ABC Rule**: Assign responses to Alone (individual contributor); Belonging (part of team); or in-Charge (as manager). Determine patterns and compare to job needs.
Character and Values (if not already answered) *Tell me about a time you were totally committed to a task.*		**Scope and Size - The 6S Rule**: During fact-finding evaluate companies and jobs according to - Span of control, Speed (pace of change), Sophistication, Standards of performance, Size, Scope and complexity of the work.
		Focus - Internal or External: Assign major accomplishments according to Building the Business - External, or Running the Business - Internal.
Personality and Cultural Fit *What three or four adjectives best describe your personality? Give me examples of when these have aided in the performance of your job and when they have hurt.*		**Breadth of Thinking**: Assign major accomplishments into Strategic (long range), Tactical (current), or Technical (process).
		Functional or Project Focus: Assign responses to task, department, function, multi-function, or total business.
Closing - Use this to create supply and determine interest *Although we're seeing some other fine candidates, I think you have a very strong background. We'll get back to you in a few days, but what are your thoughts now about this position?*		**Personality**: Look for honesty, self-awareness. **Close**: Don't go too fast. Make the job worth earning. Create competition to test true interest.

Summary and Assessment Notes	
Trend of Impact, Energy and Initiative - Up, Flat or Down	
ABC Rule for Team/Management Skills - Alone, Belonging, in-Charge	
Technical Competency and Ability to Learn - Strong, Adequate, or Weak	
Work-Type Fit - Dominant and Secondary Match, Partial, or None	
The 6S Rule Scope and Size of Prior Jobs- Comparable, too big, too	
Focus - Internal (Running the Business) or External (Building the	
Breadth of Thinking - Strategic, Tactical, Technical	
Functional or Project Focus- Task, department, function, multi-function	
Personality - Self-aware and open or misleading	

Figure 4.4 *(Continued)*

closing, one question that addresses character, and another that addresses true personality.

➤ The Opening Question—Controlling the Jitters on Both Sides of the Desk

On a recent survey we conducted with over 500 candidates, 80 percent indicated they were somewhat or very nervous. So don't dismiss candidates for nervousness during the first 30 minutes. If you conducted a phone interview or used one of the other techniques described in the previous chapter, you've already established some rapport, which will help. Some people suggest a warm-up, or get acquainted period, for a few minutes before the interview. I think this is unnecessary, although some casual conversation is appropriate. My approach is get right into the interview. Accept the fact that some candidates will be nervous, and don't judge their early responses too harshly. Work with them to provide better or more examples. Once a give-and-take rapport is established, even nervous candidates open up.

A manufacturing engineer I met a few years ago demonstrates this point. This fellow was so nervous, I thought he would fall out of his chair. It took about 10 minutes for him to calm down, but the changeover took place when he told me the specifics of an automation project. I had asked him to draw a sketch of a high-speed assembly device he was working on. Once he got into it, he was a changed person. Getting him to stop talking was the new challenge. I told the hiring manager to conduct the interview on the factory floor and talk about specific projects and problems right away. In his element—which wasn't interviewing—all traces of nervousness were eliminated.

Accept the fact that nobody likes to interview and that a nervous candidate is just a nervous candidate. Don't assume this is related to performance. If you still have a problem after about a half hour, move on to the next person on the list.

The most common opening question, "Tell me about yourself," is too big and broad. You give up too much, too soon, to the candidate. There are better approaches that establish the framework we need for both an effective performance-based interview and applicant control. We suggest the following opening question format:

As you know, we're looking for a (position). Let me give you a quick overview of the importance of this position. (Give two-minute overview of position and company.) Tell me how your background has prepared you for this type of important position.

While this is a "Tell me about yourself" type of question, it narrows the focus down by requesting only relevant background information. Further, it establishes a recruiting opening by describing the importance of the job. When you make the job compelling, applicants tell you more about themselves. They sell you, rather than your having to sell them. This establishes the framework for good recruiting. Don't spend more than a few minutes on this pitch. There's a tendency to talk too much to open an interview, which is a waste of time. One or two minutes is all that's necessary to set the tone. Remember to listen four times more than you talk. A good interview is a fact-finding mission, not a sales pitch. For instance:

We're looking for a product manager. This person will lead the implementation effort on much of our new product introduction program. This is a critical initiative for next year with new products representing 10 percent of new sales. We need someone who can coordinate the efforts of engineering, marketing, manufacturing, and sales to bring this new line out on time and within budget. Give me a quick overview of how your background has prepared you for this type of position.

This question is a great warm-up. Don't forget the fact-finding. You might not want to start this too soon, but you want to establish a communication style that allows you to get enough information to validate the candidate's initial responses. A lot will depend on the candidate's style of presenting information. Work with the candidate on this. I openly tell candidates that I'm more concerned with specific examples about a few major accomplishments than lots of broad generalities. Quiet candidates open up more when constantly asked for more examples, and louder candidates stop generalizing and start to focus.

■ UNLOCK CHARACTER—A KEY TO LONG-TERM SUCCESS

Character and personality are always revealed through performance. Sometimes you just have to probe deeply to discover it. To get at these important traits more quickly, it's best to address them directly.

My favorite character question has to do with commitment. *"Tell me about a time you were totally committed to a task."* This quickly gets at the heart of character. The ability to persevere under difficult conditions is an essential trait of top performers. It's the character component of energy. It's easier to work hard under ideal conditions than difficult situations. Real character is better observed in less than ideal circumstances. Use fact-finding techniques to understand the true extent of the applicant's commitment to the task and the underlying environment. Determine the challenges faced and the results achieved. Listen to the response and determine if the success was individual, team, or company. Find out why the candidate felt strongly about the accomplishment.

Throughout the performance-based interview, we focus on energy, self-motivation, and the ability to achieve results comparable to the job needs. Use this commitment question to validate all of the applicant's previous accomplishments. Examine the response to determine the scope and complexity of the jobs the candidate has held. Look for a pattern of commitment and the examples of significant accomplishments. While this approach doesn't cover every aspect of character, it covers the most important.

A controller candidate told me about his role in helping rebuild his manufacturing plant that was partially destroyed by the 1994 Northridge, California, earthquake. To get the plant up and running, he described two weeks of around-the-clock work and another few months of extended hours. He said this was the most satisfying experience he had ever had. The camaraderie and team spirit kept him and the others going through some very difficult times. While a strong financial type, it was this team orientation and sense of commitment that made him exceptional.

You also might use the character question if you're unsure about a candidate or have a candidate you think might be weak. Often the response to this will eliminate a marginal candidate or revive one you thought lost. This question should be used in the later part of the interview when candidates are likely to be more candid with you. You have to stay open-minded, though. If you've already made a decision, the answer will have little value. Although it's very difficult to override your own internal decision once made, always use this question on commitment to validate your judgment. The answer can sometimes be powerful enough to overcome even the most strongly held beliefs.

■ HOW TO DISCOVER PERSONALITY AND CULTURAL FIT

By the time you measure personality and cultural fit—at the end of the interview—you'll already know the answer. After the interview, you'll have explored at least five or six different accomplishments in depth. Personality, interpersonal skills, and management style will come out of this assessment. Personality in an absolute sense is unimportant. How candidates have used their personality and style in achieving results is what's really important. You'll have discovered this with the impact and leadership and anchor and visualize questioning patterns, and the fact-finding techniques we've suggested. Use this question to confirm your insight and add a few more specifics:

> *What three or four adjectives best describe your personality? Give me actual examples of when these traits have aided you in the performance of your job and when they have hurt.*

A candidate who knows himself or herself will be able to quickly list a few critical traits and provide some good examples. Many of these traits should have been discussed previously. If they seem inconsistent with your own evaluation, do some probing to uncover the differences. Raise the caution flag if the candidate seems evasive or if you notice extremes of behavior. Look for flexibility. If the person appears overly dominant, ask for examples of coaching, patience, and team skills. For the overly analytical person, probe for examples of team skills and the ability to persuade others. People who are the supportive type often have difficulty making tough decisions. Explore for this. The outgoing salesperson is often weak on details. Don't reach this conclusion without getting some examples of analytical work. Good candidates are sometimes excluded because they don't seem to fit the required personality profile. You'll get at flexibility in personality by looking for the candidate's apparently missing parts.

Also, look for growth. I often ask candidates to describe how their personality has changed over the years. This gets at maturity. A former arrogant MBA from one of the nation's top B-schools told me how he became more sensitive to others after working with a tight team on an extended crash project. Of course, I got the specific details of the project to confirm his makeover. I'm always the skeptic in the face of some smooth-talking professional.

Look for candor. It might be time to raise the caution flag if the candidate can't openly describe some failures. The second part of the question is revealing: *"Give me examples of when your personality has hurt your performance."* Don't ignore this part. Continue probing. Be concerned if you get a run-around, or some vague response. Good answers here are also a sign of character.

A few years ago, a sales manager told me he was sometimes too rough on his team, particularly when they were falling short of quota. He told me his New York personality sometimes got the best of him. He knew this was a weakness, but he said he hadn't lost any good people as a result. His solution was to work more closely with his people in developing monthly objectives, so that they were equally committed to the results. Previously, he didn't get into the details as much; therefore, he didn't understand his team members' specific strengths and weaknesses. Getting this close to the process was unnatural for him because he was more the entrepreneur, but it was helping him become a better manager and less confrontational. He became more proactive than reactive as a result. I'm sure the hard-driving personality is still there, but by adapting to a more analytical style, this manager was able to compensate for a potentially fatal flaw.

You can't really separate personality from performance. Personality is naturally revealed with the fact-finding and probing techniques discussed earlier. You might want to add more emphasis to personality if this is a major area of concern. You can even make it a SMARTe performance objective. For example, one of my clients was looking for a property manager with good interpersonal skills. It turned out that the real problem was with a very demanding owner who required 100 percent attention to his every whim. We created a SMARTe objective that stated, "Set up a quick response support program to deal with a very aggressive and demanding property owner." The candidate had to have the personality to deal with these kinds of people, but it was more than just having good interpersonal skills.

The ability to handle and resolve conflict with other departments or with difficult people is the most common type of issue we've seen that requires a real attention to personality. During the interview, get some examples of how the candidate handled similar interpersonal problems. This gets at a specific area of personality. Personality is important, but by measuring it through performance and again at the end of the interview, you'll be in a better position to understand its importance in getting the job done.

■ THE CLOSE—USE RECRUITING TO END ROUND ONE

You can use this classic ending to the first interview for all candidates, but it's essential for those that you think will make the initial cut. This starts the formal recruiting process.

Although we're seeing some other candidates, I personally think you have a very fine background. We'll get back to you in a few days, but what are your thoughts now about this position?

Three essential things occurred with this close.

First, you created supply. Good jobs are more attractive when other good people are being considered. Jobs are not only less desirable when no one else is being considered, but also you lose control of the interview, because the candidate now knows he is the only one in the loop. Create competition. Make sure you never tell the applicant you have no other candidates. This is a sure-fire way to pay more than you need to or lose the only candidate you have.

I remember an engineering VP telling a manufacturing manager candidate that she was the only good candidate he had seen. When we tried to close the candidate, she demanded, and got, another 15 percent. Everyone else on the interviewing committee knew what to say, but we forgot to give this VP the guidelines. Subsequently, the plant manager, who was the hiring manager, tried to take this unnecessary salary increase out of the engineering budget.

The second point in this closing question is that you create demand by expressing sincere interest in the candidate. A compliment goes a long way. Candidates think more about why they want a job when told they are well-liked and qualified. They think about why they're not going to get it when the ending is left neutral or flat. By itself, *"We'll get back to you in a few days,"* is the classic kiss of death; so never use it, particularly for those you like.

The reason for asking the candidate for a response to the job is to gauge true interest level. The supply and demand prefaces are used as set-ups to obtain this in an unbiased fashion. Get candidates to openly discuss their thoughts, feelings, and concerns. Suggest they call you back with other questions after they've thought the situation over. It's important to establish this open dialogue as soon as possible with all of the potential finalists. As you'll see in the chapter on recruiting, this is the key to smoother negotiations and closing.

If a candidate you like is not interested, it's important to understand his or her concerns. Most often, good candidates don't immediately see the merits of a job. They need more strategic information or just have to digest what they've heard. Don't push it. Make sure you take the time to explore their issues, but don't attempt to resolve them right away. Your objective is only to keep the lines of discussion open. Tell the candidate you'd like to get back to him or her in a few days for further discussion. Suggest that at that time, you'll be able to give a different perspective on the job, but first you want to finish interviewing all the candidates. Indicate that if the candidate does want to come back for a second interview, there will be another series of interviews. State that only after the complete assessment will the candidate truly understand the scope and importance of the position. Your objective with reluctant candidates is to get them to stay open-minded and come back for another series of interviews.

■ "JUST THE FACTS, MA'AM"— FACT-FINDING: THE MOST IMPORTANT INTERVIEWING TECHNIQUE

The interviewing approach we recommend is more a methodology than a list of clever questions. We've discovered that the questions themselves are less important than the quality of the information obtained. Get lots of information about the candidate's top five or six major accomplishments. This is all that's necessary to make an accurate hiring decision. The key for each accomplishment is to understand the results achieved, the process used to achieve the results, and the environment in which those results took place.

One of my candidates told me her greatest accomplishment was in never making a hiring mistake. She told me she clearly understood the work that needed to get done, she didn't initially care whether she liked or disliked the candidate, and she spent the first interview only getting examples, facts, and figures to verify a candidate's past performance. This is the way interviewing and hiring needs to be done.

To reinforce the point, I turned the tables on her and asked her how many people she hired, their positions, their names, how they performed after starting, the impact they made, and specifics regarding her role in their personal development. She got a laugh from this, but it was my inquisitive approach that

---

The difference between good answers and bad hiring decisions lies with fact-finding.

proved that her hiring accomplishments were real and worthy of note.

The difference between good answers and bad hiring decisions lies with fact-finding. The "most significant accomplishment" question is simple to ask. Fact-finding is what makes the answer meaningful. An added benefit is that fact-finding naturally minimizes exaggeration. There is a tendency on the part of candidates to overstate or mislead, either through outright fraud or generalizations. Fact-finding gets at reality. By asking for specific examples to support any generalization, you force the candidate to justify a response. Ask why, when, with whom, how long, and how. Get enough information for you to really understand the applicant's actual involvement in the task. Find out critical decision points, what went wrong, the resources available and how they were allocated, the strategies, the tactics, and who made the decisions. Stay low key. Don't get frustrated and contentious if the candidate doesn't immediately open up. Be inquisitive, not inquisitorial. Most interviewers ask too many general questions. A few questions with lots of fact-finding is a better approach.

Turn generalities into specifics by getting examples of everything.

Always convert generalities to specifics by using this basic question to start the fact-finding process: *"Can you give me a specific example describing what you mean?"* This should be the most frequently used follow-up question in your interviewing tool kit. Use it to get behind any generality or statement. If someone says that he or she has great technical skills, is very creative, is a real team player, or is a problem solver, ask for examples. Use this technique often. It will be the key to real understanding. While certain candidates generalize to cloud reality, some do so as a result of upbringing. Some cultures minimize the role of the individual and have been instructed to not talk about themselves. Fact-finding will help clarify this.

Fact-finding can be the bridge that improves communications and understanding. I recently met a very articulate and professional woman seeking a human resources management position. She said that her greatest accomplishment was to establish a framework and direction for the department. After asking for a clarifying example, it turned out she based this conclusion on updating the policy and procedures manual for her company. This was an important, but not glorious, task that took about three months of part-time work. A financial manager who stated he was a great manager was somewhat sheepish when asked to name the five best people he's ever hired and describe why. He could name only one over a five-year period. A soft-spoken, bearded engineering manager whom I was about to exclude because he did not seem assertive enough started to tell me about a crash program he had led to commercial success. He described the late nights and motivational talks to his engineering team. I can still hear his enthusiasm and energy. In the words of Sgt. Joe Friday on the early television show *Dragnet*, "Just the facts, ma'am." That's all you need, too.

■ PREPARATION IS THE KEY

A good part of interviewing has to do with avoiding dumb mistakes. The other part has to do with determining if the candidate can do the work. If you understand the job and can control the urge to decide too soon, the candidate assessment part is straightforward. Preparation is the key. Don't wait until the candidate is in the lobby.

If you have an upcoming interview, read the resume again, even if you've already conducted a phone interview. If you haven't conducted a phone interview, it's even more important to reread the resume. Somebody has already made the decision for you to talk to or meet this candidate. Figure out why. Circle the strengths and put big plus marks next to them. Asterisks and minus signs also help. During the interview, you'll ask for specific examples to validate strengths and clarify concerns. Don't forget that much work has already gone into the effort to arrange this first interview. It can all be lost in the first few moments if you don't carry the momentum.

Reread the performance profile and review the SMARTe performance objectives. These performance objectives cover every aspect of the job—major objectives, interim objectives, problems that need to be solved, changes to be made, team issues, management and organizational issues, and technical needs. You'll be benchmarking candidate competency against these top six to eight deliverables.

When you finally get into the interview, the candidate will know how prepared you are. Top people want to work for professionals, those who have high standards of performance, who know the job, who aren't overselling or too emotional, and who know how to listen. Floundering interviewers turn off the best candidates. Always assume you'll be meeting a top candidate. This will help get you into the right frame of mind.

I lost a great candidate once because the interviewer, the vice president of operations, was unprepared and began talking too much, asking meaningless questions, and selling too soon. Right after the interview, the candidate called to remove herself from contention. Her personality and experience level were impressive, and she felt that the hiring manager made too quick an assessment based on a few superficial facts. She told me his understanding of the job was vague and superficial, and she didn't want to work for someone who could make an important decision so quickly. This is a good warning.

The interview process we're proposing and the preparation needed to pull it off increase objectivity and validate competency. In addition, this process gains candidate interest. All three—objectivity, competency, and interest—are critical if you want to improve your hiring effectiveness.

■ THE TELEPHONE INTERVIEW SETS THE STAGE FOR THE CANDIDATE AND THE INTERVIEWER

To minimize the impact of first impressions, conduct a quick phone interview before you meet the candidate. The phone interview will help minimize the visual aspects of the first impression before you meet in a one-on-one session. On the phone, ask the candidate to describe his or her most significant accomplishments at previous jobs. Get some specific details about each. This is the impact question. Next, ask him or her to describe the biggest team he or she has managed. Ask for a description of the organization chart and specific job titles of his or her subordinate staff. Find out how the candidate built and developed this team and what it accomplished. This is the team leadership question.

Finally, anchor at least one of the most important SMARTe performance objectives. Use a little fact-finding to validate the responses. If the candidate passes this screen, invite him or her in for a personal interview. I always ask candidates to be prepared to discuss their most important team and individual accomplishments, sometimes even suggesting a written summary as an addendum to the resume. A half-page for each accomplishment is enough. This helps the candidate respond to your questions. In addition, the effort in writing the accomplishments provides some insight into interest and writing skills. The performance-based phone interview by itself will help minimize the impact of first impressions when you meet. The accomplishment write-up is an added touch that will speed the assessment process along.

■ WHAT NOT TO ASK—THE INAPPROPRIATE AND ILLEGAL QUESTIONS

At the beginning of a seminar this past year, one of the attendees complained that one of the causes of hiring problems was an inability to ask personal questions. Another person affirmed this, and in rapid-fire sequence asked what questions she wasn't allowed to ask. My response to both was that you don't ever need to ask a personal, compromising, or illegal question to conduct a great assessment. I went on to say, "if a question doesn't pertain to job performance, don't ever ask it." You won't gain any more insight. Performance is all that matters.

While this is a good general rule to follow, knowing what's illegal and what's not can keep you out of trouble. Some guidelines covering most of the basic issues follow, but contact your human resources or legal advisor for more details.

Don't Ever Ask About the Following:

> ➤ A candidate's age or anything related that can determine it, like "When were you in the army?"

➤ Race, nationality, or related issues, or anything that can determine it. Something like "Where do you live?" is an inappropriate question.

➤ Clubs, social groups, sexual preference, or religion. Avoid questions like "How do you spend your spare time?" or similar questions that pry at a candidate's personal life. It's okay if the candidate volunteers the information, but don't solicit it.

➤ Anything about the candidate's arrest record. Being arrested is not the same as being convicted for a crime, so avoid this line of questioning. You can ask about a candidate's felony convictions and the details.

➤ Children or family issues, now or in the future. Don't even attempt to bring this up. If the candidate begins talking about his or her family, it's okay to respond, but don't pry.

This is a sample of illegal questions. There are others, but they're all in the same family. Get legal advice if you're unsure, but the key is to avoid all personal questions. There are plenty of performance-based questions to ask that will give you valuable insight into a candidate's ability to perform the work. Personal questions won't give you a clue, and asking them could compromise your whole hiring program.

Don't be afraid to ask questions if they relate to the needs of the job. You're certainly allowed to ask about the candidate's academic background, if it's job related, just don't ask for the graduation date. If travel or extended hours are important, ask the candidate directly if he or she can travel or work unusual hours; however, don't ask about the family. You can inquire about professional groups and certifications. These relate to specific job qualifications and they're appropriate.

➤ To Comply with the ADA (Americans with Disabilities Act)

The Americans with Disabilities Act (ADA) prohibits discriminating against an applicant with a disability who is otherwise able to perform the essential requirements of the job.

The employer might need to make some modifications to the workplace to address some of the candidate's needs, if the person is otherwise capable, but there is no need to lower the performance standards of the job as defined by the SMARTe objectives. (This topic was introduced in Chapter 2 on performance-based job descriptions.) You may ask the person with a disability how he or she would meet these performance needs of the job given the disability. For example, asking a person who is using a wheelchair how he or she would conduct an operational audit of a manufacturing plant is appropriate, if this is a critical part of the job. Make sure these performance objectives are essential and don't generalize the physical requirements. This is something I see often. If the performance objective requires the employee to work with personal computers, don't require that he or she lift one. This has nothing to do with job performance.

■ THE PERFORMANCE-BASED INTERVIEW TIES ALL OF THE PIECES OF THE PUZZLE TOGETHER

Good interviewing skills are only one part of an effective hiring process. You need to know the work, control your emotions, have enough good candidates to interview, and be a great recruiter. All of these factors are integrated into the eight-question performance-based interview. The SMARTe performance objectives define the work in a compelling manner and reinforce the recruiting aspect of the closing question. The structured questions, when combined with good fact-finding, increase objectivity. Taking notes and listening are all essential to an accurate assessment. Practice these skills on all candidates. This is the only way you'll become proficient. The process itself will impact sourcing. You may find some great candidates you would have eliminated and some weak candidates you initially thought were stars. This is what the learning process is all about.

At some point, you'll recognize that the questions are not the important part of the interview. Objectivity, probing, fact-finding, and skepticism, combined with a thorough knowledge of the performance needs of the job, are all it really takes. You'll know your reprogramming is complete when you reach this stage.

POWER HIRING HOT TIPS—CONDUCTING A PERFORMANCE-BASED INTERVIEW

✔ Review the SMARTe performance objectives before each interview. These set the standards and guide the selection process. They're also the compelling vision of the job required for good recruiting.

✔ Read and annotate the resume. Know the candidate's strengths and weaknesses before the interview.

✔ Conduct a 20-minute preliminary phone interview before meeting the candidate. This will eliminate unqualified applicants sooner and minimize emotions for those you meet.

✔ Ask the candidate to submit a short addendum to their resume describing one team and one individual accomplishment. This quickly establishes the performance-based nature of the interview.

✔ It's the *answers,* not the questions that count. Be a fact-finder. Turn generalities into specifics. Get examples and quantify everything. Ask for facts, figures, dates, names, and measurements. This will reduce exaggeration and validate responses. It will also quickly minimize candidate nervousness.

✔ Be skeptical. Interviewing is a fact-finding mission, not a popularity contest. As long as you know what you're looking for, don't give up until you find it. As long as the job is great, great candidates won't mind.

✔ Get examples of impact and team or management projects for each past job. This lets you measure and compare the core success traits of energy (motivation, initiative) and team leadership over an extended period of time.

✔ Anchor and Visualize each SMARTe objective to determine job-specific competency. This directly measures the candidate's ability to apply past performance and talent to meet future objectives.

✔ Get examples of commitment to gain insight into character.

(continued)

✔ Find out how personality has hindered performance to better understand personality. You'll also see growth, candor, and character development.

✔ Maintain applicant control. This is important as you recruit. State your sincere interest, create competition, and then ask the candidate to state his or her interest.

Chapter 5

Work-Type Profiling: Matching Skills and Interests with Job Needs

I cannot commend to a business any artificial plan for making people produce. You must lead them through their own self-interest. It is this alone that will keep them keyed to the full capacity of their ability.

Charles H. Steinway

■ GREAT MANAGEMENT STARTS BY TAPPING INTO THE ENERGY AND MOTIVATION OF OTHERS

It's obvious that people work harder and achieve better results when they're doing work that gives them a great deal of personal satisfaction. Conversely, applying extra energy over the long term is difficult if a person doesn't find it enjoyable. To maximize the quality of every hiring decision, it's important to match the critical performance aspects of the job with a candidate's ability and true interests. This way, you tap into self-motivation and drive. This is what great management and the concept of energy[2] is all about.

We've developed a technique that directly addresses this important issue. We call it work-type profiling. With this new assessment technique, we're able to better match a candidate's

interests and competencies with the SMARTe performance objectives of the job. If you've ever hired a great person for the
wrong job, you've encountered the problem of hiring competent, but unmotivated people. These are the people who are
bright, capable, and often energetic, but exerting themselves
only part of the time. While they're praised now and then for
some great work, the missed deadlines and marginal perform-
ances on critical aspects of the job are constant reminders of a
poor hiring decision.

A painful search comes to mind. A few years ago in the tele-
com boom, we placed a marketing executive who was great at
strategy, but uninterested in management and organizational
issues. He lasted only six months. Strategy development was
the number one SMARTe objective. The candidate was great at
this, and we had examples to prove his interest and capability.
However, during the interview we accepted generalities for the
management tasks, which were number three or four on the
list of required performance objectives. He didn't like the management tasks, even though he was reasonably competent. We
didn't care; he was a great strategist. The candidate quickly got
the strategy issues under control, impressing the board and
management team with his prowess. With this problem solved,
building and managing the team became the number one performance objective. He failed miserably. Working with the
team was of little interest. He wanted to get back to more strategy issues. If we had conducted a thorough work-type profile, it
would have been obvious that the candidate was competent,
but not motivated by the management aspects of the job.

■ THERE ARE ONLY FOUR TYPES OF JOBS IN THE WHOLE WORLD

Over the past 25 years, I've been involved with hundreds of different types of jobs. These have run the gamut from the technical to the creative, and from entry level to chairman. From this
experience, it became evident that work could be divided into
four distinct and fundamentally different work-types. These
are an adaptation of the more familiar "technical, manager,
leader" or "process, tactics, strategy" categorizations found in

many management texts. Work-types combine these and address the dynamics and flow of work a little more precisely. For these reasons, the work-type categorization is better suited for our purposes. The four types are summarized next.

➤ The Creator or Strategist

All work begins with the creator or strategist, and the people who do best here are those with a future perspective. These are the people with vision, who look ahead. It's the idea phase, the world of concepts and future plans. People in these jobs do everything from developing new products to coming up with ideas for new business opportunities. We call people who are at home in this phase the visionaries, consultants, strategists, or creators. While their jobs may differ in content, they all see opportunities before everyone else.

➤ The Entrepreneur or Builder

The idea becomes reality with the entrepreneur or builder. On a small scale, it could be the salesperson closing the deal or someone starting a new business or ramping up for a major project. These are the risk takers. They tend to be more dominant and more individualistic. They're great at persuading and pushing, often in the face of insurmountable odds. We call people who like this intense world of rapid change entrepreneurs, developers, dealmakers, builders, or turnaround specialists.

➤ The Improver or Organizer

The improver or organizer runs the day-to-day business—the world of tactics, plans, and implementation. These are the managers, improvers, planners, and organizers who make the organization work better. Their focus is on upgrading and improving the processes and people that deliver the goods and services of a company. While change is gradual, the activity is broad, addressing people, systems, resources, and all of the interrelated activities. These people make companies run better.

➤ The Producer or Technician

The work really gets done with the people who produce high-quality work to sustain the business. Their focus is at the process, procedure, or transaction level. The key is the application of a skill or technical proficiency in producing a product or service. Process control, quality, technical competence, and detail drive their work. These people run equipment, design products, administer processes, and analyze results. In a broad sense, we label them producers, technicians, analysts, or administrators.

➤ The Ebb and Flow of Work-Types and Life Cycles

The four work-types represent a distinct flow of activity from the idea phase to startup, and then shifting into a managed growth phase and ultimately into a sustaining mode. The cycle then begins again. This is the normal life cycle of a product or a business as shown in Figure 5.1.

In a thriving business, all of these activities are pursued concurrently. New products or projects are being started, older ones are being updated or discarded. Some jobs and functions require all of these skills, others just one. We have taken this simple concept and applied it to the hiring process to improve the quality of the assessment. Most people tend to hire in their

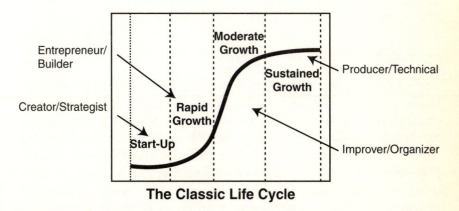

Figure 5.1 The classic life cycle of work.

own image. We intuitively match traits in ourselves as we assess candidates. Frequently, these traits fall within these four
work-type profiles. Entrepreneurs hire other entrepreneurs,
even if the job requires management skills. Managers hire
other managers, even if the job requires detailed analytical
skills. This is why we frequently hire people who are good in a
few aspects of the job, but not across the board. Sometimes
these mismatches are the cause of catastrophic failure.

Work-type profiling is a great technique to bridge the gap between the analytical fact-finding mode and the intuitive hiring
decision. It allows the interviewer to remove himself or herself
and all biases from the evaluation. This is a critical step. Only
then can the job itself become the dominant focus of the selection process, rather than the person making the assessment.[1]

■ DEFINE THE JOB USING WORK-TYPES TO BRIDGE THE GAP BETWEEN THE JOB AND THE CANDIDATE

In most performance profiles, one or two work-types stand out
as dominant. For technical jobs, it's usually the technical or
creative work-type. If there's a management component, the
organizer will stand out, usually with the technical. For senior
executives, it's typically the strategy need combined with the
manager/organizer. For sales jobs, start-ups, or a major project
launch, the entrepreneurial style dominates. Once this work-
type profile is defined, our objective is to find candidates
whose accomplishments and interests match these job needs.

A well-written performance profile, combined with good
listening skills and some talking, is all that's necessary to start
the process of work-type profiling. As you conduct your fact-
finding, listen for the specific words used to describe how the
candidate describes his or her role. This is summarized in the
sidebar for each of the work-types. Most jobs are characterized
by one dominant work-type. For example, accountants tend to
fall in the technical work-type, and artists, in the creative
work-type. Some of the examples provided in the tables will
help clarify this as you assess candidates. Use the key phrase
section as you listen to the candidate's response. You'll then be
able to assign the candidate's major accomplishments into

Assign Candidate Responses to These Work-Type Profiles

Work-Type	Producer or Technical Process Oriented	Improver/Organizer Manager
Definition	High-quality, process and procedure oriented, maintains, sustains, supervises, or executes. Conservative and detail-oriented. Technically focused. These people work from the process outward. The process determines the result. Any field that has an important technical foundation (engineering, accounting, law) tends to breed this work-type. They're more analytical and detail oriented than intuitive. Generally they want a clear picture with details of where they're going before starting. Often an individual contributor at the technical level. Can be too structured in their thinking. Sometimes they're inflexible.	Upgrades, organizes, changes and/or manages existing operations. Is a planner and team-oriented. This is the core of the "organizational man." These people have balanced egos, tend to be risk averse, they bring order out of chaos, they see issues from a pragmatic standpoint and know how to plan to meet an objective. They are better at cleaning up and running a business rather than starting something from scratch. Their focus is on improving or upgrading the infrastructure—the people, systems, facilities, and resources.
Key Phrases: Listen for these in the candidate's response	Quality, details, technical skills, craftsman, design, evaluate, analyze, probe, fact-find, test, produce, repair, supervise, sustain, maintain, learning, teach	Organize, plan, practical, budget, pragmatic, tactical, focus on existing operations, manage group/team, coordinate resources, upgrade, improve, change, persuade, compromise, realistic
Typical Jobs	Accountant, administrator, lawyer, engineer, doctor, clerical, supervisor, auditor, facilitator, teacher, machine operator, maintenance worker, mechanic, quality control, security guard, mail carrier, software developer	Manager, jobs requiring organization, planner, project manager, tactician, product manager, implementer, director

these same work-types. This is how you'll match job needs with the candidate's abilities and interests. The summary table for the Technical and Improver work-types is shown on page 133.

As you listen to the responses, you'll assign the accomplishments to work-types. Most people are strong in one or two work-types, rarely all of them. Flexibility across work-types is important for managers and team leaders. The words and phrases a candidate uses are as insightful as the accomplishments described. Look at the key phrase section. These will help guide you to the right work-type category. For example, a candidate might describe a major accomplishment as: "upgraded the manufacturing performance reporting system." This sounds like an organizer-type task. Use the key word phrases to confirm the candidate's true role. It's possible he or she did the long-range planning for the task, or liked the fact that it needed to get completed under some tight time constraints. This could change the project into a strategic or entrepreneurial job. Work-type profiling allows you to better understand the nature of work from a different perspective. This will be useful not only in hiring, but also in assigning projects to your current team members.

The summary table for the entrepreneurial and strategy/ creative work-types is shown on page 135.

■ MATCHING SMARTe OBJECTIVES TO WORK-TYPE PROFILES TO UNDERSTAND WHAT DRIVES SUCCESS

Some SMARTe objectives for a few typical jobs are shown on page 136. We've categorized the first group into work-types. Review these and then try your hand at the second group to see where they fit. This will give you practice. The answers are in the last column.

As defined, the machinist is clearly a technically oriented and individual contributor position. For the best fit, you'll want to avoid candidates who are more management focused or want to develop new methods. The CEO objectives are typical. These leadership roles usually require a forward-looking strategist with a strong manager able to build winning teams. This financial analyst needs good technical skills plus an ability

Work-Type	Builder/Entrepreneurial Rapid Change	Creator/Strategist Visionary — Consultants
Definition	Implements the big ideas or one-time projects, impatient and risk-oriented. These people like multiple projects, they're fast-paced, deal well with ambiguity and tend to be individualistic. They don't like details, and follow-up is often weak. They'd much rather build the business than run it. Jobs range from the individual salesperson hustling to make a deal, to the more sophisticated Trump-like developer. These are the people who bring ideas into reality and get them rolling, but soon they want to move on to something else. Often dominant.	Focused on long-range or future development. Idea- and concept-oriented. These people are the consultants, visionaries, strategists, R&D leaders, the creative and long-range planners. They're into new products, research, the creative side of marketing and think about the future more than the present, sometimes too much. As a result, these people can be impractical. They can take different information and see alternatives others can't see. It's the visionary part of leadership.
Key Phrases: Listen for these in the candidate's response	Sell, close, fast-paced, convince, persuade, argue, make deals, rain-maker, build from scratch, develop, promote, improvise, make-it-happen, focus on implementing ideas/concepts, impatient, risk-oriented, individualistic	Creative, intuitive, new ideas, develop, long-range strategy, conceptual, consultant, staff work, research, theoretical, focus on future
Typical Jobs	Salesman, entrepreneurs, new products manager, turn-around specialist, venture capitalist, deal makers, real-estate developers, jobs with risk or rapid change, closer, rainmaker.	Researcher, consultants, long-range planners, business advisors, R&D, strategists, creative, marketing, jobs with a long-range focus, web designers, business development

SMARTe Objectives Categorized by Work-Type

Job Title	SMARTe Objectives	Work-Type
Engineer	➤ Design hydroelectric valves.	Technical/Producer
	➤ Develop new ASICS circuit design tools.	Creator/Strategist
Accounting Manager	➤ Improve the closing process.	Improver/Organizer
	➤ Review state sales tax system for compliance.	Technical/Producer
Software Developer	➤ Debug code for complex module.	Technical/Producer
	➤ Lead team to develop new database system.	Improver/Organizer
Brand Manager	➤ Develop marketing strategy for new category.	Creator/Strategist
	➤ Launch product rapidly to meet narrow window.	Entrepreneur/Market Builder
Secretary	➤ Implement weekly mail merge to key accounts.	Technical/Producer
	➤ Maintain and coordinate all travel programs.	Technical/Producer
Sales VP	➤ Set up sales training system.	Improver/Organizer
	➤ Develop the annual sales plan and strategy program.	Creator/Strategist
Materials Manager	➤ Implement the new MRPII system.	Improver/Organizer
	➤ Evaluate and upgrade the staff.	Improver/Organizer

to interpret the results, which requires some forward-thinking, strategy component. The vice president of information systems must combine good technical skills with the vision to plan ahead (the strategist). The national accounts manager has to combine some detail fact-finding (the technical) with the actual process of getting the business (the entrepreneur) and starting a new team (organizer).

Sometimes these requirements conflict and it's difficult to find candidates who meet all the criteria. The financial analyst

Try this group out for yourself:

Job Title	SMARTe Objectives	Fill in the Work-Type
Machinist	➤ Produce high-quality molding tools. ➤ Debug molds on first article inspection.	
CEO	➤ Create a strategy to penetrate market. ➤ Build a professional team and organization.	
Financial Analyst	➤ Prepare monthly operations analysis review. ➤ Interpret impact of price changes on market share.	
VP Information System	➤ Evaluate all existing systems and processes. ➤ Develop long-range IS plan for growth.	
National Accounts Manager	➤ Identify key potential accounts. ➤ Contact and close five new accounts. ➤ Build and manage team of new salespeople.	

is a good example. It's hard to find people who are detail-oriented, yet can also understand how these results will impact the business. The same is true for the national accounts manager. This person is expected to do everything—manage, sell, and conduct detailed analysis. If you're having trouble finding a good fit, it might be better to split the job up to take advantage of strengths in one area, compensating for weaknesses in another. Think about restructuring jobs this way especially if the most important performance objectives are in different work-type categories. Although there are people who can be strong at both, finding the ideal candidate might not be worth the extra time needed.

The key is the ability to clearly define the work that needs to get done through the SMARTe objective process. Then assign each of the SMARTe objectives into its appropriate work-type.

As you interview and select candidates, make sure they are motivated by the long-term work that needs to get done. While the specific SMARTe objectives will change regularly, the work-type requirements will be more long lived. Whether selecting new candidates to hire or assigning work to your team members, work-type profiling provides a simple means to tap into personal energy and competence.

■ THREE VERY REVEALING QUESTIONS: FINDING OUT WHAT CANDIDATES LIKE TO DO

You can determine a candidate's competency to do the work using the four core performance questions. Sometimes people outgrow the type of work they've done for a number of years, so it's important to evaluate motivation. The key to good hiring is to find people who continually apply extra energy and initiative to their work. This is an essential aspect of all high performers. To tap into this energy source on a long-term basis, it's necessary to make sure that both competencies and preferences are in alignment. Three simple questions you can add to your interviewing arsenal that address this vital area follow:

1. Think about a favorite work experience, something you felt was exciting, energizing, and personally fulfilling. Please describe it and tell me why it was personally satisfying.

2. You've indicated to me that you're a real problem solver. Can you give me three examples of the types of problems you like to solve?

3. This job requires a real self-starter. Can you please give me three examples of initiative in one of your more recent positions? This would be something you did over and above the requirements of the job.

These three questions get directly at the issue of positive, sustainable, personal energy. The work described motivates and fulfills the candidate. If you can tap into that energy, the person will be unstoppable. The questions are free-choice questions the candidate is free to answer any way he or she wants by giving open examples of accomplishments. Comparing these responses to those given in the four core past performance questions allows us to match preferences and competencies. Many times the accomplishments used as examples will be the same. That's great. It means competencies and preferences are similar. If they're not, and they represent different work-types, you have a potential problem. Probe a little harder. Find out what really drives the candidate to excel. If the job can be structured to take advantage of this and not compromise some other critical area, both you and the candidate win. Let's examine each question in turn to better understand the implications of various responses.

Work Preference Question One

Think about a favorite work experience, something you felt was exciting, energizing, and personally fulfilling. Please describe it and tell me why it was personally satisfying.

The favorite work experience question is a great one. Use fact-finding to uncover the candidate's true role and the significance of the work. Conduct a work-type profile analysis, and compare this result to the candidate's other major accomplishments. If the work-types are different, find out why. It could be a big concern.

We interviewed a candidate recently for a manager position, and the applicant described a number of comparable accomplishments. His favorite work experience concerned us, though, because it was significantly different. This person described a research project during his early career that tapped into his individual and technical skills. Interestingly, the candidate became more animated and expressive when describing this task than when describing his other accomplishments. It was clear that the technical work-type was this person's dominant work-type, with the manager work-type a distant second. While acceptable for the position, we wanted a candidate who was equally motivated by the team and organizational effort, and we decided to move on to other candidates.

Sometimes the work-types are the same, but the accomplishments selected are different. Probe to find out why. It could be something as simple as the fact that the candidate didn't want to repeat himself or herself. It could also reveal something about the prior company, or even the supervisor. This is useful information as you assess best fit. Try this question out in your next interview.

Work Preference Question Two

You've indicated to me that you're a real problem solver. Can you give me three examples of the types of problems you like to solve?

People will work long and hard on problems they like to solve, so this is another question type you'll discover is very insightful. When asked about strengths, candidates often inject the stock phrase, "I'm a real problem solver." What's important, though, is the scope, scale, and type of problem. As soon as the candidate's being a problem solver is mentioned, ask for some specific examples of the problems he or she likes to solve. Assign the problems to one of the work-types.

This is a great way to understand motivation. Managers should like to solve management problems. If they don't, be concerned. If someone really likes to solve complex systems issues and he or she gives three examples to support it, that person might not be suited for a fast-paced project role. On the other hand, if a candidate for a creative marketing assignment describes overcoming a problem by coming up with the perfect ad, you've found your ideal match. Also, compare the scale of the problems solved to the needs of the job. This is another good indicator of job fit.

Here are some typical problems I've recently run across. How would you categorize them into work-types?

Depending on your perspective, there could be more than one correct assessment. My view is that assembly repair is

Typical Problems Candidates Like to Solve	Work-Type
1. Finding out why one particular robotic assembly machine is always breaking down.	
2. Determining what drives different types of customers to respond to different marketing and ad campaigns.	
3. Resolving conflict with people.	
4. Determining the best way to achieve a team objective given limited time and resources.	
5. Overcoming a customer's reluctance to buy.	
6. Debugging a piece of computer software.	

largely technical, but it could involve some creative design. The customer analysis problem requires some real creative analysis. Resolving conflict is more management and organizational. This is also true for the team objective in problem four. Overcoming buyer reluctance is the individual dealmaker or entrepreneurial work-type. Debugging the software requires detailed, analytical skills.

The next time one of your candidates says he or she is a problem solver, ask for some examples. You'll discover this is a straightforward way to better understand personal motivation.

Work Preference Question Three

Can you please give me three examples of initiative in one of your more recent positions? This would be something you did over and above the requirements of the job, or something you changed or improved.

People rarely do more than they're required to do unless they really like doing it. This is even more valid if they keep on doing it over an extended period. This is why the initiative question is such a good one. In some way, this is similar to one of our core questions. Instead of asking about impact for each previous job, you might want to ask the candidate to describe some situations in which he or she took the initiative.

As in the previous problem-solving question, get three examples of initiative. Everybody can come up with one example of anything, but few people can quickly describe three unless they've really done it. This is especially true with initiative. If the third example of initiative is as credible as the first two, you have found a high performer. These people consistently do more than required. They like to change and improve things. Then assign these changes and improvements to work-types and compare to your job needs. If they're comparable, you've probably found a top candidate.

Following are three examples of initiative a controller candidate described to me many years ago.

1. Helped set up a new accounts payable system.
2. Upgraded the monthly financial statements.
3. Researched tax compliance.

This is one of the few interviews I ended early. The examples chosen were superficial, none took more than a few weeks to complete, and the candidate had been working at this job for over three years. I even had to pry the third one out of the candidate. In responding to the second one, the candidate was more general, less interested, and the answer was much shorter than the first one, less than a minute compared to about three. Furthermore, the job I needed to fill was a manager's role, not a staff accountant's. With one simple question, I learned all I needed to make an informed "no."

When the responses to these three questions overlap responses to the four core performance questions, it means preferences and competencies are the same. Sometimes the examples used are different, but the type of work is the same. The problem arises if the preferred work is different.

This happened in the marketing executive example mentioned earlier in this chapter. The job required both a strategic focus and strong technical product management effort. The candidate described great examples for both. From his references, we got the sense that there was a preference for the long-range, strategy-oriented aspects of the job. While we brought the candidate back in for a panel interview, we didn't take it far enough. We accepted his assurances of interest in the product management work, which he described only in general terms. He outlined his plans to address this area, but we didn't push hard enough to get multiple examples. He was a bright, articulate visionary who could do the management and team-building task, but he was not motivated to do it.

If we had asked these three preference questions, we would have observed that his answers all dealt with long-range marketing and strategy development. It's important that competencies and preferences match the job needs. Whenever they don't, you'll probably wind up with a short-term success story. In retrospect, I should have advised the company to hire an outside consultant to handle the strategy work, because this kind of work wasn't ongoing. A strong manager work-type would have been a better choice for the long term.

A similar mismatch can happen when the great salesperson is promoted to, or hired into, a sales manager position. If you want a sales manager, get examples of sales management accomplishments. Don't accept plans or ideas as substitutes, no matter how clever they sound. Many technical people want to get promoted into management. Not all succeed. With technical managers, you need to get examples of technical management. These include activities like meeting launch dates, controlling budgets, persuading other technical people to modify their work, and working closely with other functions. Good technical managers need to be good at all of these skills. Look hard for examples of these skills during the interview.

People who are excellent in one area often fail in another, because they were hired for a job with the wrong emphasis. Frequently, this results from mismatching among work-types and has to do with motivation as much as competency. You want to hire people who are both motivated and competent. Using the four core questions in combination with the three preference questions, you have the key tools needed to assess both. As long as you're aware of how these mismatches can happen, it's unlikely you'll become prey to this classic hiring error.

■ AVOIDING FAILURE: MEASURING WORK-TYPE RESISTANCE

People tend to work hard at work they like to do. This is the motivation factor we've been stressing as a key to hiring accuracy and job success. However, some people sometimes work equally as hard at avoiding work they don't like. Few people like every aspect of their job, but this aversion can be serious if what a candidate doesn't like is a critical job need. This was the problem with the marketing executive described earlier. He liked the strategy aspects of the job and did a great job with them, but avoided the detailed product management component. This resistance can be a cause of failure. Work-type resistance is a reasonably common problem. Many of these people make great first impressions and have a series of significant accomplishments under their belts. But, if these don't match all of the job needs, you're headed for a potential failure. Watch for these clues:

1. Voids in the work-type profile might indicate resistance. In an interview for a customer service director, we had a

candidate who did not indicate an interest or preference for any fast-paced project-type or entrepreneurial work. This was an important area, and we checked it out thoroughly on a follow-up interview. Similarly, ask the great salesperson to give examples of an ability to handle complex order transactions, if this is important. Salespeople in the printing industry need to have a strong attention to detail to make sure press runs don't result in expensive scratch pads. Not all great salespeople can fill this need. For Verizon Information Services, we had to specifically address this area for their Yellow Page sales reps. Their best salespeople could handle the printing details and a frenetic pace, and work with their clients helping them design customized marketing plans both in print and online. Checking out all of the work-types was essential in putting a complete interview together.

2. The candidate's telling you he or she doesn't like one aspect of his or her job is a great clue that's sometimes ignored. Ask why he or she doesn't like it, get examples, and look for patterns. Assign the disagreeable work to a work-type. If it's an important part of the job, don't hire the person. You could prevent a costly error this way. You might also ask, "Tell me about a work experience that you didn't find particularly interesting," to force the issue. A candidate told me she didn't have the patience to deal with the myriad of people problems her management job entailed. It turned out she was better suited for the entrepreneurial life. She was great at launching new products, and she ultimately landed a more appropriate individual contributor job in this field.

3. The candidate's answers to one type of questions seem shorter or shallower than others. I asked one candidate to describe his most significant management problem, because I sensed he was more an individual contributor. While he professed otherwise, his response was more general and the example chosen was superficial compared to his individual accomplishments. I had to interrupt this candidate when he was talking about work he enjoyed, but I had to wring a one-minute response out

of him about work he wasn't interested in. The length of an unprompted response is a clue to interest and competency. This is especially true if the candidate has answered other questions at some length.

If actual examples of performance seem to be concentrated in only one or two work-types, use forced-choice questions to test for the other types. For example, ask the candidate to give an example of his most significant accomplishment in the area that concerns you, whether it's technical, management, a fast-paced project, or some long-range or product development activity. This type of questioning will enable you to paint a profile of the candidate's competencies across all of the four work-types.

Use the information in this section to better understand personal motivation. You might want to start with yourself and maybe some of your team members to get some practice. Keep track of the type of work that you and your team members seem to enjoy more and work harder at. Where do you do your best work? What's your favorite work experience? What types of problems do you like to solve? Where have you taken the initiative lately? Keep track of shortcomings the same way. What don't you like to do? Where are you weaker? Assign the answers to specific work-types and look for patterns. You'll learn more about yourself and, ultimately, the types of people you'll hire.

If you have a tendency to hire in your own image, work-type profiling will help you prevent future hiring problems. It's always better to match the candidate to job needs rather than to ourselves. Work-type profile your entire staff. It will help to broaden your understanding of their strengths and weaknesses, and the types of people you need to hire to fill in the gaps. Knowing the work-type preferences for each of your team members will help increase their motivation when they are assigned projects that tap into their specific strengths and interests. When you look at work-types this way and get comfortable with the approach, you'll be able to quickly recognize sources of strength and areas of resistance when you're meeting candidates. This is how you will build both a competent and highly motivated team of talented people.

■ BEYOND THE WORK-TYPE MATCH: COMPARABILITY OF JOBS

On a recent senior engineering management search, my client was concerned that the top candidate was more a technical expert than a manager. The job was split evenly between technology and management, with some solid long-range product development needs. The candidate was great at the technical side and the long-range development, but lighter on the management side.

The candidate actually brought much more capability to the job than hoped for but still appeared short on the management side. References confirmed this. However, the issue resolved itself when we looked at comparability. The size and complexity of his previous management task was enormous when compared to the new job. In his previous position, the candidate was thrown in over his head and was judged too severely by some of the sales references we spoke with. The candidate had supervised over 80 engineers through 3 directors and 5 managers. In fact, he built most of the team after inheriting the job during a rapid ramp up. In the job we were considering him for, the staff size was about half as much, with the growth rates comparable.

When everything was put together, the jobs were quite close. The staff size was somewhat smaller, the pace was the same, the complexity of the products was slightly less, allowing more forward-looking thinking, and the business issues and decision-making needs were very similar. Overall, he was perfectly suited for the job.

Just because someone meets the work-type profile, it doesn't automatically mean he or she can do the work. You still have to consider comparability—the jobs have to be reasonably similar in terms of management scope, sophistication, scale, complexity, and standards of performance. This is usually rather obvious. For example, you can meet a great organizer/improver who has managed only five people and the job requires 50. Much of this information will surface in your fact-finding, but the following list will help you quickly sort through this comparability issue:

➤ Have the candidate draw an organization chart and compare job needs according to total size, number of direct reports, types of people and functions managed, the pace of change, the standards of performance, and the level of sophistication of the systems and support functions.

➤ Use the ABC rule to evaluate interpersonal skills. Assign the responses to the different accomplishment questions to the following three interpersonal skills categories: **A: A**lone or individual contributor, **B: B**elonging to a team, or **C:** in-**C**harge, or a management role. This analysis will quickly reveal the candidate's preferred interpersonal role. Compare this analysis to the needs of the job. Don't put individual contributors into important management roles if the analysis is inconsistent with all of their previous significant accomplishments. Be concerned if individual contributors have few team projects. The opposite is equally true. Don't put great team players into individual roles, if this is critical to job success. Get some examples if there's an apparent void.

➤ Consider the complexity of individual and group assignments. Look at the scope of the assignment, technical needs, decision-making differences, the expectations and the results achieved, the pressure, and the available resources. On the surface, a candidate might have a comparable job title, but one job might be maintaining a functioning group, and the other might be creating one from scratch.

➤ Understanding that company environment provides great clues regarding fit. This is the "e" in SMARTe. Compare your company culture and environment to the candidate's. Consider the sophistication of the systems, the pace, the rate of growth of sales, the pressure, the demands of the job, the quality of the staff, the quality of the reporting systems, and the expectations of senior management.

➤ Consider the financial issues and business issues. Comparability can be easily measured in dollars. Are the budgets comparable? Consider sales growth, headcount, the number of products, the number of facilities, receivable and payable levels, debt levels, financing needs, and the quality of outside professional support, including CPA and legal firms used.

There are many ways to determine comparability. The worst is to hire people with the same type of experience in the same type of job in the same industry. While this is easy to do and logically comfortable, you'll continually underhire. People who are willing to do the same old things repeatedly are just cruising along. These aren't the top performers. The best people want new challenges and a chance to grow and develop. Work-type profiling is an alternative. It considers comparability from a new perspective based on the real content of the work, not just the titles. It also meets the top candidate's need for growth, while minimizing the hiring manager's risk.

POWER HIRING HOT TIPS: USING WORK-TYPE PROFILING TO IMPROVE JOB FIT

✔ There are only four different types of jobs and all work falls within these work-types:

- The *Creator/Strategist* is the forward-looking visionary or consultant. This is the person with the new ideas, products, and strategies.

- The *Entrepreneur/Builder* brings ideas into reality. The person is usually an impatient fast-paced person willing to take risks and earn the rewards.

- The *Improver/Organizer* is the manager who brings people, systems, and resources together to improve, upgrade, and change the way things are done.

- The *Producer/Technical* is the person who sustains the business, gets into the details, designs and makes the products, delivers the goods and services, and maintains the quality.

(continued)

✔ People apply more energy toward work they like to do. The work-type profile analysis allows the hiring manager to quickly identify these areas.

✔ You can increase hiring accuracy by assigning each SMARTe performance objective to a work-type. Compare the candidate's major accomplishments the same way to these job needs.

✔ Listen to the words, especially the verbs, and examples a candidate uses to describe his or her accomplishments. Assign these to work-types.

✔ By anchoring each SMARTe objective, you can determine a candidate's competency within a narrow range of work-types.

✔ Get examples of each work-type to paint a complete profile of the candidate's competency across all of the job factors. Balance and flexibility across all work-types is an indicator of upward potential.

✔ Ask candidates the three questions that elicit their favorite work experience, examples of initiative, and problems they like to solve. This highlights preferences and underlying motivation.

✔ Be concerned if preferences and competencies don't match. You might have a candidate who is competent, but unmotivated.

✔ Watch for clues for resistance at the work-type level, especially if it's a critical job need. Raise the caution flag if the answers to some questions are shorter or more generalized and for those lacking specific details. Watch out for philosophic statements that sound good, but have no substance.

✔ Use the ABC (**A**lone, **B**elonging, in-**C**harge) comparison to determine fit based on preferred interpersonal style.

✔ Evaluate job comparability even if the work-types are a strong match. Consider the types of team members and staff size, company size and growth rates, sophistication of the systems, performance measurement issues, decision-making needs, and complexity of the job.

Chapter

After the First Interview— How to Make Sure You Have a Great Candidate

Far more crucial than what we know or do not know is what we do not want to know.

Eric Hoffer

■ STAY OBJECTIVE: THE FIRST INTERVIEW REPRESENTS LESS THAN HALF OF THE TOTAL ASSESSMENT

Additional interviews, reference checks, and testing are all invaluable. Frequently, these important steps are ignored or minimized. Once a candidate is on the short list, most managers use the added time to look for information to confirm a yes decision. Because so much time has been invested in the candidate and momentum is building for an offer, a "no possibility" is only passively being considered. Once someone passes muster during the first round of interviews, there's better than a 50 percent chance an offer will be made. Positive data is magnified, and negative data is rationalized away. This is a major cause of bad hiring decisions. Objectivity must prevail throughout the assessment. Negative information must still be sought as aggressively as positive data.

There are some great tools available to increase the accuracy of the assessment. They're especially valuable when used in conjunction with the POWER Hiring interviewing process. Alone, the performance-based interview can consistently achieve a 70 percent to 80 percent accuracy rate. When combined with some of the other tools suggested in this chapter, accuracy can increase to 80 percent or 90 percent. Good hiring takes work, but not as much as bad hiring.

If you're serious about a candidate, conduct reference checks. Here's a basic rule about reference checking that's probably not 100 percent true, but you should follow it 100 percent of the time.

Strong candidates have strong references who will openly tell you about them. The lack of good references is a sign of a potential problem.

Although there are very few exceptions to this rule, once in a while, a candidate's job search is extremely confidential. Under these circumstances, it's sometimes hard to find a colleague willing to vouch for the candidate if he's been there for a long time. Even in this case, look for someone who has recently left the company. Since 1978 when I became a headhunter, I've never had a problem getting a reference from a good candidate. Once a candidate is serious about a job, a reference check is in order. Good candidates expect it and will find some good references for you. This is a great sign. It means the candidate is serious about the position. I become very anxious if a candidate can't give me a few people to call.

Recently, at one of our seminars, a buttoned-down human resources vice president vehemently disagreed with my contention about references. She told me she would give only the bare minimum of information about an employee who had left her firm, fearing potential legal reprisals. I then asked her about one of her coworkers we both knew very well and asked if she would give me an open reference about her. She said, "Of course, but that's different; I know her." And that's why there are no exceptions to the basic rule. Good people know other good people who will tell you openly about them. Weaker people come up with excuses about why they can't give names to you.

■ REFERENCE CHECKING—HOW IT SHOULD REALLY BE DONE

Conduct the reference just like the interview by getting specific examples to prove a generality, and then by fact-finding. You can ask the reference any performance-based question you want. Don't ever ask any personal questions, especially those that involve family, age, or racial issues. Although the laws differ by state, the reference has to give only minimal data, but you can ask any performance-based question. This minimal information guideline was established to protect employers from lawsuits from their former employees if they gave negative or less than stellar references. Many companies are now stating that employees can give open references if it's clearly stated that the reference is personal.

It's important for the hiring manager to personally check at least one or two references. It doesn't matter when you conduct the reference. Sometime after you've established intent and before the last round of interviews is best. Don't quickly delegate this important task. The human resources department or the recruiter has a vested interest in placing the candidate, so they won't be as inquisitive as the hiring manager. Plan on at least 20 minutes for each reference. This gives you time to do some fact-finding. The key to good interviewing and good reference checking is to ask many questions and get examples. Use peers, subordinates, and supervisors as references. Subordinates are sometimes the best references, so don't ignore these.

Although not getting a reference is a sign of a weak candidate, getting flowery, glowing comments is not the sign of a good candidate. References, even from strong candidates, need to be validated, which is done in two ways—by determining the quality of reference and by getting the reference to give specific examples to validate the hyperbole and generalities.

➤ 1. Qualifying the Reference

The Reference Check checklist that follows is divided into two distinct parts—Qualifying the Reference and Qualifying the

Candidate. The quality of the reference is as important as what the reference tells you about the candidate. We address this first.

All of this information will allow you to place the reference's subsequent comments in context. Don't accept a reference's comments without some benchmark for the reference. If the reference is personal, ignore it. If you decide to use it for some strange reason, you then must get great examples of exceptional, above-the-call-of-duty activities. From nonwork-related references, you must determine why the candidate is special and how this relates to on-the-job performance. Volunteer work, especially useful for candidates just starting their careers, would apply here.

Knowing what criteria a reference uses to rank performance provides additional insight into the quality of the reference, and is also a means to validate the reference's comments. The reference might value traits differently than you do, so this could be important. Some of the more common value systems include teamwork, interpersonal skills, results independent of methods, intelligence, commitment, character, and loyalty. You

---

REFERENCE CHECKING CHECKLIST
Part 1 Qualifying the Reference

- ☐ First determine the relationship to the candidate. Find out the titles of both the reference and the candidate, how long the working relationship lasted, and their most recent contact.

- ☐ Obtain the reference's current title, company, and the scope of the job in comparison to the job when the reference knew the candidate.

- ☐ Determine the reference's scope of responsibility. Ask about the size of his or her organization and the number and types of people on the staff.

- ☐ Determine what the company environment was like—pace, standards of performance, quality of the people, and the quality of the processes and systems.

- ☐ Ask the reference how tough a rater he or she is, and why.

can get many different answers about accomplishment depending on the rating system used.

➤ 2. Qualifying the Candidate

Use Part 2 of the checklist to qualifying the candidate. You'll rarely obtain all of this information but the checklist will help guide your thinking when you're on the phone. The key to good reference checking is to get details and examples to back up general statements about the candidate's competency. For example, if the reference states that the candidate is "really committed," ask the reference to give you an example that best demonstrates this trait. Probe like this a few times and the reference will realize you're serious. Most reference checkers just want to check boxes. When you show professionalism, the reference will be more open and frank with you.

Start the second part of the reference check by asking for an overall summary of strengths and weaknesses. You can then "cherry pick" your way through the balance of the reference items. The key is to ask for a specific example demonstrating the skill or behavior the reference mentioned. For example, if initiative was mentioned as a key strength, follow up by asking for a specific accomplishment demonstrating initiative. Do this for weaknesses also. Don't form judgments about the candidate based on generalities from a reference. Get proof with good examples. This is the most important aspect of good reference checking.

Ask the reference to compare the candidate to others at the same level. *"How would you rank this person among other people you know at this level?"* is a good opener. Ask how many are in the group and what percentile the candidate falls in; for example, top 10 percent, top 25 percent, or top 50 percent. Then find out the basis for this ranking, like team skills, energy, or technical competence. Ask what it would take for the candidate to move into the top 10 percent or 5 percent. This will get at weaknesses.

The key to good reference checking is to get details and examples to back up general statements about the candidate's competency.

REFERENCE CHECKING CHECKLIST
Part 2—Qualifying the Candidate

☐ Please give me a summary of (candidate)'s strengths and weaknesses.

☐ Get examples of accomplishments to support major strengths and weaknesses.

☐ How did the weaknesses affect job performance?

☐ Can you give me some examples of where the candidate took the initiative?

☐ How would you rank this person as a manager?

☐ What was his or her biggest management accomplishment?

☐ How strong was this person in building/developing teams?

☐ How would you rank this person's overall technical competence in (job specific) area? Get specific examples.

☐ Is technical competence a real strength? Why?

☐ Get example of best work for top 1 to 2 SMARTe objectives.

☐ Team and interpersonal—get examples of group projects.

☐ Determine timeliness—get examples of meeting deadlines under pressure.

☐ How strong are his or her verbal and written communications? How were these measured?

☐ Find out ability to handle pressure, criticism. Get examples.

☐ How strong a decision maker is he? Can he give some examples and how the decisions were made?

☐ Can she give you an example of commitment?

☐ What single area could the candidate change to be more effective?

☐ Would you rehire the candidate? Why or why not?

☐ How would you rank this person's character and personal values system? How did this affect performance?

☐ How would you compare this candidate to others at the same level you know? Why is the candidate stronger (or weaker)?

☐ How would you rank overall performance on scale of 0 to 10? What would it take to move up 1 point?

Ask where this person excelled, and again get an example for proof.

Here are a few other good ways to uncover weaknesses. Ask the reference to describe the one single thing the candidate could do or change to be more effective. Then find out how the lack of this affected performance. At the end of the interview, ask the reference to summarize the candidate's overall performance on a scale of 0 to 10. Usually you'll get a number from 6 to 9. Then ask what it would take for the candidate to move up one point. Asking if the reference would rehire the candidate and for what type of position is also revealing. Probe to confirm previous statements.

Use the reference to confirm the information obtained during your actual interview of the candidate. Throughout the interview, you obtained numerous examples of the candidate's greatest accomplishments. Ask the reference to validate this information. Get examples of core success traits, and see if the traits and examples are the same as the candidate described. If different, find out why. Get the candidate's actual involvement in the major accomplishments. Compare this to what the candidate has stated. It's easier to correlate information if you focus on the most exceptional work the candidate has done in each job.

Conduct the reference check with an open mind. If you really want to hire the candidate, you might unintentionally avoid asking the tough questions. Many years ago, a senior executive at one of the large health care companies told me he was asked to provide a reference for a candidate we both knew. The candidate was solid, but not a star, more an individual contributor than a manager. The senior executive intimated that the candidate in question was a superb analyst, but only an average manager. He said that once he mentioned this, the human resources person conducting the reference did not ask any further questions about management and tried only to reinforce the strengths.

You can get any answer you want conducting a reference check this way. If you don't have an open mind and are not willing to change your opinion, it's a waste of time to even conduct the reference check. It's hard and always embarrassing to admit you've made a mistake in judgment, and eliminate a candidate at the last moment. It's a much bigger mistake to go forward and hire someone you shouldn't hire no matter how important it seems at the time.

Reference checking allows you to validate the candidate's true role in each major accomplishment. Concerns about style can also be addressed. Weaknesses can be validated with other references. As the hiring manager, you'll also get some great tips on how to better manage or motivate the candidate if hired. You can prevent more hiring mistakes with a good reference check than with any other method. But we've seen hiring managers ignore negative data because they were too sold on the candidate. This is another important reason to stay objective until the whole evaluation process is completed.

■ THE SECOND ROUND—HANDLING SUBSEQUENT INTERVIEWS AND ADDITIONAL INTERVIEWERS

You'll never have enough information to make a foolproof hiring decision. Use a second interview to confirm core issues and address new important issues. Make use of other interviewers the same way. Telling them what you want them to look for will make their interviews more meaningful. Courtesy interviews can wind up being popularity contests. Little real investigating goes on. Following are some ways to get maximum benefit from these subsequent interviews:

➤ The Complete List of Things You Need to Know Before Making a Hiring Decision

The list represents all of the information you need to collect before making a final hiring decision. Use the second round of interviewing to collect whatever is missing. Assign specific responsibility for obtaining this information to all of the interviewers involved.

☐   Level of drive, energy, initiative, and self-motivation.

☐   Trend of growth based on examples of major accomplishments in last two to three positions.

(continued)

(Continued)

☐ Ability to work in comparable team projects.

☐ Motivation to do the type of work at peak levels.

☐ Technical competency and ability to apply the knowledge to achieve the desired results.

☐ Ability to meet all the SMARTe performance objectives— anchor and visualize each one.

☐ Managerial, team, and organizational responsibilities of the job.

☐ Experience and education compared to job needs.

☐ Problem-solving and analytical skills using real problems as tests.

☐ Thinking—technical, tactical, and strategic—using visualization of SMARTe objectives.

☐ Goals—get examples of major past goals already achieved.

☐ Commitment and responsibility.

☐ Character, values, and integrity.

☐ Personality and cultural fit.

☐ Confidence and positive attitude.

☐ Ability to deal with the environment—the "e" in SMARTe— pace, professionalism, standards of performance, resources, decision-making, span of influence.

☐ Process compatibility—what aspects of the process does the person do better than others compared to what's required.

➤ Conducting the Second Interview

Before the second round, make sure you have written down everything you still need to find out about the candidate. The previous checklist will help you sort this out. The questioning and evaluation techniques already introduced, combined with fact-finding, are suitable for any stage in the interviewing process. In fact, this is often all you'll need to conduct additional interviews. Simply ask the candidate to give you an example of an accomplishment that best demonstrates the desired skill, behavior, or trait. Then validate the response with good fact-finding.

Anchoring and visualizing all of the SMARTe objectives are best done over two or more sessions. Format the second interview around some of the SMARTe objectives you haven't yet evaluated. It's also a good idea to assign these performance objectives to other interviewers. If your boss is involved in the interview, make sure he or she anchors and visualizes at least the most important SMARTe objective.

Have peers anchor and visualize the SMARTe objective most relevant to their work. For instance, we had an engineering manager ask a potential marketing manager about the development of product requirement documents[1]. This tightened the focus of the interview. Candidates don't mind this line of questioning, even though it appears that you're asking similar questions repeatedly. The process of anchoring SMARTe objectives and fact-finding always results in a different line of questioning, because the trail followed is always different. As a result, you'll always get different answers and different conclusions. By controlling the breadth of the interview, you can obtain useful and more objective information from each interviewer. Request written summaries from each person involved.

Spend time in the second interview on management, team, and organizational skills. The team leadership core question addresses this directly. Make sure you consider this question for at least the past few jobs. The focus of much of the first interview is on individual contributor traits, so use later interviews to restore some balance. Later interviews are a useful means to ensure a strong match between job needs and abilities and interests. Look for extra motivation and effort on similar projects. Frequently, a candidate will tell you he or she will do certain aspects of the work that are less exciting, but once on the job these are often done poorly or ignored. This is a classic problem. Be cynical. If a candidate needs a job, he or she will say anything to get it. This is how competent but unmotivated people get hired. To overcome this problem, obtain recent examples of the candidate going the extra mile to complete the type of work required. Raise the caution flag if you don't find some recent evidence.

You can download a comprehensive interview that summarizes all of the questions presented in this book from

POWERHiring.com. Select questions from it to use in subsequent interviews. The interview includes the eight basic
questions, some work-type matching, and some additional
questions on character and personality. In addition, there are
a few universal questions, which are explained next.

➤ All Purpose Performance-Based Question

*(Trait, desired skill, or characteristic) is important to suc-
cess in this position. Can you tell me about a time when you
had to use this trait to achieve a major objective? Please give
me a specific example.*

Spend 5 to 10 minutes on this, if the trait is important. Obtain the major objective achieved, the circumstances at the
beginning of the task, what was changed or improved, the environment, the dates, the names of the people involved, the
importance of the task, and the impact on the company and
the candidate. This is the classic behavioral interviewing
question converted into a powerful tool to better understand
true performance.

➤ The Two-Step Questioning Pattern to Better Understand Motivation and Values

First Step: *What two or three things are you looking for in a
new job?*
Second Step: *Why is having (A) and (B) important to you?*

The first question is the setup. The second question gets at
underlying motivation and values. Look for the source of motivation or goal setting. This question gets at how values were
formed. The preface is important, and it's a good question only
if you've established a strong bond with the candidate. You'll
get a superficial response if you haven't. The candidate has to
explain his or her answers with this one. He or she will be
more open if there has been some trust developed earlier in
the interview. Look for insight and congruity in the answers.

➤ Value Formation Question

Values are usually formed through an early youthful experience, sometimes painful or uncomfortable. Do you have any experiences like this that helped shape your values and character?

This question is not required in every interview. I suggest it only when the person you're hiring is critical to your success or the success of the project or business. If you try it, don't speak after asking it. Let the candidate open up. This underlying source of motivation and character can sometimes reveal the true measure of a person. Attempt the question only when trust has been established between the candidate and the interviewer. Be sensitive to this. An emotional bond is often created when a candidate answers this question. If you get a superficial response, it usually means the candidate was unwilling to reveal his or her innermost feelings. Answer the question for yourself first, so you have a sense of how important this question is. Make sure only the hiring manager or a senior level human resources person asks this question.

■ THE PANEL INTERVIEW—A GREAT WAY TO LEARN MORE AND NATURALLY CONTROL EMOTIONS

I'm not very fond of interviews by subordinates, who often have hidden agendas. If they're weak interviewers, the information obtained is questionable, making matters worse. One way around this is to include subordinates in a panel interview, which eliminates most of these problems.

In the late 1980s, a potential client asked me about panel interviews. "They're intimidating, cold, a poor recruiting tool, and unwieldy," was my instant reply. The CEO looked at me and said, "That's too bad, because that's all we use here, and if you want the CFO search (which at the time would have been our biggest assignment), you'll have to use them." Without hesitation, I indicated that I'd be willing to try them. You should, too. They're a great tool. I was totally wrong.

As long as they're organized well, panel interviews provide a much truer picture of a candidate than the one-on-one interview. Here's why:

➤ They're more objective because there's less personal interaction.

➤ You have a chance to think more about the candidate's responses. You're more an observer than a participant. This increases the validity of the assessment. In most one-on-one interviews, you're often thinking about what you're going to ask next, rather than listening to the candidate's answer.

➤ You don't judge answers as much during the response, because others are asking for clarifying information. More in-depth responses are possible this way.

➤ The interviewer's body language isn't as meaningful. Even if one of the interviewers doesn't like an answer, the physical clues (slumped shoulders or glazed eyes) aren't so obvious to the candidate.

➤ It's a great way for subordinates to meet the candidate without the typical awkwardness. Because it's less of a personality-based interview, their hidden agendas stay hidden.

➤ Strong candidates like panel interviews if they're not held too soon in the process. You see more of the candidate's true personality in a panel interview, especially if most of the questions are about how accomplishments were achieved.

➤ Panel interviews save time. It takes only three or four people one to two hours to know a candidate, rather than a whole day.

➤ Panels allow weaker interviewers to get into the act. This is especially important if the weaker interviewer is the hiring manager. I later discovered that the CEO who liked panel interviewers considered himself a weak interviewer, so the panel was arranged with him in mind. He felt he always talked too much, because he didn't know what questions to ask, and the panel interview eliminated this problem.

➤ The assessment is more accurate and consistent. Because everyone is using the same information to make an assessment, consistency is achieved. If the panel interview is led by a good POWER Hiring interviewer, the information obtained is insightful. This is something the other interviewers couldn't have obtained on their own.

The panel should include no more than three or four people; otherwise, it can be both intimidating and unwieldy. Make sure all interviewers have read the SMARTe objectives for the job before convening. Have one or two people lead by asking the major performance-based questions. Make the thrust of the interview a discussion of major accomplishments. Get many examples and have everyone on the panel use fact-finding for follow-up questions. It's okay to ask the candidate to come prepared to discuss a few of his or her most relevant major accomplishments. This will improve the information exchange. Consider individual contributor, team, and management projects. At the end of the interview, get the group together to summarize their findings. This process offers a good check and balance. Strengths and weaknesses are tempered, resulting in a much more objective assessment. Personality naturally takes a second position behind performance when evaluated in a panel session.

Recently, one of my manufacturing clients excluded a great candidate for an operations management position because he was too chatty during the first interview. My client was annoyed by this superficial banter, most likely caused by initial nervousness. Our client was a typical entrepreneur—bright, fast-paced, prone to make instantaneous decisions, and strong-willed. These are not the traits of good interviewers. The candidate was top notch, though—a perfect match for the entrepreneur to build the solid infrastructure to maintain his fast-growing import and distribution company.

We didn't want to let this one die, so we arranged a panel interview with one of my associates leading the session. There were about four people in the room, but we orchestrated the questioning. It lasted about 90 minutes and covered everything, focusing largely on comparable past accomplishments dealing with rapidly changing environments. The candidate passed this much more grueling session with flying colors. After a subsequent three-hour, one-on-one interview with the entrepreneur, the candidate was offered the position and accepted. During this interview, the group created the operations plan and budget for the next twelve months. My client recently thanked us for intervening and indicated that job performance is as expected: top notch.

The only potential problems with panel interviews are that they can be intimidating to the candidate, and they need to be well coordinated. Review everyone's role beforehand or you'll wind up with a bunch of people asking a bunch of miscellaneous questions. You'll ease the candidate's fears if you describe the format of the session a few days beforehand. Put the candidate in the middle, not at the end of the table. This way, the candidate will feel like one of the team. One of the leaders should ask all the leading questions, with the rest of the panel members following up with fact-finding questions. Don't make it seem like an interrogation. It's better to be low-key by requesting more information in a neutral tone of voice.

■ THE TAKE-HOME CASE STUDY: DON'T JUST TALK ABOUT THE JOB, HAVE THE CANDIDATE DO IT!

You'll see instant results with a panel interview—more agreement and fewer hiring errors. The process can be made even stronger if you give the candidate a take-home problem to present in the panel session.

The take-home project is discussed at a subsequent meeting. Topics run the gamut from reviewing reports, solving problems, evaluating new products, and assessing tactical or strategic plans to providing consulting advice on a mini-project. The take-home project is effective because the candidate is required to do real work, not just talk about it.

The take-home case-study approach has a number of tangible benefits. It reveals true motivation and desire. Candidates won't spend time preparing if they're not truly interested in the job. It does a better job of revealing competency through direct observation, as opposed to opinion, gut feeling, or second hand information. Also, the open interaction with the candidate allows true character and personality to come out.

A few years ago, a CEO called me about three months after we placed a vice president/controller at his company. He wanted to tell me how pleased he was with the candidate. He said that the candidate's performance, sense of humor, and interpersonal skills were exactly as demonstrated in the panel interview. This was not his initial assessment, though. After the first interview, the CEO thought the candidate was not confident enough for the job, that he had some quirky mannerisms, and that he was unsure of the candidate's technical competence. He thought the two other contenders were far stronger.

I knew all three candidates very well and knew that this person was the best of the three, although he was nervous in the interview. I suggested the CEO conduct a panel interview coupled with a take-home problem. Each candidate was asked to assess a potential acquisition. After reviewing the financial reports, the candidates made a 15-minute presentation about the merits of the opportunity. This was followed by a 45-minute open discussion. During the panel session, this candidate wowed everyone. He explored the financial impact on taxes and earnings. He raised serious questions about costing and financing. He was confident, funny, and insightful. In this element, which was much more natural for the candidate than the interview, he had a chance to demonstrate his true capability.

Unfortunately, most of the time great candidates don't get a fair chance like this, because they're eliminated too soon in the process. In this case, I personally intervened to bring a dead situation back to life, but this is rare. You can preclude the possibility of missing a great candidate by exploring accomplishments in great depth, rather than assuming competency based on presentation skills.

One of our clients in catalog distribution went a bit overboard with the panel interview idea. The day after the first interview, our candidate for a marketing manager position was asked to come in for a panel interview with a few people. The candidate was not 100 percent sold on the job, so this type of panel session was premature. After arriving, she was told that there would be six people on the panel, and she had to present her solution to three marketing problems. She was given 25 minutes to prepare an evaluation of these problems, which weren't very relevant to the job.

Although the candidate handled it well, the problems could have been avoided. If you're going to use take-home projects, give the candidate a few days to prepare, and then only if the candidate has expressed a desire to be considered a finalist. Make sure the issues explored are relevant and job specific. If you have more than three or four people in the session, it can be both intimidating and unwieldy.

Here are some specific ideas for the take-home project. You don't need to have a panel session to review these, but if you do, you get the benefit of both assessment techniques.

Some Take-Home Project Ideas

1. Review reports, financial statements, studies, or plans.
2. Give the candidate a SMARTe objective to study. Have the candidate first describe a significant anchor. Then have the candidate tell you how he or she would accomplish the task (visualize). Use a flip chart and get into serious give-and-take discussions. This is how you'd discuss the task after the candidate starts. Why wait?
3. Give a loan officer a credit application to assess.
4. Have an engineer assess a design, and then present some alternative solutions or approaches.
5. Describe a problem in a process (order entry, logistics, manufacturing, or accounting, for example), and have the candidate describe how he or she would come up with a solution.
6. Have a salesperson tell you how to penetrate a big account.
7. Have a product manager describe how to develop and launch a new product.

The types of issues are endless. The key is to make them job-specific. Situational questions that don't directly relate to the job and what needs to get done are a waste of time and will give misleading results. Always get examples of comparable accomplishments during the panel interview; this makes the take-home project an expanded anchor and visualize exercise. It reveals true job competency by applying the candidate's knowledge in solving job-specific problems. In addition, the amount of time spent on the assignment directly reveals real interest.

■ BACKGROUND VERIFICATION: CHEAP INSURANCE YOU MUST HAVE

Many reliable firms conduct background checks. Most check degrees, employment, credit, driving, and criminal records for a relatively inexpensive amount, around $50 to $200 per candidate. Hire Right (www.hireright.com) does a great job at this online, making it even easier. Do it for every finalist. While most resumes describe the basic truth, many do a great job of camouflaging the sand traps. The background verification will help sort this out.

Of late, I've become a real cynic with respect to trusting resume content. This sad story makes the point. A few years ago, we were looking through our main database (consisting of everyone we had met personally in the past 10 years) for some candidates for a material control manager's position. We found some strong candidates, and we called them personally to determine interest. Three were interested and sent in their current resumes. They must have forgotten we had earlier versions. One was identical, other than updated for the current period. Another falsely added a master's degree in an earlier time period. The other eliminated a job from the earlier resume to minimize turnover. The latter two candidates were eliminated from contention without further contact. This is disturbing. I believe it reveals a trend of candidates falsifying resumes. Think about the Notre Dame football coach who recently lost his one-week-old job. His resume cited three college varsity football letters (he had none), and a nonexistent master's degree.

Caution is advised. Remember that resumes are marketing tools only. A clever layout is okay; fraud is not. Spend the money and wait the two days it takes to conduct a background check to separate fact from fiction. It's cheap insurance.

On your application forms, you can state you'll be conducting a background check and ask the candidate to validate the truthfulness of the information, affirmed by his or her signature.

This will minimize fraud. You can also use the background check as part of the close to test both interest and truthfulness. Before the second or third interview, tell the candidate you'll be conducting a rigorous background check. Ask the candidate to reconfirm that everything on the resume and application is 100 percent consistent with the facts. If the candidate says yes and agrees to come in for another interview, he or she is demonstrating sincere interest and honesty. You can learn a great deal about the candidate by using this conditional approach to move forward.

■ TESTING TO CONFIRM, NOT PREDICT, COMPETENCY

I've been interviewing candidates since 1978, and I'm still not sure about the validity of testing. Some tests are better than others. In this section, we provide a review of the tests we have used and explored over the years. Tests can be divided into two broad categories—those that test competency and those that test personality. Competency tests measure ability in some way, whether intelligence or some specific job-related skills. Personality tests measure traits and behaviors.

Any test that accurately measures a specific job-related skill is a useful indicator of subsequent performance. Some of these include testing software knowledge, equipment usage, and PC skills; solving job-specific problems; and testing manual dexterity. If the job is narrowly confined to this specific area, the test should weigh more heavily in the hiring decision. For most jobs, it's the application of these skills that ultimately determines success; and in these cases, the testing will give the wrong conclusions. But, it's not because the testing is invalid. The real problem is that the true job is ill defined. That's why the most important component of good hiring is the performance-based job description and SMARTe objectives.

Despite these drawbacks, some tests are useful tools if used to confirm a strong performance-based interview. Raise the caution flag if the results of the test don't confirm the information obtained during the one-on-one interview.

Following is a rundown of the most common tests and some tips on how to get the most out of them.

➤ Cognitive Ability

Cognitive ability tests measure intelligence. Intelligence is a good predictor of ability to learn; therefore, this type of test is frequently used to screen candidates. The most commonly used intelligence tests are the Wonderlic Personnel Test and the Thurston Test of Mental Agility. Profiles International and ePredix offer similar tests. There is a strong correlation between ability to learn and on-the-job competence, but it's far from 100 percent. Professors John Hunter (Michigan State) and Frank Schmidt (University of Iowa) have done much research on this topic. A recent study they conducted of common selection methods indicated that 25 percent of a candidate's subsequent performance can be measured with this type of test.[2] Next to work sampling and structured interviews, this is one of the best predictors of subsequent success. We use this type of test as part of an overall performance-based evaluation process to confirm our judgment, but not predict performance. When used this way, it's an invaluable tool and highly recommended.

You may recall a few years ago that a candidate for a police officer position was denied the opportunity because he scored too high on the Wonderlic. The community leaders felt he would have been bored by police work because his score exceeded their norms. This is where I think the test is wrongly used. My suggestion would have been to get examples of work the candidate had recently done that best duplicated the routine nature of police work. If the work was similar and the candidate was motivated by it, I would discount the high Wonderlic score as meaningless. On the other hand, if the past work required a higher degree of intellect than police work, then the high Wonderlic would confirm that the candidate was indeed overqualified. This is how an intelligence test should be used.

Here's a potential problem that can occur on the other extreme. Many years ago, I was working with a top-notch candidate for a human resources manager's job. She seemed great, but scored very low on the Wonderlic. The score was totally inconsistent with her track record of success based on our personal interviews and her reference checks. Checking further, we discovered that English was her third language! She grew up in Italy, lived in Quebec as a young adult, and went to school in the United States. Surprisingly, she had no noticeable accent. Many of these tests rely on knowledge of the idiomatic expressions of the language and others are timed. If English isn't the primary language of the candidate, then these tests can give flawed results. The woman was ideally suited for the job and was subsequently promoted to an executive position. If we had relied on the test for guidance, we would have eliminated a top-notch candidate from consideration.

The problem with these tests is that they're relied on too heavily as predictors of performance. They should not be used as a substitute for a good performance-based interview. Someone who scores low on the test might be a top producer, substituting work ethic for talent. Someone very bright might get bored with the job or try to get by without working hard enough. These tests should be used to tell you where to look when the results are inconsistent with your expectations.

➤ Personality, Style, and Behavioral Traits

Personality-style tests measure traits and behaviors. There is some correlation between these tests and subsequent performance, but it's less than the test for cognitive ability. One problem is that these tests measure preferences, not competencies. This is an important distinction. If you prefer to go to a party rather than read a book of poetry, you will be classified in a certain way. You might be competent at neither. In fact, the party goer might be able to offer more insight into Frost, and the poetry reader might be a more effective leader of others. Another problem is that most of these tests present an "either-or" choice. You might like to read poetry and go to parties, but the test lets you select only one. This forced-choice distinction doesn't give a true reading of personality balance.

For these reasons, personality tests should be used only to confirm, not predict, performance. If the test indicates an inconsistency with the performance-based interview, further investigation is mandatory. Use panel interviews, take-home tests, and additional reference checks. The best means to predict future performance is past performance. If a specific test raises concerns, use examples of past performance to address the issue.

A recent situation illustrates this point. One of our candidates for a marketing position did well on the creative portion of a personality-style test, but she scored quite low on detail orientation. Our client was concerned. On further investigation, we found that the problem was the way the test was used and interpreted, not the candidate. The test our client used forced the candidate to indicate a preference for the creative over the analytical work. The job required solid database marketing skills to supplement the creative aspects of the job, and our client was correct in raising this issue. To address the concern, we gave her the Wonderlic Personnel Test for intelligence and she did well on the math component. In addition, we contacted a number of references to confirm her analytical abilities by getting specific examples of some of her analytical projects. Finally, the client had her interpret some of their database reports and present her findings at a panel interview. With this added insight, it was clear she had the ability to handle the analytical aspects of the job. In this case, the personality testing was used correctly— only to raise the concern, not to predict performance.

The following tests are useful tools if used to confirm past performance as described in the previous example.

The Wonderlic Comprehensive Personality Profile

We often use this test. It addresses typical personality traits and indicates best fit for some classic jobs. It adds test-taking honesty to the list of traits. This is unusual. It's inexpensive, about $30, including self-administered, computer-based scoring. The results for this test vary; therefore, reliability is a question. Because we use it as a confirmation tool, this is not a problem, but it can add confusion. The automatic write-ups at first seem great, providing much apparent insight. The problem is that the advice is too broad. The same advice covers many different profiles. Despite this flaw, the test provides good tips for both test taker and the hiring manager; for this alone, it's worth looking at.

Predictive Index (PI), the DISC Instrument, and the Myers-Briggs Test

These tests are based on the early work of Hippocrates regarding the four temperaments. In the first part of the twentieth century, Carl Jung developed this concept into a theory of human nature based on the four personality types, which led to the Myers-Briggs test. The DISC and Predictive Index instruments arose from the style and behavior analyses work conducted shortly thereafter by Dr. Bill Marston. Both of these tests are quantitative, describing the degree to which a person is **D**ominant, **I**nfluencing, **S**teady, or **C**ompliant. Figure 6.1 provides a quick overview of the four types.

The primary style is determined by a person's tendency to be active or passive (the horizontal axis of the graph), combined with his or her thinking or feeling orientation (the vertical axis). Plot yourself to get a quick sense of your primary style. Through word choices, the tests quantify how strong you are in each of the four styles. From my use of these tests, I conclude they have great value in team building and improving communications within a group. I'm less convinced of their ability to predict job competency. Nevertheless, if the test results are inconsistent with past performance, we always conduct more reference checking or have another round of interviewing. As a checkpoint, the tests are great.

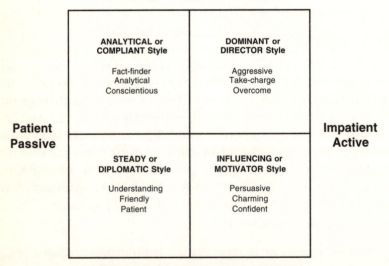

Figure 6.1 The four primary personality styles.

The Myers-Briggs is based on similar behavioral theory, but the output is more qualitative than quantitative. You end up with 16 different personality types by classifying people as **I**ntroverted or **E**xtroverted, **S**ensing or i**N**tuitive, **F**eeling or **T**hinking, and **J**udging or **P**erceiving. By mixing and matching the four fundamental behavioral traits, you can wind up at one extreme being an ENTJ, the natural leader; or at the other end of the spectrum, you could be one of nature's observers, the ISFP. This test is a useful tool to understand people better, but, in my opinion, it doesn't add much to the hiring process. I've met many supposed ENTJ leaders who are incompetent and some great leaders who are introverted and quiet.

The classic logic argument, *asserting the consequent,* addresses this situation. The phrase means that specific truths are often incorrectly generalized for all conditions. The result is bad guidance. For instance, let's assume that a test revealed that seven out of ten leaders are extroverted. Some would conclude two things: First, you probably need to be extroverted to be a leader, and second, all extroverts are leaders. Both generalizations are untrue, but the underlying details get lost somehow. This is why I think all of these personality style tests are flawed. Look for the leader first. He or she will be either introverted or extroverted.

The Enneagram

Although based on the same behavioral underpinnings as the tests discussed previously, the Enneagram[3] adds the dynamics of personality change to reveal healthy and unhealthy personality types. These correspond to different styles, ranging from leaders and thinkers to artists and helpers. You can find a number of Enneagram tests on the Internet. I like this concept very much because it reveals how personality style changes over time, but it's not any better as a predictor of subsequent performance than other personality tests.

The Profile

The Profile is a combination of tests published by Profiles International of Waco, Texas. In addition to asking more questions (which offers a higher reliability), The Profile measures what they call "Thinking Style" (a kind of general/cognitive ability).

The Profile also adds a measure of occupational interests, which most assessment tools ignore. The personality section is based on dynamic business traits. Because it is multidimensional, it stands out as more of a "whole-person" assessment, something the Department of Labor likes. The Profile test takes about an hour to complete and is worth the added time because it covers so much. It can be administered via booklet, computer, or the Internet.

As a preemployment hiring tool, it does a good job of predicting and confirming behavior in potential applicants because it covers both cognitive ability and personality style. We recommend this test highly because of this combination. Another important feature of this tool is the ability to benchmark top performers in a specific job function. All current employees take the test to establish the benchmark of performance. Applicants are then compared to the top performers in the current employee group. Candidates who have been interviewed and seem strong, but fall out of the top range, are then examined in more depth before an offer is extended. Sometimes marginal candidates are also pulled back in because they do surprisingly well on the test. The test costs about $100 per person in reasonable volumes, which is cheap insurance if used for the final two or three candidates. This type of external validation also helps keep the interviewing team honest. You tend to conduct a more thorough assessment when you know a test will be used later on.

If you use the POWER Hiring interview methodology, you'll soon discover that your assessments and the test results will yield similar results. Over the past 20 years, 80 percent to 90 percent of these types of tests tended to confirm what I observed during the interview. When the tests don't match up with your interview, it's important to conduct more in-depth probing to better understand why the two differ. The difference could be attributed to a problem with the test, a problem with your interviewing methods, or a flaw in the candidate, possibly a fatal flaw. These typically include extremes in behavior—too smart, too aggressive, too warm, or too intense. The Enneagram is good for sorting out some of this.

While all of these testing instruments offer insight into personality, none are substitutes for a detailed performance-based interview. Personality and character are clearly revealed in a person's past performance. By getting the best examples of compatible past performance in the interview, we have ensured a correct personality and behavioral fit. Testing can only confirm this. If it doesn't, it means either the testing was bad, our interviewing wasn't as exhaustive as it should have been, or we didn't clearly understand the needs of the job. Any one of these is quite possible. That's why it's important to reassess the candidate if the testing indicates something is amiss. Many managers use the test to replace a good interview. It can't. It's a great tool when used to confirm the results of a well-conducted performance-based interview.

■ PUTTING IT ALL TOGETHER

Although the one-on-one performance-based interview represents the heart of the hiring decision, it needs to be supplemented with other tools. If you use the POWER Hiring techniques described throughout this book, you'll be about 70 percent to 75 percent accurate, maybe even as high as 80 percent. You'll get close to 90 percent if you add the other techniques described in this chapter. The percentages shown in Figure 6.2 indicate the relative importance of each assessment technique.

The quality of the input of others and of the references correlates directly with the quality of the job description. If the

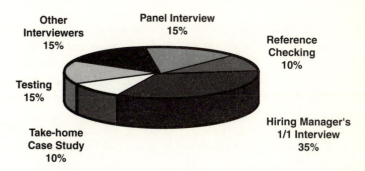

Other Interviewers 15%

Panel Interview 15%

Reference Checking 10%

Testing 15%

Take-home Case Study 10%

Hiring Manager's 1/1 Interview 35%

These techniques are not substitutes for a performance-based interview. They're complements to it.

Figure 6.2 A summary of candidate assessment techniques.

performance objectives are clearly known by all members of the interviewing team, the assessment approach we recommend will work smoothly. It falls apart if the interviewing team is unclear about the job. Then there's a tendency to substitute emotions, stereotypes, personal biases, testing, and more reference checking to compensate for a weak performance-based interview. Problems arise if the supplementary techniques overshadow the interview itself. In this case, it's time to reassess your complete assessment approach.

My philosophy is this: You should try anything, and everything helps. Just conducting your one-on-one interviews with the candidate at different times of the day in different situations will help. I know one CEO who conducts three different interviews—one in the office, one during a meal, and one in a social gathering. He gains something from the change in settings. Personality and style are revealed in natural fashion this way. I learn a great deal about my candidates during casual phone conversations scheduling meetings and negotiating offers, even when talking with a spouse or children. Don't base the hiring decision on one interview by one person. Use the combination of all of the techniques presented in this chapter to increase the accuracy of the assessment.

POWER HIRING HOT TIPS: EVERYTHING YOU NEED TO KNOW TO MAKE AN ACCURATE HIRING DECISION

✔ The one-on-one interview is not a complete means to get all the information you need to make an objective hiring decision. Use reference checks, panel interviews, take-home projects and tests to better understand competencies, motivation, and preferences.

✔ Always conduct reference checks and don't accept any excuses from candidates that the don't have any. Good candidates always have good references that will talk openly about them.

✔ Make sure references give lots of examples to prove every positive statement. Also ask references to describe the candidate's biggest accomplishments providing details and examples.

(continued)

✔ Get at weaknesses by asking the reference how the candidate can improve in the technical, team managerial, and decision-making areas.

✔ Use second interviews and other interviewers to gain more facts about past-performance. Get additional examples to support the critical SMARTe objectives. Forget courtesy interviews. Have other interviewers get useful examples of past performance as it relates to their specific function and need.

✔ Use panel interviews for every candidate on the short list. They minimize emotions, allow you to think rather than judge, they save time, and they allow subordinates and weaker interviewers to participate. Candidates like them since they're more performance and less personality dependent.

✔ Use take-home case studies to test job-specific competency and candidate motivation. The typical interview relies too much on spontaneous responses. The take-home project taps into reasoning, judgment, and motivation. The quality of the take-home case is a better indicator of ability, since it demonstrates real work, not just the talk about it.

✔ Background verification is a must. Resumes are prone to misrepresentation. The background check will uncover most of it.

✔ Cognitive and skills testing are very useful predictors of performance, but they're not foolproof. There are some people without all of the skills who are top performers. For example, think about all of the top internal candidates promoted into bigger jobs. Skills tests would have knocked some of them out.

✔ Personality testing is fine, but use it to confirm, not predict performance. These tests sometimes indicate areas for additional performance-based interviewing questions or reference checking.

✔ Use a combination of interviewing and tests as part of an overall assessment process. The more you use, the more accurate the whole system will become.

Chapter 7

The Ten-Factor Candidate Assessment

There is something rarer than ability. It is the ability to recognize ability.

Elbert Hubbard, American Author

■ BALANCE IS THE KEY

Accurately assessing candidate competency is the key to better hiring decisions. Unfortunately, given the busy schedules of managers, there is a natural tendency to short circuit the hiring process. In the rush to decide, managers often overvalue one piece of data or the input of one influential person. We assume a candidate we initially like with a few good traits can do it all. This is how the partially competent get hired. A somewhat nervous candidate missing something is cause for exclusion. This is how the great often get overlooked.

The hiring decision should not be based on a few narrow traits. It must cover all job-related performance factors. Every decision needs to consider a candidate's competency, capacity, and desire. Competency is the raw ability to do the work. Capacity is the ability to learn and apply these skills to deliver results in a variety of different circumstances. Desire is about motivation. Without it, all the competency and capacity in the world sit idle. You have to want to do the work or it won't get done, no matter how good you are at doing it. An accurate

178

measurement of these factors requires information from various sources, including the interview, different interviewers, test results, and reference checks. Consider everything in balance. Don't stop just at competency.

I learned the value of balance a number of years ago during a search for a director of quality for a chemical solutions manufacturing company. The final candidate had a low-key personality, and I was concerned about her ability to lead change. While otherwise qualified, during the interview process she just didn't seem dominant enough. We didn't have many candidates, so we reluctantly sent her to meet the client.

A phone interview with the CEO and human relations vice president the next day set me straight. Their first interview was a combined three hours. They got detailed examples of complex quality improvements the candidate instituted, team-building efforts, and projects she led when working with government agencies in developing industry standards. Her values and character were explored at subsequent meetings, as well as technical competency, motivation, and critical thinking skills. This was a superb, well-rounded candidate with tremendous upside potential. She is still with the company, now a senior vice president, and an industry-recognized expert. This was our first search of many with this company, and this person established the ongoing standard of quality for top candidates. Without the company's thoroughness in seeking balance, it is unlikely this person would normally have been hired. It's an important lesson we can all learn from.

It doesn't take any extra time to complete the candidate assessment across all of the critical factors. The eight-question interview, especially the four core performance-based questions, will be enough to uncover most of the information you need to make a well-reasoned hiring decision. The rush to judgment is what causes most of the problems. Here's a case in point.

Many years ago, a vice president of finance at one of the entertainment companies let a top-notch candidate slip away. The vice president was an intuitive interviewer and liked applicants who were smart, socially confident, and assertive. We sent in a great candidate who had all three traits in spades and more, yet tended to be a little tongue-tied early in the interview. I knew this and suggested to our client that he wait at least 30 minutes before making any judgment. Unfortunately, the advice was ignored; and within 15 minutes, this very promising young man was eliminated from consideration. He subsequently took a job at one of the competing entertainment companies and now, 15 years later, is one of their senior executives.

You can't afford to lose great people for the wrong reasons. To prevent this from happening, you need to keep an open mind and carefully measure all of the critical factors before reaching any conclusions. If you're getting input from others on some of these factors, make sure they also conduct a thorough interview. The quality of your interviewing and assessment skills is as important as the quality of the candidate in getting to the right answer.

■ THE TEN-FACTOR CANDIDATE ASSESSMENT— WHAT YOU NEED TO KNOW TO MAKE AN ACCURATE DECISION

The POWER Hiring Ten-Factor Candidate Assessment template in Table 7.1 on pages 182 and 183 will help ensure balance. The ten traits shown can easily be ranked on a 1 to 5 scale right after the interview. Delay the hiring until you've measured all of the ten factors accurately. It helps to take notes during the interview. If a candidate is particularly strong or weak in one category, make sure you indicate why in your notes. These notes will help you make the necessary trade-offs later on when you begin comparing candidates. Sometimes there are major strengths that can offset what initially appears to be a deal-breaking weakness. Sometimes major strengths don't appear as important in the face of a critical void. Try not to make the final decision until each factor has been considered. With the rush to hire, there is always a tendency to make premature decisions without all of the facts.

While the descriptions on the template are self-explanatory, it's important to understand how each of these ten traits can be measured during the interview.

➤ 1. Energy, Drive, and Initiative

This is energy^2 described in the POWER Hiring formula in Chapter 4. It shows up as passion, desire, and self-motivation. Don't ever compromise on this. It's the universal trait of success. Look for it in every job. During the fact-finding, get examples of initiative and extra effort. People with energy^2 show it in many ways. An extroverted personality is not proof. Have the candidate provide examples with specific facts, dates, and quantities. You'll be able to eliminate a number of those candidates who are socially assertive, but not necessarily motivated on the job. Similarly, don't assume the calm or quiet candidate lacks energy^2. These people can often be more proactive on the job than outgoing people. Still, get proof.

Don't forget that the anxiety of the interview can put a damper on even the most confident. The process of fact-finding and getting examples will help you get through this temporary condition and allow you to find energy^2.

Look for special projects, extra effort, and major accomplishments even in recent graduates. This could be in the form of schoolwork, extracurricular activities, or in part-time jobs. Highly motivated people always do more than required, and this trait is evident early in a career. The work might not be comparable to your needs, but that's secondary. Here's a personal example. My son spent the last semester of his senior college year putting together a CD for his singing group under a concert deadline. This took a number of 12- to 14-hour days for about eight weeks; and while his grades suffered, he got some great experience. He and his team, in what I first considered an ill-advised project, went the extra mile in dealing with vendors, printers, publicists, and a recording studio 150 miles away. All this, while rehearsing for the major year-end concert. Both were successes. Extra effort, wherever applied, is an important characteristic of all successful people. Look for it in every person you hire, and match the work to your specific job needs.

If the candidates have no big projects, look for smaller successes. In this case, always ask for three—three examples of initiative, three examples of exceeding expectations, or three examples of projects in which the candidate did more

Table 7.1 The Ten-Factor Performance-Based Assessment Template

Trait/Factor	Scale—Weak (1) to Strong (5)					
	1	2	3	4	5	Score
1. Energy, Drive, Initiative	Little energy shown in any previous job. Passive work performance.	Generally consistent performance, but never exceeds expectations.	Consistent level of performance with some periods of high levels of energy.	Generally highly motivated, but a few periods of average performance.	Consistent self-starter. Always delivers more than expected.	
2. Trend of Performance over Time	Growth trend is spotty and inconsistent with the needs of the position.	Trend of growth down, but canidate meets the basic needs of the position.	Trend of growth has flattened, but still consistent with needs of position.	Trend of growth is upward and/or direct hit with needs of position.	Upward pattern of growth and increasing track record of performance.	
3 Comparability of Past Accomplishments (Anchor SMARTe Objectives)	No position needs are directly met. The gap is too wide to overcome.	Only one or two SMARTe objectives are met, with too many voids to handle.	Key SMARTe objectives are met with few voids that can be addressed.	Most SMARTe objectives are met with little compromise needed.	Past accomplishments directly compare to all SMARTe objectives.	
4. Experience, Education, and Industry Background	Weak fit on all standard measures: not enough experience or education.	Adequate experience and education. A stretch to meet minimum standards.	Solid education and experience, consistent with needs of position.	Direct education and experience exceeds current position needs.	Very strong comparable experience with good industry and educational fit.	
5. Problem-Solving and Thinking Skills (Visualize Objectives)	Structured thinking. Inability to adapt knowledge to new situations.	Some ability to upgrade and modify existing methods and processes.	Able to understand issues. Can develop some alternative solutions.	Has ability to understands most issues and can develop new solutions.	Understands all issues and can develop and communicate solutions.	
6. Overall Talent, Technical Competency, and Potential	Little direct technical competence and inability to learn within reasonable time.	Some technical ability and talent, but might take too long to come up to standard.	Technically competent. Reasonable ability to learn. Narrow focus on job only.	Technically strong, smart, ability to learn quickly. Broader focus. Sees related issues.	Very talented, learns quickly, strategic, tactical, and technically focused. Broad perspective.	
7. Management and Organizational Ability	Little relevant management experience or unable to organize similar projects.	Some management ability, but insufficient to make contribution soon.	Reasonable management experience consistent with needs of position.	Solid manager and organizer. Exceeds the needs of the position.	Outstanding ability to manage and organize groups of similar size and staff.	

Table 7.1   (continued)

Trait/Factor	Scale—Weak (1) to Strong (5)					Score
	1	2	3	4	5	
8. Team Leadership—Persuade/Motivate Others	Little evidence of persuading or leading others. Tends to be more individualistic.	Some evidence of team skills, but inconclusive. Generally more individualistic.	Solid team leadership skills or potential. Consistent with needs.	Seems to have very strong team leadership. Exceeds needs.	Strong track record. Clearly the ability to motivate and develop others.	
9. Character—Values, Commitment, Goals	Questionable values and integrity. Self-serving. Misleading.	Reasonably solid values and ethics, but some questions remain unclear.	Appropriate values and ethics. No significant problems observed.	A committed person. Good character, values, and attitude.	High integrity, committed person with strong values and ethics.	
10. Personality and Cultural Fit	Fatal flaw or some imbalance or poor attitude and fit with existing team.	Adequate fit, but could cause some conflict or negative impact.	All around solid person. Will fit with group without causing much conflict.	Generally positive attitude. Personality will help in performance of job.	Has balanced ego, positive attitude, flexible, and can work with others.	
Total Point Score	Rank each trait on a 0–5 scale. Reinterview the candidate if insufficient information is available for any of these categories. Multiply total score by two (× 2) to compare with 100.					

than required. Everyone can come up with one or two. Few can come up with three good ones. Those who do are the ones you want to hire. You know you have a problem if the second or third example is pretty lame.

During her initial job interview, I asked our secretary to describe three things she started on her own in her previous job. She promptly told me about learning and writing a number of complex Word macros, setting up an open-invoice tracking system on Excel, and reorganizing large mailings with an outside production company. This is what the best do. We hired her in the mid-1990s, and she's still working for us today.

Rank the candidate a 5 if you observe a pattern of consistent and high energy in every job. Average people do just what's expected of them; a 2 or 3 is appropriate for this group.

➤ 2. Trend of Performance over Time

Examine the candidate's team and individual accomplishments over time. These accomplishments show how the candidate has grown and impacted the organization. The ideal candidate is one who has had comparable jobs and is still showing signs of upward growth. Rank this person a 5. Rank the person a 4 if he or she is still highly motivated to do high-quality, excellent work, even if the growth has flattened.

Jobs don't need to be identical to get a high ranking. Consider instead staff size, complexity of the issues, standards of performance, pace, environment, and level of sophistication. Combine these factors when evaluating comparability.

On a recent engineering management search in the telecommunications industry, we had a close match with staff size, growth rates, the product development process, and the level of systems support and sophistication. The candidate was weak on the technology side, though. He compensated for his weakness by demonstrating an ability to learn new technology very quickly and by hiring great people. By taking a balanced look at strengths and weaknesses, we looked for engineering managers who demonstrated an upward trend of management growth, independent from the technology. This allowed us to find a great candidate who might otherwise have been overlooked.

If the growth pattern had been flat for this candidate, we would have required him to be stronger on the technology side. Give a 2 or 3 if the trend is flat and the comparability is a little weak. Use your judgment because there are many factors to consider. A pattern of upward growth is always more important than experience. People with this pattern get promoted, so look for this in the people you hire.

I recently met a VP of finance candidate who had a strong work ethic, was highly energetic, and always seemed to be taking on new projects. I ranked him a 5 in energy[2], but only a 3 in the trend of performance category. While he was a very self-motivated person, he had been at the same management level for the past ten years, an indication that he had plateaued in his career. I still recommended that the company consider him for the position because his skills were consistent with the needs of the job, but I didn't expect him to ever take on a significantly bigger job.

➤ 3. Comparability of Past Accomplishments

Anchoring SMARTe objectives allows the interviewer to compare a candidate's past accomplishments to the required performance objectives of the open position.

The VP of finance candidate mentioned previously is a good example. The company needed someone to guide its long-range planning process and bring business advice to a relatively young management team. The candidate was adequate in this area, but did not bring the leadership qualities the company needed. Because he was so strong in all the other areas—systems, performance reporting, internal controls, and financing—I still ranked him a 4, downgrading him slightly for one deficiency. The CEO ranked him a 3 because he felt the lack of the strategic focus was a critical void. He weighed this one SMARTe objective higher than all of the others combined. When everyone knows the real performance needs of the job, it's easy to resolve these types of differences. That's why it's important to get every member of the interviewing team to agree to the performance objectives.

Be concerned about mismatching. While energy[2] is a prerequisite for success, it's sustainable only when the candidate's natural passion is consistent with real needs. For example, a highly energetic designer might be ineffective as a manager. The bright consultant might be a misfit for a technical, rather than strategic, position. These people might sound great, but they often flounder when they have to do the work, not just talk about it. If management skills are important, make sure you hire someone who has a track record of proactive management accomplishments. The same is true for entrepreneurs. While they exude energy, don't assume it can be applied equally to all tasks. A mismatch can often be confirmed by the lack of comparable anchors.

Give a 5 if the candidate has a comparable accomplishment for each SMARTe objective, and a 1 if there is only a slight match. The accomplishments don't have to be identical to match. Look at the scope and complexity of the task against the needs of the job. In a recent assignment, I considered a logistics position in a food packaging plant similar to a materials manager in office products. Both positions had about 12 people in the department, the systems issues were similar, and the needed changes required the same type of organizational and team skills.

➤ 4. Experience, Education, and Industry Background

Consider "Experience, Education, and Industry Background" in comparison to your ranking on "Past Accomplishments." Strong experience and education can often partially offset a weaker accomplishments rating, if the environment is comparable. This is the "e" in SMARTe objective. Consider the pace, style, and standards of performance of the companies to assess the quality and comparability of the experience. Ten years of seemingly relevant experience doesn't mean much if the candidate's previous company had lower standards and the pace was much slower. Likewise, two years of experience can be worth ten if the candidate performed at stellar levels in a world-class company going through rapid change.

Give the highest ranking to those with accomplishments and experiences comparable to the job needs, especially if they took place in more challenging environments. Give very strong rankings to those who have done well in the more challenging environments, even if the jobs don't seem as big. Assign lower rankings to those candidates who seem to have comparable experience, but in less stellar organizations. Of course, don't ignore candidates from these organizations if they've been able to rebuild and upgrade their organizations. Consider both the experience/accomplishments in combination with the environment. You'll learn a lot about the real competence and quality of the candidate.

Give some credit to direct industry experience and education. Add a point or two to the score if the experience and education add significantly to the candidate's ability or improve the job fit. Subtract a point or two if they detract from the experience and the environment.

➤ 5. Problem-Solving and Thinking Skills

Somebody asked me how smart a person should be to be effective on the job. My response was "just smart enough," but any less and you're in trouble. A strong candidate needs to have the ability to understand the work, solve job-related problems, and anticipate what needs to get done. Collecting and processing information to make appropriate decisions is part of it. So is the ability to apply previous knowledge and experiences in solving new problems. You're directly testing for problem-solving and thinking skills when you have the candidate visualize the SMARTe objective. His or her responses, discussions, and even questions will give you direct insight into this important area.

How the candidate organizes a job objective or evaluates a current problem requires insight and understanding. The quality of the questions the candidate asks is a strong indicator of thinking and reasoning skills, adaptability, communication skills, logic, decision-making, knowledge, and problem-solving ability. This is great insight. At the end of the interview, you'll really know if the candidate is smart enough.

The quality of the candidate's questions forms a part of the visualization component. Ask the candidate what kinds of questions he or she would ask to get the information needed on one of the performance objectives. Asking many great questions, even with limited experience, is a good sign of a high potential person. Raise the caution flag if the candidate's experience is strong, but the questioning is weak. These people have difficulty adapting to new situations. Don't give more than a 3 in this case if the candidate is not good at visualizing. Selecting candidates often becomes a trade-off between experience and potential. My favorite mix includes high potential, just enough comparable experience, and a track record of learning quickly. Ask candidates to describe their greatest accomplishment with the least amount of experience. You'll get at all three of the mix with this answer.

On an assignment for a marketing director for a direct mail company, I asked each of the candidates to describe how they would re-layout the company's catalog. About a third of the candidates knew exactly what to do. They spent a few minutes reviewing the catalog, asked me some insightful questions, described what additional information they needed, and then suggested a number of courses of action based on different alternatives. This group deserved a 5 in this category. Another third of the candidates asked some good questions, but didn't take them anywhere. Their ideas regarding what to do were vague and too general. This was worth a 3. The remaining third didn't even ask relevant questions. They seemed to be clueless as to what to do. This group barely deserved a 1.

Sometimes we hire very bright, capable people for the wrong job. Different jobs require different types of intelligence.[1] During my executive search work, I've observed three broad categories of intellect—technical, tactical, and strategic or creative. Being competent in one category doesn't imply being competent in another. Review these categories to see where your candidate fits based on real job needs.

Technical Intelligence

Technical intelligence includes analysis, processing of detailed information, and systematic thinking. Those ranking high in math do well in this area. Have the candidate give you examples of this type of problem solving to assess technical competency. For a visualization question, ask the candidate to describe the process he or she would use to solve an analytical problem. For someone in financial analysis, you might ask for a description of the process he or she would use to find out why costs have increased in a certain area. In manufacturing, find out why a certain process has gone awry. Match needs with competency and rank the candidate high in technical intelligence if the job demands this type of analytical thinking.

Tactical Intelligence

Tactical intelligence is oriented toward marshaling resources, getting team results, coming up with practical solutions, and being focused on the bottom line. These organizational skills are found in some of the best managers, or those with a more practical attitude. People with high tactical intelligence have the ability to adapt to the situation at hand. Get the candidate to give you examples of trade-offs that had to be made, or have him or her prioritize the list of SMARTe objectives. To test this trait in a copy center manager, we asked candidates to describe how they would prioritize and schedule five different types of documents. Look for a commonsense approach to thinking and decision making. It takes the real world into account, recognizing the need to balance competing objectives.

Strategic or Creative Intelligence

Thinking about or planning the future or being able to understand long-range consequences of current actions is one aspect of strategic or creative intelligence. This also includes creativity, conceptualizing ideas, seeing the big picture, and coming up with new products or approaches. Get examples of related accomplishments to validate competency. To test for this type of intelligence, I asked a functional vice president to describe the strategic impact on the company of her department's new role. She did okay, but it was clear she had a more functional than business perspective, and I ranked her a 3. The key is to get examples of creativity or strategic thinking. This is an important skill for all vice president-level positions. Be careful. Some candidates possess this skill, but not much else. We often hire bright people like this and are later disappointed when they don't deliver on other aspects of the job. Don't be overwhelmed by a bright, creative mind, if that's all he or she has.

Good thinking and problem-solving abilities require a combination of skills. Rank the candidate a 5 for a clear understanding of the work requirements, insightful questions, and strong responses. Drop the candidate down a point or two if there are too many questions, too few, or if the questions are widely scattered. Too many is a sign of good reasoning, but lack of experience; too few is a sign of structured thinking; and widely scattered is a sign of floundering. Listen carefully and take notes. The candidate's responses to the visualization questions will help validate your assessment. Look for crisp responses. Assign a 1 or 2 when a candidate doesn't know how to even begin a project or what to look for in solving problems.

➤ 6. Overall Talent, Technical Competency, and Potential

This broad category encompasses the interaction of different competencies. The score given should represent the candidate's ability to grow and take on bigger roles. To get a 4 or 5 in this category, candidates need to have a broader focus than demanded by the current job. I look at three areas to gauge this ability:

1. Thinking skills—technical, tactical, and strategic/creative.

2. Breadth of business understanding—an understanding of how different functions interact.

3. Application of technical skills—the ability to achieve results.

The first category addresses the same technical, tactical, and strategic thinking described in the previous problem-solving section. Rank a person high in potential when good thinking skills are combined with execution and true business understanding.

I met a great financial analyst in the late 1980s. He was very technically competent; even though he was only a few years out of school, he was already managing small groups. In addition, he really understood the strategic impact of all the financial advice he was providing. He was insightful and a great problem solver; he clearly understood the role that finance could play in helping each function operate more effectively together. I lost track of him for almost ten years, but was not surprised to discover that he became the president of a midsize, fast-growing, medical products company. He demonstrated all the traits of high-potential thinking and competency long before they were used. At our luncheon meeting, I could tell he still had the capacity to continue his rise up the corporate ladder.

The second area of potential is breadth of understanding and business perspective. Candidates who see beyond their own functional requirements to the broader needs of the business add real strength to an organization. Good product managers have the ability to understand the competing needs of engineering, sales, marketing, and manufacturing. That's why many people with this ability move into general management. I recently interviewed a candidate who was very strong in systems and cost accounting for a manufacturing position. While she didn't have all the direct experience needed to handle the manufacturing job right away, I was comfortable recommending her and ranking her a 5 in potential because she added more to the job in other important ways.

CPAs get the bad rap that they're too focused on the internal process accounting issues and don't appreciate the needs of the other functions. It's frequently true, but you need to confirm that with the visualization questions, rather than stereotype all CPAs. MBAs in finance and accounting tend to be weaker technically, but broader in focus. As a result, they have more of an ability to balance competing business needs. Look for this broader perspective when evaluating potential. It's the prerequisite for upper management.

The third area is the application of technical competency in getting practical results. Instead of looking for someone who already has technical skills, I am more concerned about a candidate's ability to learn and apply those skills. A minimal level of technical knowledge plus the capacity to learn and deliver results is a better trade-off. For example, if you need products designed quickly that rely on specific technical skills, it's better to get examples of comparable products the candidate has designed and under what circumstances. The technical skills, while important, are secondary to the environmental and business conditions.

I've seen lots of technical people miss the mark here by focusing too much on technical issues and not enough on their practical application. A number of years ago, we had a search for a CFO of a Fortune 500 company. The CEO insisted that the candidate must have hands-on experience as a cost accountant and be good at it. This was his number one priority. I asked how this skill would be used on the job. The CEO said the CFO would need to set up a multiplant performance reporting system, evaluate each manufacturing plant's performance, and hire good plant controllers. As he listed these requirements, he recognized that the cost accounting skill wasn't important, but the application of the skill by preparing and evaluating reports, and hiring people with the skill was. This then became the job requirement.

When ranking talent and potential for management positions, be more concerned with the broader thinking skills, the ability to execute, and general business understanding. Give a 5 to those strong in all areas. Give a 4 for strength in two, and a 3 goes to those who are solid in all, but not superior in any. For technically intense positions, bias your ranking depending on the candidate's technical strength. A great technical person still needs to have business understanding to move up. Be careful of a great technologist who doesn't have a practical side or who doesn't understand some of the related business or management issues. These will become detriments to his upward growth. Under this condition, a score of 3 or less is appropriate.

➤ 7. Management and Organization

Most interviewers focus too much on individual, rather than managerial, competency, which is a major cause of hiring errors. If the management and organizational aspects of the job are important, spend as much time as necessary to validate the candidate's competency. Rank candidates high if their management track record compares favorably to the needs of the job. This means they have managed, built, and developed groups of similar size and have achieved similar results. Be careful not to measure individual contributor skills as you assess this factor. This is a common mistake.

Use projects to determine organizational skills, even if the candidate doesn't have a big staff. I recently met a candidate for an operations position that required organization of a number of small teams over many facilities. The job required strong communications, coordination, and planning skills. At first, I didn't think the candidate possessed the necessary management skills to handle the job because he seemed too technical.

To better understand his organization skills, I asked him to describe the most complex project team he had led. He told me about an eight-month crash project to get a very complex piece of automation equipment debugged, installed, and operational. He took over when the project was severely behind schedule. The successful completion of the task required the coordinated efforts of a dozen engineering and manufacturing personnel, plus balancing the competing needs of his own company, the customer, and two other major vendors. Budgets were tight, tempers were on edge, and the credibility of his company was on the line. He won an award for his efforts and the appropriate kudos. There was no doubt he could handle what now appeared to be my client's pretty tame management need.

Have the candidate prepare a team chart for the last few positions, listing coworkers, subordinates, vendors, customers, and superiors. This allows for a span of influence comparison to your current job needs. Have the candidate rank the performance of each key staff member. Look for a pattern of building, managing, and developing strong teams. Ask the candidate to describe his or her most significant management accomplishment. Compare the insight, enthusiasm, and detail provided to the individual contributor accomplishments. Even the length of the response is important. These differences can reveal a candidate's preferences for individual contributor or management projects.

Rank the candidate high if he or she is a proactive manager with a track record of managing similar-sized groups, handling similar work, and comparable projects. This kind of record, plus demonstrated performance building top teams wherever he or she went, would earn a 5. I give a 3 for solid, basic comparable management experience. These people can adequately run the department, but not grow it into anything special.

Be concerned if the candidate has high turnover in the group, complains about his or her staff, and seems to talk less or in more general terms about management successes. Score this a 1. Score a 2 if the candidate has solid management skills but those skills are too light for the current job. You still might want to consider this person if there are some offsetting strengths, especially team leadership and strong organizational skills. Get references from subordinates to validate any of your conclusions. Subordinates have the best perspective on someone's management skills.

For nonmanagers, look at team projects to get at this trait. Give high rankings to those who have taken on extra duties in getting team results. Make sure you check out the results in detail, the steps taken to achieve them, and any challenges the candidate had to face along the way. People who become strong managers have the ability to persuade and motivate others, possess very strong organizational skills, and go the extra mile for the good of the group. These people are ready to be managers when the circumstances warrant it.

➤ 8. Team Leadership—The Ability to Persuade and Motivate Others

Team leadership is a component of both management and the interpersonal skills part of personality. It's important enough to consider separately. Team leadership represents the ability to tap into and harness the energy of others. Getting someone to do something he or she wouldn't normally do, without threats or coercion, is a wonderful skill.

Team leadership has two dimensions: one organized around the subordinate team and the other involving coworkers. Whenever a person has some degree of power over another, the team leadership component gets clouded. Motivating a subordinate is easier than motivating someone who doesn't work for you. Look for managers who have a track record of developing their staff. They can point to a number of people whom they have personally helped become successful. They are proactive with respect to this staff development issue and take great pride in it. As a result, they have the ability to inspire their own staff to exceed expectations. When you ask about these issues, get names and examples of how they helped their subordinates become better. Give high rankings to those who consistently go out of their way to hire superior people and then help upgrade the skills of each team member.

Team leadership is also important in dealing with people outside a person's own department. The ability to persuade and motivate people who don't work for you is a critical component of leadership. Examine this area for managers and nonmanagers alike. Get examples of major team projects and use fact-finding to uncover the candidate's true role. Get examples of how he or she dealt with conflict and persuaded others to change their positions, and determine how compromises were made. Ask how he or she coped with difficult people in other functions. People who rank high in this aspect of team leadership are often selected to lead groups, always do more than they're required to do in the group, and understand how to develop real win/win situations. They are sensitive to the needs of others, and they can describe numerous examples of similar team leadership roles.

Extroverted people have an easier time with this team leadership trait but don't make quick conclusions. Not all extroverted people are strong at team leadership. Those who are too individualistic or have overblown egos create more problems than solutions. Introverted people can be great team leaders; you just have to work hard to get them to open up.

Another aspect of team leadership is attitude and confidence. Don't be fooled. Social confidence in the interview is not the same as real confidence in getting the work done. Confidence and a positive attitude of a "can do" optimism go hand in hand. Together, they can inspire individuals and teams. A positive attitude is an essential trait of all continuing success. In his book *Learned Optimism,* Martin Seligman describes the importance of a positive attitude and shows how to measure and develop that trait.

Having a positive attitude doesn't ensure success, but not having it is certainly a step toward failure. You can get some direct sense of positive attitude and confidence by examining the candidate's greatest challenges and even failures. The ability to bounce back from defeat, or successfully handle conflict and pressure, is a strong indicator of a positive attitude. Find out how the candidate dealt with adversity. I heard Paul Westphal, the former NBA and college basketball coach, say that the strongest trees weather the strongest storms. This is good interviewing advice. Find candidates who have weathered tough storms.

Rank candidates a 4 or 5 if they can manage, develop, and inspire teams composed of their own staff members and coworkers. Rank the candidate a 3 if you're concerned about attitude, don't get as many examples as you'd like, or conclude that the candidate is just adequate. Weak communications skills, a bad attitude, lack of personal confidence, and faulty logic are clues to weakness in this category. Rank the candidate a 1 or 2 if you observe these clues. Adjust these rankings to reflect the degree of leadership required on the job. This trait is more important for companies going through significant change, less if you just want someone to maintain the status quo.

➤ 9. Character Values, Commitment, and Goals

Character is a deep-rooted trait that summarizes a person's integrity, honesty, responsibility, openness, fairness in dealing with others, and personal values. Don't address this trait until the end of the first interview, or for the second interview. Not only is it more relevant then, but also candidates will be more comfortable and open with their responses. A person's character is revealed through his or her on-the-job performance, so you'll learn a great deal about character during your performance-based questioning.

Ask the candidate the basis of his or her personal value system and how it was developed. Be sure to listen carefully. If you've developed an open relationship with the candidate, this answer can be very revealing. At one presentation, I asked a similar question to a volunteer. His response was heartwarming. He told the group he was once a drug addict and had lost everything. While rebuilding his life, he learned the value of relationships and personal commitment, which were far more important to him now than material possessions. The relationship between him and the rest of the group changed instantly because of this revelation. This is what can happen when true character is revealed.

Ask why the candidate wants to change jobs and what aspects of work the person finds important. This will help determine both fit and satisfaction. If the basic needs of the job are incompatible with the candidate's motivational needs, you'll only create problems later on. Understanding a person's value system allows you to predict how he or she will react under various work-related circumstances. If work is a secondary priority in the person's life, you could be in trouble if you need to rely on him for a crash project coming up, even if he agrees to it.

Having goals is an important part of character and personal motivation, but the typical questions can be misleading. Everyone has goals, many of them very lofty, but few are actually achieved. A better approach is to first ask the candidate to describe one or two major goals already achieved. Look for a pattern of goal setting and achievement. Once this is established, ask about future goals. If they're consistent with the pattern, you've got a winner. It's easy to talk about future goals, but it means little if nothing has ever been achieved. Compare the size of the goals already achieved to any future goals and to the needs of the job. Ask if the goals are in writing. This helps validate the candidate's real, versus stated, philosophy. Goals always require a series of substeps before they're completed. Ask about this progress.

If the candidate wants to be promoted to the next level, ask what he or she is doing to get ready. Only a few are doing something proactively, usually in the form of continuous outside education, volunteering for new work, or taking the initiative on expanding the role of the job without expectations of any reward. Goals are meaningful when there is a pattern of personal growth, self-motivation, self-sacrifice, and a track record of goal setting and achievement.

Commitment is a critical component of character that complements energy[2] and potential. Ask the candidate to give you an example of when he or she was totally committed to a task. Some high-energy people are great starters, but poor finishers. Look for a pattern of meeting deadlines. Get related examples. Find out when the candidate missed an important target. Determine the recovery response. While important, a one-time commitment just sets the stage. It's the consistent pattern that counts. Determine the source of the commitment and the reasons for failure. Was it an internal factor like a personal commitment to another person or a desire to achieve a long sought-after goal? Was the failure because of the lack of resources, knowledge, or personal commitment? This is an important topic with many possible outcomes. You might not find the complete answer, but you'll always learn more about the candidate if you look carefully.

When assessing character, look for frank and open responses, especially regarding the failures. Does the candidate take responsibility for both the successes and the bombs, or is it all one-sided? Be concerned if the answers become vague, too short, or too general, which is a sign of misleading or avoidance. Rank the candidate a 5 in character when you observe the combination of sincerity with a sense of commitment, strong values, and a pattern of goal setting and achievement. Look for honesty, actions, and decisions based on right and wrong, and an ability to openly express a point of view.

Rank the person a 3 if you have no strong sense about character and values, either strong or weak. Rank the candidate a 1 or 2 if something disturbs you about the candidate, you feel you're being mislead, the resume is fraudulent, or if answers don't ring true. A low ranking on character should always eliminate the candidate from any further consideration.

➤ 10. Personality and Cultural Fit

A person's true personality is best measured through his or her accomplishments. Look for flexibility, interpersonal skills, and decision making in different situations—as a team member, leader of the team, and individual contributor. Be concerned if every accomplishment relies on the same strengths. I met a vice president/controller candidate who relied on his strong analytical and negotiating skills in each major accomplishment. He sounded good during the first half hour of the interview while describing significant financing roles and discussing his identification of operating problems of a major company. Soon, however, the real pattern emerged. He was weak in building and developing teams. He was excluded as a candidate because his individual contributor style wouldn't work well either in managing others or in dealing with the senior management of the company.

You can discover a person's preferred relationship pattern by categorizing his or her accomplishments according to the ABC scale—**A**lone, **B**elong to team, or in-**C**harge of the team. Ask the candidate to describe favorite work experiences or give you examples of problems he or she likes to solve. Keep track of these responses by putting little tick marks on the top of your notes. When the candidate describes an individual contributor task, put a tick mark under the A column. Put a mark under the B column for team-related work, and under the C for a management or leadership role. By the end of the interview, a definite and revealing pattern will emerge.

The use of *I* or *we* is not indicative of an individual contributor or team member. Consider the project described, not the use of *I* or *we*. For example, you might get too many "We did . . ." for an individual project, or many statements starting with "I did . . ." regarding team projects, so listen carefully. At the end of the interview, this collection of tick marks will provide some real insight into the candidate's preferred way of working. Lots of As means an individual contributor. A manager inclination would have more Cs. The real team player would have a majority of Bs.

How someone scores depends on the needs of the job. If the job is an individual contributor role (salesman, technician, analyst, or consultant), make sure you hire someone who likes to work independently. If you need a manager to lead a group, make sure you observe this pattern. Be concerned if you see little balance or someone too one-dimensional. Most jobs require some mix of all three. A pure individualist is as much of a concern as a dominant director or a consummate team player. Remember that no pattern is bad; it all depends on the needs of the job.

A number of years ago, I conducted a phone interview for a sales manager for a high-tech product line. The candidate was very aggressive and all of his major accomplishments were related to his closing major deals. The *I* word was in every sentence. The A column had 75 percent of the tick marks. In this case, the person was a very strong, persuasive, individual contributor. While a top-notch salesperson, he was someone I couldn't recommend for a sales management position. Toward the end of the interview, I asked him what he thought his greatest strength was. A "people person" was his immediate response. Although I wouldn't have categorized him this way, he believed a strong "people person" meant having the ability to persuade and sell others. For me, someone has to have at least one-third of the ticks in the B column to merit this description. You'll learn a lot about interpersonal skills and flexibility by keeping track of accomplishments according to this ABC classification.

Personality should be used to exclude candidates rather than to include them. Personality problems are a frequent cause of problems on the job. Conflict, ego, inability to work with others, and immaturity all result in friction, inefficiency, loss of morale, and turnover. These fatal flaws should immediately eliminate a candidate from consideration.

Most people are easy enough to work with; therefore, if they don't have any fatal flaws, rank them at least a 3. Rank the person higher when personality helps him or her do the job better. For customer service and salespeople, this is a critical need, so don't compromise here. A strong personality plus an appropriate ABC balance deserves a 4 or 5. For most positions, it's best to remember that you're not hiring a best friend—just a coworker. Personality tests and reference checks will help you sort through this.

The Ten-Factor Candidate Assessment is as much a checklist of what a good interview needs to address as it is an evaluation tool. Use it as a roadmap to uncover the traits of top performers. If you've measured all of these ten factors during the course of the interviewing process, your assessment will be extremely accurate. Don't exclude or include candidates too soon. This approach will lead you to a balanced assessment, considering strengths and weaknesses in an objective manner. If your assessment is based on feelings rather than specific examples, you should re-interview the candidate.

Complete the Ten-Factor Assessment form immediately after you meet the candidate, but consider it a work in progress. Update your evaluation of the candidate based on reference checks, subsequent interviews and phone conversations, testing, and the inputs of other interviewers. All of these factors should be considered before the assessment profile is finalized.

■ SPOTTING FATAL FLAWS

Don't overlook the fatal flaws. These are the less obvious traits that can cause an apparently great person to fail once on the job. An abusive personality, intolerance in some form, or an inability to make critical decisions under pressure are some common fatal flaws. These sometimes go unrecognized during the interview, either overlooked or masked by an offsetting strength. Clues abound, but you must be observant and vigilant. Raise the caution flag if you discover one of these tendencies or traits on the following lookout list:

Clues to Some Fatal Flaws

➤ Great communicator, with self-confidence, but his or her management role doesn't seem to be growing. You might have found a great individual contributor or consultant-type person, but a weak manager.

➤ High drive and ambition, but maybe too assertive. This could relate to ego problems, immaturity, or an inability to work in cross-functional teams.

➤ A dominant or stern personality. This might relate to the previous point or be indicative of a negative attitude, lack of patience, or an inability to persuade and motivate others.

➤ Extremes in any behavior—too analytical, too assertive, too friendly, or too persuasive. This usually leads to problems regarding lack of flexibility or balance.

➤ High energy, great personality, but answers are too general, or vague, doesn't volunteer details, even with urging. This is the classic—lots of sizzle, but little substance.

➤ Too many *I*s or *we*s might indicate someone too hung up on himself or herself, the classic individual contributor, or in the *we* instance, a person who hasn't accomplished much on his or her own. The previous section discusses how to probe for this trait.

If you observe any of these signs, you must get proof to overcome the potential concern. The best way is to get a significant example that disproves the potential fatal flaw. For example, if lack of team or management ability is the concern, get the candidate to describe his or her most significant management or team project. Get more than one example and make sure you get many facts, figures, dates, and names to substantiate the example.

For extremes in behavior, get examples of the opposite trait. Someone who is too friendly might not be strong willed enough and vice versa. Likewise, someone who is always selling might not be detailed enough. Get these people to describe some projects that required details or analytical work. Get the overzealous analyst or individual contributor to describe some important team projects. Then get specific examples of how he or she persuaded or motivated others to take actions against their better judgment. Reference checks and testing can help here. Do not ignore these caution flags. They can mean the difference between a great hire or a big problem.

A few years ago, we placed a very bright, assertive candidate who was a great communicator. His references confirmed these qualities, but they also indicated that he was only an adequate manager. He had the ability to hire strong people, and then let them manage themselves, but even this wasn't high on his list. It turned out to be true. Unfortunately, he didn't even want to spend the management time necessary to build a team. We were so excited about getting a candidate that was superb in all but one critical dimension, we ignored a potentially fatal flaw. As a result, the company asked him to leave within four months. You must do your homework with an open mind, or else you'll miss or ignore the obvious.

■ THE PROFESSIONALISM AND QUALITY OF THE INTERVIEW COUNTS

Sometimes a weak assessment occurs because of poor interviewing skills rather than because the candidate is weak. You need to be a good interviewer to evaluate the candidate properly. In the process, you'll attract a better class of candidates. The best candidates want to work for great managers; good interviewing skills, especially knowledge of the job, is one aspect of this. Candidates judge the quality of the company and the quality of their potential supervisor by the quality of the interviewing process.

The quality of the assessment process is only as good as its weakest interviewer. This is especially true if every person has an equal vote. If you rely on the weak assessment skills of others, the whole process is compromised. I've seen many strong candidates lose out because one or two interviewers missed the mark. The hiring manager has to be confident enough to override these flawed inputs. One way to minimize this problem is to give partial voting rights.

On a vice president human resources search, the CEO of a large financial organization wanted to reduce the scope of the inputs of a few members of the interviewing team, while still giving them the courtesy of having input. We told these interviewers that the CEO and CFO had already decided that one candidate was the best of the five presented. Their only role was to detect any fatal flaws in the candidate. By limiting the authority of other interviewers this way, you can minimize the problems associated with weaker interviewers.

A different tack is required if the other interviewer is the hiring manager's boss. If the boss is a weak interviewer, or just wants to conduct a personality and fit interview, it's best to list the reasons you want to hire the candidate beforehand, and ask the boss to validate one specific area. The number one SMARTe objective is a good choice. By narrowing the scope of a less reliable interviewer, you can easily turn a personality contest into a mini performance-based interview.

If the weak interviewer is the hiring manager, you could conduct a panel interview with some good interviewers taking the lead. This allows the hiring manager to participate. Time is wasted and bad hiring decisions are made when incompetent interviewers influence the final decision. These problem people must be identified and alternative procedures established ahead of time. There's too much riding on every hiring decision to allow controllable error to affect the outcome.

Following is a quick checklist to gauge the quality and professionalism of an interview. We've found these five conditions essential for an accurate assessment. Weakness in any of these areas by anyone involved in the hiring decision compromises the whole process.

Assessing the Professionalism of the Interview and the Interviewer

Level of Preparation. A strong interviewer has read the resume, is very familiar with the performance profile, and knows how to ask the four core questions and assess competency. Weak interviewers wing it.

Length of Interview. An hour or more is not unreasonable for any critical position. Less than 30 minutes is a waste of time. It's impossible to judge competency in this short period.

Basic Interviewing Skills. A strong interviewer knows how to ask the four core questions using fact-finding. Weak interviewers rely on emotions and gut feelings.

Time to Decide. Strong interviewers stay objective for at least 30 minutes whether they like the candidate or not. Weak interviewers make decisions too early in the interview, sometimes in as little as a few minutes.

Success Factors Considered. The strongest interviewers know how to accurately assess competency, the capacity to grow, self-motivation, and the ability to motivate others. Weak interviewers guess at this based on interviewing personality and what's written on the resume.

Address each of these areas if you want to improve the quality of the assessment. Asking for a written assessment is one way to ensure that other interviewers have conducted a thorough evaluation. Have them use the Ten-Factor Candidate Assessment as a guideline. For any rating other than a 3, have the interviewer provide some added substantiation. This should be written information citing actual examples to support the weak or strong rating. On these written assessments, have the interviewer indicate the length of the interview. In our half-day training session, we suggest that the interviewing team prepare the SMARTe objectives together and then divide them up. As a substitute, send a copy of the resume with the SMARTe objectives and a rating sheet to each interviewer before meeting the candidate. This, along with the written assessment, will act as a catalyst to improve the value of the input of other interviewers.

■ MAKING THE HIRING DECISION

Merely deciding to delay the assessment until you've collected enough information about each of the ten factors will lead to a better decision. If you decide to take a shortcut or eliminate any of the factors from consideration, accuracy will decline. As you conduct the assessment, watch for fatal flaws. These can easily sneak up and bite you when you're not looking.

These assessment and interviewing techniques, while not hard to use, take some practice. The best opportunity is with those candidates you wouldn't even think of hiring. Every now and then, don't be surprised if you find a great candidate in this group.

Collectively, the ten traits will measure competency, capacity, and desire. Balance is essential. That's why it's important to measure all of the ten factors before excluding a promising candidate who is weak on one or two traits or before hiring someone who seems great on just a few traits. If you hire someone without capacity, you have little future. If you hire someone without desire, the present will be compromised. If you hire someone without all of the skills, but with everything else, all you lose is a few months.

POWER HIRING HOT TIPS:
THE FINAL CANDIDATE ASSESSMENT

✔ Don't short-circuit the assessment. Minimize conclusions based on gut feelings and emotions.

✔ Use the 10-Factor Candidate Assessment template as a checklist. Get detailed examples of past performance for each of the factors.

✔ Be prepared. Before the interview, read the resume, know the job, know the four core questions, and stay equally inquisitive whether you like the candidate or not.

✔ In each candidate look for self-motivation (energy^2), the ability to motivate others, the ability to deliver comparable results, and the ability to solve job-related problems. These are the four core traits of success.

✔ Look for a upward pattern of personal growth and development. Be concerned if growth has flattened or declined along with motivation.

✔ Match the performance needs of the job by anchoring each SMARTe objective. Look for comparable, not identical, accomplishments.

✔ You'll be able to determine potential, talent, and thinking ability through the use of visualization questions. The best candidates can anticipate the needs of the job or project before starting it.

✔ The application or use of similar technical skills is a better predictor of success than the absolute level of technical skills.

(continued)

(continued)

✔ Compare the environment (complexity, growth, standards, pace, level of bureaucracy) of the candidate's prior companies to your needs to determine real compatibility.

✔ Great managers show a pattern of proactively building strong teams and developing strong people.

✔ Character and personality reveal themselves through performance and developing others.

✔ Use external means to validate your assessment. Reference checks, background checks, and testing strengthen your evaluation.

✔ Watch out for the fatal flaws—too bright, too dominant, too analytical, or too clever. Too much of anything can be a clue to a problem.

✔ A professional, well-run interview is as important to you as it is to the candidate. Strong candidates judge companies and managers based on the quality of the interviewing process. Unless the interview is thorough, the conclusions obtained will be less reliable.

Chapter 8

Recruiting, Negotiating, and Closing

To be persuasive, we must be believable.
To be believable, we must be credible.
To be credible, we must be truthful.

Edward R. Murrow

■ RECRUITING IS NOT SELLING, AND OTHER MISCONCEPTIONS ABOUT THE MOST IMPORTANT PART OF HIRING

Recruiting is the most important part of the hiring process. Everything is a wasted effort if a top candidate doesn't accept a reasonable offer. We start this chapter with some fresh ideas about what recruiting is and isn't to make sure that we get it right.

➤ Recruiting is not something you do at the end of the interview. It starts at the beginning of the hiring process, when you write the performance profile and post the ad.

➤ Recruiting is more about buying than selling. If you sell too soon, you stop evaluating.

➤ Recruiting is more about consultative needs analysis than heavy-handed selling. For the candidate, accepting an offer is a long-term strategic decision, not tactical, and can't be rushed.

➤ Recruiting is more about career counseling than negotiating salaries. The candidate will evaluate your job against all competing career opportunities. The best always have multiple opportunities.

➤ The best candidates always seek advice from others before accepting an offer. Good recruiting must provide enough information for the candidate to persuade others as well as himself or herself.

➤ In the Beginning

Recruiting starts when you first contact the candidate, whether it's a compelling written ad or verbal pitch. Recruiting then continues through the interviewing process from the first phone screen to the final interview. It does not begin after you've assessed the candidate and decided that you want to move forward. This is too late. Interviewing and recruiting must take place in tandem. The compelling nature of the opportunity must be presented up front. This way, the best candidates join the initial pool of applicants. If you wait, the best will either not apply, or they'll filter themselves out during the course of the assessment.

While you need to start at the beginning, don't rush it. Just because you think you've found a hot candidate, don't start selling within 15 minutes. Some managers think they can sell or charm a candidate into taking a job. This is not recruiting. This is selling in its worst form (e.g., think about the overzealous used car salesman). It not only demeans the job, but it also drives the best candidates away. It they do stick around, you'll wind up paying unnecessary premiums. Recruiting is more about career counseling and solution selling. The key to recruiting: Create a compelling opportunity, present it early and often, and make the candidate earn the right to have it.

The key to recruiting—create a compelling opportunity, present it early and often, and make the candidate earn the right to have it.

To do this right, the hiring manager needs a complete understanding of the job, a thorough knowledge of the candidate's competency, short- and long-term motivation, and compensation needs. A balance among these competing issues is the key in bringing a fair deal together. This takes time and strong recruiting skills. Open and honest communication is a prerequisite. None of this happens when you're selling.

Recruiting is as much about the buying process as it is about solution selling. Many managers stop the evaluation and begin the selling process as soon as they find someone they like. The interviewer talks more and learns less. From this point onward, nothing new is learned about the candidate other than what he or she wants you to know. Complete control of the interview is lost and handed to the candidate. This cheapens the job and makes the candidate more expensive. Even if the candidate is good enough, you'll never know until he or she starts. Then you'll wonder how you blew the interview. This is why staying the buyer is essential. Good recruiting requires a carrot and stick approach during the interview. Dangle the opportunity out there for the candidate to see, but still ask all the questions to make sure the candidate is both competent and motivated. Just because you're favorably impressed with a candidate doesn't mean you're ready to start selling or stop evaluating.

Many years ago, I worked with a very strong candidate on an assignment with a company that had a very rigorous selection process. The candidate was excited about the prospect and went to each interview ready to sell himself on why he was the best person for the position. He didn't get it, but he tried like heck. The job became more appealing the more difficult it was to obtain. This same candidate was turned off by another client who started selling him within 15 minutes of the first interview. This provides a valuable lesson—*if you make it too easy to get the job, the candidate doesn't want it as much. If you make it challenging and difficult to get, he or she wants it more.* You've increased the value of the job by making it more difficult to obtain. This is a basic principle of human nature and the very heart of recruiting. A job has more value when it has to be earned. It has less value if it's too easy to get, and you have to pay more, too. Top candidates are excited by competition, real challenges, and an opportunity to grow. Candidates sell you when confronted with

---

If you make it too easy for someone to get the job, they don't want it as much. If you make it challenging and difficult to get, they want it more.

---

opportunity. Strong candidates are proud of their accomplishments and want their potential new boss to know all about them. This is how you attract top people without selling them.

A job is never perfect. You never have enough money, the location is bad, the best candidates generally have multiple opportunities, and you're always vulnerable to counteroffers. A good recruiter can level the playing field. Attractive opportunities need to be presented in an open, give-and-take manner. Every step of the way requires persuasion and understanding to overcome the natural resistance to move forward. At the same time, you need to collect additional information about the candidate's competency. The first step is to position the job to take into account the candidate's long-term motivational needs. This will increase the likelihood of getting a top person to join your team, despite the typical roadblocks, restraints, and hurdles you'll encounter along the way.

■ WHY CANDIDATES TAKE JOBS— UNDERSTANDING AND MANAGING MOTIVATION

Understanding candidate motivation is the first step in putting together an effective recruiting program. Candidates take offers because of two fundamental reasons. The first we call a "going-away" strategy. It usually has to do with leaving a bad job situation. This could be the result of a layoff or a spouse's relocation. Recruiting is relatively easy if the candidate's current situation is weak and future options are limited. Standards are lowered based on these personal circumstances. If you find strong candidates in this position, move fast. You have a good, but temporary, advantage. Their future opportunities will change for the better very quickly.

The "going-toward" strategy is the more common reason good candidates take other positions. These people need some very compelling reasons to leave an already strong position or to compete with other opportunities that are very attractive. For most candidates, the underlying motivation to change jobs is usually a combination of these two strategies. The interviewer's job is to determine the degree of both and which one is most important.

Quickly find out which strategy is dominating the candidate's job-hunting efforts. Early in the interview, ask why the candidate is considering a move now. This gets at the going-away strategy. Later on in the interview, follow up with a question asking what he or she is looking for in a new job. This gets at the going-toward strategy. To get at underlying motivation, ask the candidate why having these conditions is important in accepting a new position. This requires an applicant to think at a deeper level and often reveals true motivation. You may need to use this later in presenting the merits of the job. Compare the consistency between the going-away reasons with the going-toward strategy. For example, it makes sense if a person wants to leave a chaotic situation for more security. It doesn't seem logical, though, if someone is leaving this same chaotic situation for more growth opportunity. Look for congruity at every level. Understanding motivation will help you make an insightful decision.

If the candidate is currently in a good situation or has multiple opportunities, you must be extra diligent. The candidate will need something very attractive to pull him or her away. This is when you'll really need strong recruiting skills, especially if the candidate is one you think you want on the short list. Candidates with a going-toward motivating strategy take a new job for three reasons:

1. The quality of the company.
2. The quality of the hiring manager.
3. The challenge and excitement of the position.

You have to be able to address each of these during the course of the interview. You need to develop a recruiting pitch around all three areas. Ask yourself why a strong candidate would want this job. Be specific and insightful, not general and superficial. Come up with four or five good ideas for each category. Base the company opportunities around the strategic plan—new products, new markets, and new systems. This will form the basis of your company's recruiting pitch, but don't present it as an opening ten-minute talk. It's better to break it into one-minute sound bites. You'll use these before you ask your questions. This creates interest and keeps the momentum of the interview at a high pace.

For example, telling a candidate how you're planning to grow in a certain area has great appeal if you relate it directly to the importance of the job. Such statements establish the foundation for long-term growth and opportunity. By creating excitement, you challenge the candidate to rise to the occasion. Well-written SMARTe objectives are sufficient to address the position needs. During the questioning, state the strategic or tactical importance of the objectives to make them sound even more appealing. For example, *"The new IS system will help us get control of our rapid overseas expansion programs. Can you give me some examples of when you took the lead in setting up new complex systems like this?"* This type of question makes the job more important and more interesting. This is the carrot and stick approach to recruiting and interviewing in tandem.

Good candidates want to work for strong managers because this increases the likelihood that they'll grow, develop, and improve themselves by taking the job. The best evidence of this is the quality of the hiring manager's interviewing skills. Knowing the job, having high standards, asking tough questions, and openly listening to the responses in a nonjudgmental way provide insight into your leadership qualities. Make sure you understand what motivates the candidate; then suggest how this job will help him or her grow in this area. Give examples of what you've done for other people who have worked for you. Give their names and describe how they have advanced in the company. Allow the candidate to talk to them. Recruiting is much easier if candidates want to work for you because you're a strong leader. This is one of the best ways to overcome many typical recruiting problems.

If done right, this three-pronged recruiting approach will overwhelm all competing opportunities. It needs to be planned beforehand and integrated into the performance-based interviewing process. While there's a tendency and a need to attract and pursue great candidates, going overboard will usually misfire. Good recruiting provides the balance by making the job worth having and worth earning.

Before you start meeting candidates, prepare a table like this one we did for a marketing manager of a software company. This sets the stage for the three-pronged recruiting information you'll need during the interview.

Recruiting Pitch—Software Manager

The Job	The Hiring Manager	The Company
Critical game-breaker position—Own the product line.	Strong leader and background with one of the top software companies in the United States.	Well-funded start-up with charismatic leader at the helm.
Establish strategic direction and distribution channels.	Great leadership style and allows subordinates to take on new challenges and grow fast.	Well-positioned in market space with new technology.
Develop new skills in the area of negotiating and business development.	A real team player, has demonstrated ability to build great teams everywhere.	Strong executive team ready with lots of relevant experience.
First multifunctional management job.	A high potential person who's going places.	Big equity play to offset the inherent risk.
Learn new distribution channels in software.	Warm and personable, but with high standards.	Top-notch technical team that's been together.

This information must be presented in small pieces throughout the course of the interviewing process. Some of it can be told directly while you're asking questions, and some can be presented indirectly—in the form of literature, an informative Web site, conversations with others who have worked for the hiring manager, or a tour. Surprisingly, most companies do a very poor job with this. If you don't constantly build up the importance of the job, the quality of the company, and the strength of the hiring manager, all you have left is the offer package. This is not the best way to attract top talent.

If everything else is compelling, the financial aspects of the position become less important. This is how you overcome salary constraints and other typical problems. The candidate makes a personal strategic decision about all aspects of the offer, rather than a tactical one that relies on just a great compensation package.

■ RECRUITING AND CHALLENGING QUESTIONS CAN STRENGTHEN YOUR POSITION

You can increase candidate interest in a position through the use of recruiting and challenging questions. Recruiting questions are no more than using the recruiting sound bites we mentioned earlier as prefaces to the standard questions. For example, *"We're creating an advanced line of industrial lubricants that will dramatically reduce machine maintenance costs. This will be backed by an extensive advertising campaign. We're looking for some top industrial salespeople to handle the Fortune 100 market. Can you give me some examples of your most comparable sales accomplishments?"* It's important to state the strategic or tactical importance of a task and then ask the candidate to describe a related experience (the anchor) or how the task would be accomplished (visualize). Recruiting questions are effective because they create interest and pull the candidate toward the job.

Challenging questions create interest by pushing the candidate away. For example, *"I'm concerned you don't have enough experience in developing international accounting systems. Have I missed something?"* This slight challenge increases the importance of the skill and requires a candidate to sell you. This approach, used judiciously throughout the interview, can increase a candidate's interest in a job. If the concern is valid, it demonstrates areas where the candidate can learn and grow if he or she were to get the job. Often, applicants self-select this way. If the job is worthwhile, you'll sense the candidate's excitement and tenacity by how hard he or she pushes back. If the job is too challenging, the candidate will exclude himself or herself from consideration.

Challenging can be abrasive when carried to an extreme. When combined with a compliment, it works very well. *"While you have great experience in consumer marketing, it appears you haven't been exposed to industrial products. Is this true?"*

Recruiting and challenging can also be combined. Mentioning the importance of a task and then expressing concern about the candidate's apparent lack of skills raise the standards of performance. A candidate needs to overcome a negative belief and sell harder if it's a critical area. *"Developing the international market is essential for us in achieving our three-year plan. From your resume, I'm concerned you don't have enough European experience to handle this. What are your thoughts on this?"*

For practice, try this recruiting process with some candidates you wouldn't normally consider and observe their reaction. See how they push back. Recruiting and challenging questioning techniques are essential tools if you want to attract the best. These techniques allow you to maintain balance with the strong candidates you want to attract by creating interest, determining motivation, and opening up the lines of communication.

■ END THE INTERVIEW ON A POSITIVE NOTE

The hiring manager should use the following as the last question at the end of the first interview. It's a must for all finalists.

> *Although we're seeing some other fine candidates, I believe you have a strong background, and we'd like to get back to you in a few days. What are your thoughts now about this position?*

For those candidates you like, this is a good way to test their interest at the end of the first interview. By stating that you have other strong candidates, you create supply, which makes the job more desirable. Candidates get nervous about a job if they're the only one being considered. This strengthens your eventual bargaining position and improves the open flow of communications.

A positive affirmation also is important. This feedback tells the candidate he or she is in contention. The candidate will think more about why he or she wants the job, not why he or she is not going to get it. This push-pull technique sets up the candidate interest question. This is what you really want to know. You want to hear about interests, concerns, and objections. If any are voiced, acknowledge the issues and suggest that they will be discussed at a later meeting or discuss them briefly at this point. Give the candidate the opportunity to call you back later. This open two-way exchange of information will be important as you move forward.

If a candidate balks at some point and does not want to move forward, it's okay to try to convince the candidate using traditional sales persuasion techniques. Once persuaded, go back to a buyer's position. Tell the candidate that while you want to convince him or her this is a great chance, you still need to complete your assessment. This approach allows you to present your position strongly, while maintaining underlying control. Often an interviewer will move too fast after a candidate has been persuaded in the traditional way. We forget that the evaluation process is not yet completed.

■ HOW TO REALLY NEGOTIATE AND CLOSE OFFERS

We're now ready for the second interview. One of the short-listed candidates will ultimately be getting an offer; therefore, you have to take care every step of the way. Use the techniques in the following section to make sure that the closing process moves along as smoothly as possible.

Don't start too soon or wait too long to talk about salary. The best time is when both parties are somewhat serious. This usually requires at least a 15- to 20-minute good phone screen, or it could be discussed at the end of the first interview. Sometimes it's best to wait until you're scheduling the second interview. Never wait until the assessment is completed. By then, the candidate will know he is the finalist, giving him the upper hand. As a minimum, wait until the end of the initial phone screen to mention salary. Otherwise, it's just a yes/no filter based on no knowledge.

The financial considerations are rarely the reason that a deal falls apart. In the past 29 years in more than 1,000 different salary negotiations, less than 5 percent fell apart because of compensation. My rule is to keep people talking about the importance of the job. Candidates are always more realistic after they understand the opportunity, and companies are always more flexible when they meet a strong candidate. One of my candidates for a COO position in a $500-million company wanted 50 percent more than my client was prepared to go. We discovered this at the end of the first interview. By then, the job was so appealing and the candidate so perfect that both parties agreed to split the difference. We would never have gotten to this point if salary had been discussed first.

We suggest presenting components of the offer package throughout the assessment before the candidate is the only finalist. For example, *"Our comp structure is heavily based on bonus, with low base salaries. Is this something you'd consider as we move to the second round of interviews?"* This type of approach minimizes the awkwardness of the typical negotiating session when everything is put on the table at once. The key is to negotiate the offer and get concessions along the way, when you have leverage and something to offer. You can negotiate every aspect of the offer in this way, rather than leaving it all to the end. This is a great way to test sincere interest at each step. Using this parallel approach, you'll be assessing the candidate's competency at the same time you're recruiting and closing the deal.

One of my associates used this approach recently in negotiating an offer with a product manager for a health care products company. The candidate was very interested in the position after the first interview, and our client wanted to move quickly. We told the candidate that she was one of three people being invited back for a second round of interviews and the salary range was only slightly more than her current level. The job was an excellent career move for her, and she agreed to go back knowing that if she were to get an offer, it would be only a small increase. After a few more rounds of interviewing, it was clear she was the finalist; at that time, she upped her financial demands. We held firm, though. We indicated to her that one of the reasons for proceeding was her prior agreement to continue the interview process knowing the tight financial situation. Although we didn't have any other candidates, we told her she would have to drop herself from consideration if she wanted to push the salary issue. She relented and accepted an offer consistent with our earlier discussions. This deal would have fallen apart or become very uncomfortable if we hadn't discussed salary right after the first interview.

You must have the candidate's salary history before you invite him or her back for a second interview. If it's too high or if you have little room to maneuver, state your concern and ask if this is a serious issue. If you don't know the salary history, state your salary range and say that you hope this fits with the candidate's needs. In either case, balking is a good clue you might be light. A little probing helps. Keep your options open. Unless there's too much resistance, urge the candidate to come back in. Tell the candidate that while the salary could be an issue, there might be other things you can do to compensate, or that there are other significant opportunities worth exploring.

If the candidate agrees to come back, you know you've just established the condition of a potential offer. For candidates who are still reluctant, you can dangle some more carrots. A salary review in three to six months is one approach that works well. Don't go overboard. Salary, bonus, and equity opportunities can often move a reluctant candidate forward, but you don't want to play these cards too soon. I like to suggest to the candidates that they not make long-term career moves without all the facts. Great opportunities can always offset short-term financial constraints. The key is to make the strategic opportunities overwhelm the tactical issues.

Use each subsequent interview session to gain more buy in. If you sense sincere interest after the second interview, mention to the candidate what still needs to happen to get to an offer stage. This could consist of background and degree checks, reference checks, psychological testing, additional interviews, and a medical exam or drug testing. Going forward is tacit acceptance to these conditions and the high likelihood the candidate is being honest about his or her interest and background.

Describing the benefit package can be used either as a lure or a way to relay nonpositive information if the benefits are weak. Much of these discussions can be part of casual conversations as you're arranging other meetings. *"Because we're growing, our benefit plan isn't as comprehensive as some of the larger companies."* This way, by the time you're ready to make an offer, many of these potential deal-breaking contentious details have already been addressed.

A few years back, I had a strong candidate for the CFO position at a southern California-based retail store chain. After his second interview with the CEO, I told the candidate what the range of the offer would be (only a few percent over his current package) and the next steps in the evaluation process. This consisted of a meeting with two board members on the East Coast, a half-day session with an industrial psychologist in the Midwest, and then a dinner with the chairman. This was before the medical and drug test, and a final meeting with the CEO. The candidate was very interested, but when he agreed to continue this arduous process, I knew the deal was done. Three weeks later, we finalized the package exactly as described. The candidate's decision to go forward under the conditions described was ample evidence of commitment and interest in the job. This is a great model of how all offers need to be tested.

■ STEP BY STEP THROUGH THE OFFER

Even though some of the components of an offer have been discussed, you don't want to rush into presenting a formal offer after the interviewing has been completed. You have fewer options if the candidate responds with an *"I have to think about it."* The applicant is now the buyer and the company is the seller. Open communication stops. Candidates stop thinking about why they want the job and start thinking about why they don't want it. Thinking about an offer is fine, but before a formal offer is extended, you get unbiased information. Afterward, your same attempt to find out interest and what's happening comes across as harassment, pushiness, or overselling. Negotiations are awkward and stressful. Neither party wants to lose face. Deals often fall apart at this point for petty reasons.

Never make a formal offer until every aspect of the offer has been tested and agreed to beforehand. First, test for general interest. This question allows you to differentiate between the job and the offer. *"Assuming an attractive offer, how does the job and*

Never make a formal offer until every aspect has been tested and agreed on beforehand.

---

challenge appeal to you?" This allows you to address any concerns about the job first. You'll eliminate a lot of bad fits this way.

Bad jobs are often accepted because of great financial incentives. This is not the way to build a great team. By starting with job fit, you'll also be able to make the financial consideration a secondary component of the offer. Salary negotiations are usually easy if the candidate wants the position for personal growth reasons. Go back to this throughout the negotiating process if you get in trouble later on. Find out why the candidate really wants the job, and be sure to remind him or her about these points often.

"We're thinking of putting an offer together for you, but we'd like to know your thoughts now about the job," is a good way to make a preliminary offer test. Use a trial close to get more specific. Something like, *"What do you think if we could put a package together in the range of $_____ to $_____?"* works well. You'll need to go back and forth with the candidate to test this range, but this gets both parties to start talking in an open manner. Add some competition. *"Although we're still seeing other candidates, I believe you'd make a great addition to our team. What do you think about something like . . . ?"* Competition allows you to be a little stronger during the negotiating phase and makes the candidate more realistic.

Use the table on page 221 as a checklist as you test the offer.

Hesitation on any item means there are other issues to be considered, so continue probing. Objections at this stage often result from lack of information. Don't move forward until these objections have been addressed. You can make trade-offs at this time. Give something else if you can't meet a particular need, such as a signing bonus instead of a higher salary. Find out if this issue is a deal breaker if you can't accommodate the candidate. *"Does this mean you don't want to move forward if we can't resolve this issue?"* Work these points until you obtain agreement. You'll discover this give-and-take process is easier if a formal offer is not on the table.

Offer Summary and Checklist

Target Offer	Summary Details	Test/Agree	Objections/ Comments
Salary			
Bonus			
Car			
Other Cash Comp			
Title—Position			
Benefit Package			
Options			
Relocation Package			
Next Review			
Other			

■ THE CLOSE—PUTTING IT ALL TOGETHER

Once all the aspects of an offer have been agreed to, you're ready for a preliminary close. Don't make the offer formal yet. Use a close that gets the applicant to indirectly agree to the terms of the offer. Ask, *"If we could formalize this package in the next few days, when do you think you could start?"* In classic selling terms, this is called a *secondary close* because giving a start date indicates total acceptance. There are other big issues to resolve without a specific start date—such as competing offers or counteroffers. If the candidate is reluctant to provide a start date, you can probe to uncover any other issues and give yourself time to address them. If you get a start date, but still have doubts about sincerity, ask the candidate about his or her company's termination process. Find out how he or she will tell the boss, the likely reaction, and possible counteroffers. Leaving a company is a difficult process for many, so provide some guidance and a helping hand.

Now you're ready for the final close. You're still testing, so don't hand over the offer letter quite yet. As you review the final terms of the offer with the candidate, ask, *"If we could put this offer in writing today or tomorrow, when would you be in a position to give formal acceptance?"* Anything other than "immediately" is of concern. By this time, you've negotiated all the terms of the offer, the job scope, and provided streams of information on every point. Acceptance is assumed and any back-tracking now needs to be met with serious concern. Find out the problem and attempt to address it using all the points noted previously. You can certainly give the candidate until the next morning to officially accept if the reaction is positive, but never agree to more than this.

The approach we recommend is an open, natural, give-and-take process. If the offer is fair and mutually agreed to, there is no reason for the applicant to need to think about it. This thinking process should have already taken place by the time you get to this point. There is a serious problem if the candidate still needs to think about it for more than one day. Step back and withhold the offer. Hesitation at this late stage typically involves counteroffers. If you sense this is the case, tell the candidate that you are very concerned, and that you would like to understand what's happening. It's best to put every issue on the table so that it can be discussed in an open and frank manner.

This testing process is not a high-pressure approach. Making an offer and taking a job is a critical decision for both the candidate and the company. We want to give the candidate as much time as necessary to make a well-informed decision. That's why the informal offer and testing process is effective. It allows the candidate to do research and consult with spouse and other advisors throughout the interviewing process. By delaying the formal presentation of the offer until acceptance is guaranteed, the company keeps the lines of communications open and stays in a stronger negotiating position. You'll gain more unbiased information this way and have more flexibility. Once the formal offer is extended, candidates are not as revealing in their comments, and you have less opportunity to respond.

Of course, there is no guarantee that all offers will be accepted or that everything will go easily. Our experience has been that more offers are accepted using this process, and difficult problems often get resolved more easily—largely because of the open communications aspect of the process. Neither party loses face with the testing and give-and-take discussion of all issues.

■ OVERCOMING OBJECTIONS—WHAT TO DO WHEN THINGS GO WRONG

Occasionally, the closing process hits a snag or two. In this case, you'll need to use one or more of the following advanced recruiting techniques:

➤ 1. Close upon an Objection

Use this technique with any objection. Just ask, *"I assume if we can resolve this issue, you're in a position to accept all the other terms of the offer."* This narrows down any other possible objections to this issue. If the candidate hesitates, you know you have some other problems. It's best to get all of the objections on the table before you negotiate any of them.

We had a candidate who hesitated to accept an offer, stating he was concerned about the relocation package. We then asked if he would accept the rest of the package if we could meet his relocation needs. He still wouldn't commit and later reluctantly admitted the problem: His wife had a good job and really didn't want to move. We couldn't resolve this issue, and we were forced to drop an excellent candidate. Without this technique, we would have spent many more hours on a useless cause.

➤ 2. Not Enough Money

There's never enough money. This is why you must test all offers before finalizing the financial package. If the candidate balks at any time before you've made a formal offer, it's easy to just ask the candidate how flexible he is on the salary point. If he's open to discussion, your objective is to switch his interest in the job to the more strategic aspects. This could be better growth opportunities, more challenge, or more impact. An early review (less than a year) is one way to compensate for a lower than desired starting salary. Sign-on bonuses are always popular and special bonuses can also meet some compensation targets. Review in detail the benefit package, which is often overlooked and sometimes includes some real gems.

If the candidate doesn't appear to be flexible on salary, stop the process. Because you haven't made a formal offer, it's easy to state that the compensation discussed is your limit. *"I don't think we can go any higher."* Get confirmation from the candidate. *"Are you suggesting that if we can't meet your salary needs, you're withdrawing yourself from consideration?"* If the answer is yes, you can either say, "I'll see what I can do," or terminate the process. Often the candidate will acquiesce.

Another way to negotiate salary is to introduce competition. Even if you don't have other strong candidates, you can still use the concept of indirect competition. A few years ago, I created a salary cap on a production manager's position in the food industry by telling the candidate that if we were to go any higher on salary, we would be forced to look at candidates with more experience. The salary the candidate wanted was excessive. We had enough data to show him that the higher level was more consistent with directors than managers, and he had a few more years to go before he could get to this level. With this information and our strong stance, the candidate agreed to proceed in the salary range we targeted.

Presenting an experience gap is a great way to overcome salary problems and to create a compelling opportunity at the same time. A few years ago, I was working with a strong candidate for a CFO position at a small company. She had some great Fortune 500 corporate experience that drove her compensation up. A move to a smaller company with a broader focus would have been an essential career move for her, but she had to give up some salary to make the move. The company let her know that they were willing to risk her lack of experience in some important areas because she had so much potential, but they could not meet her initial salary requirements. She recognized the opportunity and agreed it was a fair trade-off. From her perspective, she was getting something more important than salary if she were to get the job. She did get the job, and she's still there and still excited about the opportunity.

➤ 3. Counteroffers

You need to confront the candidate early if you sense the possibility of a counteroffer. Be wary if the candidate hesitates to commit to a start date or is vague about getting back to you with a final acceptance. Ask the candidate about the chance that the current employer would present a counteroffer after he or she gives a resignation. Be concerned if you receive shallow or general responses. Ask the candidate how he or she feels about counteroffers in general. Explore the character issues. You defuse the threat of a counteroffer by exposing it as an inappropriate means to keep an employee. The long-term relationship is often weakened when an employee threatens to leave and is then lured back with a counteroffer. Cite examples as proof. Also ask how she would feel if one of her employees had to be coerced with a counteroffer to stay. This is an indirect way of exposing the lack of integrity associated with accepting a counteroffer.

Counteroffers must be handled in a frank and direct manner. Most counteroffers occur during the period after a formal offer is presented, but not yet accepted. It's what happens during the *"I have to think about it"* time period. Testing the offer minimizes this problem. Because the formal offer won't be presented until all objections are addressed, the candidate is less likely to be pressured into a difficult counteroffer position by the current employer. The candidate will have to either discuss the resignation beforehand without a formal offer, or state that a formal acceptance has already been given.

➤ 4. Apparent Lack of Promotional Opportunities

Every good candidate wants a chance to grow and develop. Don't promise a promotion, though. This can get you in trouble if the candidate isn't as strong as expected or if business conditions worsen. Good recruiting comes into play here because you've been describing many of the long-range opportunities in the company as part of your one-minute recruiting sound bites. To reinforce this, you can say that candidates will be given as much responsibility as they demonstrate they can handle. Follow this up by stating that promotions are given to those who meet their performance objectives. If both the company and candidate meet their objectives, these promotional opportunities will certainly develop and the candidate will be in a great position.

Describe other people under your direction who have been promoted. This demonstrates that you're the type of manager who can develop people. Your personal mentoring is an important reason that a candidate might take your offer despite other problems. Good people want promotional opportunities. If the candidate believes you'll be strongly supportive and that there are realistic opportunities in your firm, you'll do well on this point. Bring this issue up even if the candidate doesn't mention it during the course of the interview. Presenting a realistic picture of how a candidate can grow, develop, and get promoted is the heart of effective recruiting. It is also the difference between building a good team and building a great team.

➤ 5. Job Isn't Big Enough or Not Enough Challenge

If a candidate contends the job isn't big enough, make it bigger. This doesn't mean you need to give a bigger title or larger staff. Just add more work. Adding special projects works well. Assigning one-time projects of a critical nature is a great way to expand the scope of a job. These one-time efforts provide real meat to a position and can often help sway a candidate. Find out what really motivates a candidate to excel. Then assign projects that complement this. You can also tell the candidate that you'll assign special projects as soon as he or she gets up to speed. Be specific, because these projects are often the reason that candidates accept jobs. If they're challenging, important, and offer high exposure and learning, they become great means to expand a job's scope.

You need to discuss the strategic and tactical importance of the position if the candidate believes it to be beneath his or her competency level. This is a very important issue and must be dealt with directly. It affects the candidate's self-worth, so don't minimize it. Titles are important. If your title is not comparable to the candidate's previous title, make sure the comparability of the job is discussed. Higher visibility, exposure, and impact on the organization can offset an apparently lesser job. Make sure you use this technique to clarify a job's scope if it's perceived to be too small. Of course, if the job is in fact a lesser position, you could have a real problem.

➤ 6. Hesitating to Move on to the Next Step

A candidate's hesitation to come back is an obvious sign of a problem. If the candidate is a strong contender, it's worth the effort to have him or her reconsider. Find out the problem or concern. Often it's lack of information about a specific issue or some rumor the candidate has heard. Frequently, candidates remove themselves from consideration for the wrong reasons. Get in the habit of testing interest. You'll uncover issues that can be easily addressed before they become deal breakers.

Try this. At the end of the interview, ask, *"Although we're still considering a few other strong candidates, I believe you're an excellent fit. From what you now know about the position, how would you rank your interest level on a scale of 0 to 10?"* If it's in the 6 to 7 category, ask what it would take to get to an 8 or 9. This will tell you what you need to work on. The key to good recruiting is an open back and forth exchange of information. Losing a strong candidate for the right reasons is acceptable, but often great candidates get away because nobody bothered to find out and address their concerns.

The same problems can occur when you're inviting a candidate in for the first interview. Significant objections can often be overcome with great opportunities. Always position the new opportunity in such a manner that the candidate will explore it objectively. I remember a great candidate who wasn't interested in a top job closer to downtown Los Angeles because it would involve a move. I knew if I could just get the candidate into the first interview, it was a done deal. The job would have been a significant career move that would put the candidate into the big leagues. The job, the company, and the hiring manager were all representative of a world-class opportunity. I told the candidate he obviously wouldn't move unless this was a top 1 percent opportunity, so it was at least worth exploring. He agreed. He called me the afternoon after the interview and loudly complained. It was a great job and he knew he was going to be moving away from the home he loved. Strategically, however, it was the right move. He's now the number two person at a multibillion-dollar company.

➤ 7. Lack of Apparent Long-Term Opportunity

You can minimize this problem by including some strategic objectives in the performance profile. If you include a SMARTe performance objective like, "Prepare a long-term facilities plan to support annual growth of 25 percent," the candidate instantly recognizes the strategic importance of the job and the potential promotional opportunities. A good preplanned recruiting pitch can also help. Ask yourself why a top candidate would want this job. Forget the "mom and apple pie" stuff and be specific. Things like increasing market share by five points, introducing new technology, or a chance to rebuild after a fall are meaningful reasons why good candidates take jobs.

These performance objectives are part of the recruiting plan suggested earlier. As you interview the candidate, describe how the job relates to these strategic needs. Again, it's best to break down this recruiting pitch into short sound bites to use as prefaces to your actual questions. For example, here's a recruiting preface used at the beginning of a question for an accounting manager: *"The company is planning to enter Europe in a big way later this year. We see enormous growth potential in this market. In fact, we expect it to represent 25 percent of our business in three years. This is why we need a strong person to set up our complete international accounting system. Can you please describe some of your international accounting projects?"* This is a much better way of forming a question than the more common, *"Tell me about some of your accomplishments in the international accounting area."* Not only do you send a great message about the job, but also the candidate will talk more openly as he or she sells you on his or her qualifications for the position.

➤ 8. The Take-Away to Address Hesitation or Resistance

When it looks like a deal is about to break apart, take the offer off the table. If the candidate has many significant objections or seems to be drifting away, it might be time for some drama. *"I don't think we'll be able to overcome your objections on these issues; perhaps we should just agree to stop discussing a possible offer,"* might do the trick. If the candidate is seriously interested in the position and wants to really work something out, he'll pull it back. This could take the form of modifying his position or just agreeing to talk some more. Because you haven't made a formal offer, the take-away technique is a great way to test a salary cap or overcome some unreasonable objection. If the candidate still expresses interest, he or she has basically accepted your package, with modest changes. Don't use this approach more than once with any candidate, and don't use it too soon. Use the take-away when it looks like the negotiations are about to fall apart. It can be the key to breaking a stalemate.

We used this approach once with a hot product marketing prospect from a top consumer packaged goods company. The candidate was good and knew it. He kept on ratcheting up his offer demands until the situation got tenuous. I called the candidate and told him he just broke the bank. My client had just taken the offer off the table and wouldn't go any higher. The candidate called back within four hours to accept the previous offer.

➤ 9. The Push-Away to Demonstrate Growth Opportunities

This is a good approach to convert a tactical weakness into a strategic strength. By raising doubt about competency in a certain area, you can often get the candidate to push back. This demonstrates an opportunity for growth and makes a job more appealing. For example, if the financial package is a little tight, tell the candidate this is because of his or her lack of skills or experience in a certain area, like international marketing. Here's an example, *"As mentioned during the course of the interview, we're a little concerned about your lack of international experience. This is a critical area for us and will represent a great area of personal growth for you. As you develop, we'll certainly compensate you accordingly, but right now we believe the offer is fair."*

Candidates will view this as a great trade-off for giving up a little salary. By setting high standards, the candidate views the job as both a good growth opportunity and as a source of added compensation, once the skills are mastered. Balance both of these aspects as you put together a complete offer package. This is an area missed by many managers in the rush to the close. When you don't know enough about the candidate and ignore this vital area, you're left with compensation as the only negotiating lever.

■ DON'T STOP RECRUITING—FROM BEGINNING TO END

Don't forget the candidate after an offer has been accepted. There's a natural tendency to let your guard down at this point. Instead, be extra vigilant. The best always have multiple opportunities.

Recently, an applicant called one night leaving an urgent voice mail: "I've got a problem. We need to talk." Since this candidate had already accepted an executive-level engineering spot but had not yet started, it was an unsettling call. It seemed that the candidate was getting a tremendous counteroffer that matched the salary and included a promotion. The candidate wanted my advice. The new position was a strategic move into a smaller company, but in a more influential position. The counteroffer was a bigger individual contributor role in a large bureaucracy. The candidate knew this, but wanted reassurance. It was after 10:00 P.M., but I got my client, the CEO and hiring manager, to call the candidate and discuss all the issues again. We re-closed the deal without any changes to the offer, just constant attention. It's important to keep on recruiting until the person arrives on the job. It probably doesn't hurt to keep it up after he starts (but that's a different book).

Make sure the candidate stays closed by getting the person involved in the job right after the offer is accepted. A few ideas follow:

➤ Jointly prepare the formal transition program before starting. Meet a few times to review the performance profile and prioritize activities. This clarifies the expectations before starting. This is something all great managers do.

➤ Give the candidate an assignment before starting. One of my Silicon Valley clients had a candidate review the strategic and annual plan to better understand department objectives.

➤ Meet and call the candidate regularly and update him or her on what's happening. This will give the new employee a strong understanding of what needs to get done before starting.

➤ Let the candidate see the new office. This allows the candidate to visualize his or her role and strengthens the bond to the company.

➤ Have the candidate meet all of the other staff members either in a formal or informal manner before the start date. This makes him or her part of the team right away.

➤ Send plenty of reading material and new positive information. Get your new employee up to speed as rapidly as possible. He or she will stay excited and be ready to make an impact right away.

➤ If convenient, send the candidate to a seminar or company event. We placed a sales manager who went to a company sales meeting before starting.

➤ Have a social event, like a dinner with spouses. This loosens tensions and is a good way to build understanding and a working relationship.

These things will help even if there's little likelihood the candidate would renege on an accepted offer. It's important to stay in touch with your new employee before starting. This sets the stage for a great working relationship once on the job.

■ HOW TO SHOOT YOURSELF IN THE FOOT AND OTHER RECRUITING BLUNDERS

It doesn't take much to lose a great candidate. Recruiting is important, challenging, and difficult. Don't lose all of this effort with some dumb mistake. There are enough land mines around without your having to create your own. Some of the biggest blunders I've seen in the past 20 years are shown in the list on page 232. This is a good checklist of what *not* to do.

■ RECRUITING BRINGS IT ALL TOGETHER

Recruiting is vitally important. First, by opening the flow of communications, it allows you to learn more about the candidate than you normally would. Second, it allows you to control the terms of the offer. Finally, it allows you to better position

RECRUITING MISTAKES TO AVOID

☐ Don't put a damper on the job. Don't tell a candidate that there are few long-term opportunities or that they'll have to stay in the same job for at least 2 to 3 years. Maybe you think it's true, but jobs always grow and change. The best employees always seem to see their jobs expand regardless of the situation.

☐ If you're unprepared, appear unprofessional and ask stupid question, you'll drive away even average candidates. The best candidates want to work for great managers. If you know the job, ask tough questions, and listen more than talk, you've set yourself and the company up as a place where top people work.

☐ Don't sell too soon. You'll sound desperate if you start talking about the merits of the job within 10 minutes. This cheapens the job, you, and the company.

☐ Don't talk about money too soon, or too late. In the beginning, money is only used to filter in or out candidates. In the end, it's just a negotiating point. It's better to start with small steps by the second interview. By the time you make the offer official, it will be already done.

☐ Stay away from personal, ethnic, or family matters. They're against the law and in bad taste. If in doubt ask your human resources department for advice. Candidates frequently cite these *faux pas* as reason to withdraw themselves from consideration.

☐ Don't wait until the end of the interviewing process to make an offer. You've given up your bargaining position, because the candidate knows he's the only one left

☐ Don't wait until the end to recruit. Start the recruiting process with the first question in the first interview. Make the job compelling and the candidate important.

☐ Don't stop recruiting after the offer is made. These are tumultuous times. Great candidates are getting counteroffers and competing offers. Don't stop recruiting until the candidate starts.

your open job against all competing opportunities. This is why you have to be good at marketing. To recruit the best, you need to market yourself, the company, and the job, as something valuable and worth having. The candidate needs to learn enough about the job to be in a position to trade off this opportunity against all others and against short-term financial needs.

Being a good recruiter is an essential component of good hiring. It's the key to building a strong team and the first step to becoming a top manager. Every college sports coach is rated primarily on being a good recruiter. If you can get the talent, being the coach is relatively easy. But even a great coach can't compensate for weak talent. The hiring manager must proactively take on the responsibility of recruiting. No one else is going to do it. A manager's personal success hinges on the ability to first build the team. As Jim Collins points out in his book *From Good to Great* (HarperCollins, 2001), no company becomes great without first building the team. It starts with good recruiting.

POWER HIRING HOT TIPS—RECRUITING: THE HEART OF EFFECTIVE TEAM BUILDING

✔ Use the performance profile to create a compelling job. A compelling job is the foundation for the recruiting process.

✔ Recruiting is not selling, it's career counseling and marketing. It must begin the first time you phone and interview a candidate.

✔ The best candidates make strategic decisions when considering an offer. Long-term opportunity is more important than short-term compensation.

✔ Use the interview to conduct a needs analysis to determine what motivates a candidate to excel. This will allow the interviewer to create an opportunity gap showing a clear growth path.

✔ Unless leaving a bad situation, top candidates accept jobs for three reasons—the quality of the company, the manager, and the job. Make sure you present all three during the interviewing process.

(continued)

(continued)

✔ Stay the buyer throughout the interviewing process. You don't learn anything new if you're selling.

✔ Assess, recruit, and negotiate at the same time. If you wait until the end of the interview, the candidate knows she's the finalist.

✔ Use a push and pull technique. Ask challenging and recruiting questions to stay in control, create interest, and test motivation.

✔ Maintain competition. A job has more appeal and you'll have a stronger negotiating position throughout the negotiations if there are other candidates still in contention.

✔ Test all components of the offer before it's formalized. Candidates won't openly talk once the formal offer is in hand.

✔ The testing process is a great tool to identify and overcome objections. If you make the offer too soon, you'll never really know the candidate's other options.

✔ Don't shoot yourself in the foot. Move slowly. Keep an open mind. Don't sell too soon. Listen more than talk.

✔ Recruit from beginning to end. Stay in touch with the candidate after the offer has been accepted, and until the candidate starts. Great candidates will get pursued heavily once you stop the contact.

Chapter 9

Sourcing—How to Find the Best

"Begin at the beginning," the King said gravely, "and go till you come to the end; then stop."

— Lewis Carroll, *Alice's Adventures in Wonderland,* 1865

■ YOU CAN'T HIRE THE BEST, UNLESS YOU'RE SEEING THE BEST

The quality of a company's hiring process hinges directly on the quality of its sourcing efforts. You can do everything else right, but if you're not finding enough top people, you won't be hiring very many. The emphasis of a sourcing program should be on getting the best talent to openly explore your company and the career opportunities available. Unfortunately, most sourcing programs concentrate on filling many jobs quickly and cheaply, while managing a high volume of incoming resumes. The concept of hiring top talent is somehow lost in this rush of activity.

This chapter helps you refocus your sourcing effort. If you want to hire the best people, you need to first attract their attention. To attract their attention, you must understand that there is a fundamental difference between the best candidates and ordinary candidates. As we review these differences, follow this basic rule:

235

The Basic Rule of Sourcing

You can't use the same techniques to find ordinary people as you do to find the best people.

The second rule of sourcing helps clarify the first rule:

Sourcing and Human Nature

Candidates will only explore career opportunities that meet their personal needs.

The third rule of sourcing puts it all together:

It's a Matter of Perspective

The best people want careers, not jobs.

If you're offering just typical jobs, you won't get many takers from the top group. The best have needs different from ordinary candidates. That's why you can't use the same techniques to attract their attention. To make the situation a little more challenging, recognize that fewer top candidates use job boards than do ordinary candidates. This is especially true in good economic times. Therefore, if most of your sourcing is based around job boards using traditional messaging, you won't find many top candidates.

It's commonly recognized that the best candidates are found through referral programs and networking. The best sourcing programs should, therefore, combine an emphasis on personal networking with career-oriented messaging.

■ OFFER CAREERS, NOT JOBS

Before you write another ad or speak to another candidate, it's important to note the distinction between top candidates and ordinary candidates. Top candidates, whether they're active or passive, are motivated by different things than are traditional candidates. When accepting a job offer, compensation is *not* the primary consideration. The opportunity and challenges inherent in the job are. What the person will learn, what the person will do, and what the person can become are far more important than compensation. The best candidates always have multiple opportunities. For these people, accepting another job is a strategic decision based on opportunity and growth. It's the beginning of a new career. The best candidates take longer to decide. They seek the advice of friends, family, and business associates. For the typical candidate, accepting a job is a tactical decision based largely on job content, compensation, and geography. For them, getting the job is the end of a difficult job search. They make the decision quickly and with little outside advice because there's less to consider. For the typical candidate looking for a job, getting back on the payroll or leaving a situation that's not very satisfying is a dominant need. Understanding and managing candidate motivation is the key to successfully sourcing and hiring top candidates. You need to offer careers, not jobs.

Most advertising and sourcing programs are ineffective because they are targeting the wrong audience: those who *need* another job, not those who *want* a better job. This is why you get too many unqualified candidates. Top people will respond to clever ads that are easy to find and that describe challenges and opportunities to grow. Frequently, top candidates don't have all of the skills a job requires. So, if you filter on skills, you run the risk of eliminating the very candidates you want. If your ads focus more on skills than challenges, you worsen this problem because the best candidates won't even consider applying. If your ads have boring titles and are hard to find, only those desperate for another job will even look.

■ UNDERSTANDING MOTIVATION IS THE KEY TO SOURCING

Most sourcing programs ignore the differences in candidate motivation. The best are motivated by issues different from what motivates the typical candidate. Even if a top person needs another job, he or she will always have the opportunity to compare various alternatives. Top people always consider the challenges and growth opportunities over the compensation, skills required, or location.

Don't ignore these motivators if you require candidates to take an online test. For one thing, don't put up tactical eliminators (skills, years of experience, relocation, compensation) too soon. If the job is great, the best will consider a relocation or take a lesser salary. Make sure you constantly reinforce the opportunity in the job if you make the application process difficult. A carrot-and-stick model is a good one to follow. The best won't put the effort in unless the reward is great. If you're not getting enough great candidates from your sourcing programs, you might be ignoring this vital aspect of motivation.

Take these differences into account as you design and build sourcing programs. A great Web site with boring jobs won't attract great people. A sophisticated applicant tracking system that filters out the best candidates is just an expensive reporting system. A referral program that eliminates high-potential candidates lacking a few years' experience is soon ignored. It takes a great job to hire a great person. Whether you're hiring one person or a hundred, this fact must be advertised, discussed, understood, and paraded about by everyone involved in the hiring process, especially hiring managers. It needs to be built into every system, ad, process, letter, e-mail, and form. Hiring the best is hard enough. Make sure you're not precluding the best candidates from applying in the first place.

To hire the best people, you need first to find them. Next, you need to attract their attention with the right offer. Most sourcing efforts ignore both these concepts. It's like fishing in the ocean for trout and getting angry that you're having no luck.

■ ACTIVE VERSUS PASSIVE CANDIDATES, COST PER HIRE, AND THE ECONOMY

An *active candidate* is a person proactively looking for a new job. A *passive candidate* is a person who already has a job, is not looking, but will be open to consider an opportunity if personally contacted. It's generally assumed that the quality level of active candidates is lower than passive candidates. In good economic times, this is a safe assumption. In weaker economic times, even good people lose their jobs, so you'll find some top candidates using the job boards more frequently. However, in weaker economic times, passive candidates become more passive. Because there are fewer good opportunities around, they would rather wait for the economic storms to pass before considering a move. In tough times, it takes a much better job to attract the attention of a passive job seeker. Understanding this economic shift is important in designing sourcing programs.

The following table compares the cost per hire of common sourcing programs to their effectiveness in hiring top people:

Sourcing Program	Effectiveness	Biggest Problems
Advertising—job boards	Inexpensive, but marginal results.	Too many unqualified, not enough top candidates, process problems.
Advertising—media	Modest cost, but better for entry level. Good as part of employer branding program.	Long time delay.
Resume databases	Low cost up front, but marginal results.	Too much time to call. The best get jobs quickly.
Referral and networking programs	Moderate cost, targets the right audience, and very good potential.	Very effective if managed properly.
Career fairs, events	Moderate cost with fairly good results.	Lots of competition, so differentiation is required.
Internal contract recruiters	Moderate cost, quality is inconsistent.	If untrained, then you're overpaying for performance.
Third-party recruiters—contingency	High costs, but fair if getting good candidates.	Unprofessional, random results, weak control.
Third-party recruiters—retained	Very expensive, but well worth it if you're hiring great candidates.	Time to hire is long.

You'll obtain comparable results as you work your way through these options. If you can overcome the obstacles noted in the "biggest problems" column, you'll be able to dramatically improve your effectiveness with very little cost increase. Much of this chapter is devoted to overcoming these inherent problems. Try these techniques first. You'll see improvements very quickly.

Cost per hire and time per hire are not the best measures of sourcing effectiveness because both ignore quality. An "A" candidate is easily worth a 33 percent search fee from a return on investment (ROI) standpoint. This fee will be paid back many times in cost savings in the first year, productivity improvements, new products, increased revenue, and improved leadership. However, you're not always sure you're getting an "A" candidate, so this is one concern. In the rush to reduce search fees, don't compromise on quality. This is a poor trade-off, but one most companies make. Quality should always be the number one measure of a staffing department's effectiveness. Cost and time per hire are distant seconds. In the McKinsey consulting group's book *The War for Talent,*[1] the authors describe developing a "talent mind-set" as the required first step to hiring great people, which means: Never compromise on hiring the best. We call the concept "creating a talent-driven culture." This chapter describes how you can keep building the front end of this talent-driven culture. Many of these techniques are applicable whether you're using inexpensive job boards or working with third-party recruiters. The goal of hiring the best should never be replaced by some other short-term measure of performance. The long-term cost is always higher.

■ FIFTY PERCENT OF YOUR SOURCING PROBLEMS HAVE JUST BEEN ELIMINATED

Before you look for another person, define what top talent looks like, and then get every member of the hiring team to agree to this definition. This is the P in POWER. If you've already done this, at least 50 percent of your sourcing problems have already been solved. If you haven't, then more great techniques on finding the best won't help as much as they could.

If you're using a performance profile as the job standard and you're measuring a candidate's ability to do the job, rather than just get the job, the foundation for good sourcing is in place. This change alone eliminates many of the sourcing problems noted on the previous table. Good hiring is about hiring candidates who can achieve comparable results and are motivated to do it. Define great results and stop filtering out candidates for lack of skills. This eliminates many top performers who have 60 percent to 70 percent of the skills, but 150 percent of the desire and potential. By advertising for performance rather than skills, you'll increase the number of qualified candidates. By basing your selections on performance rather than personality, you won't inadvertently exclude a great person. If you don't have these basics in place, better sourcing techniques won't result in better hires.

Here's one example. Recently, I spent a day with a group of outstanding engineering managers, who are developing the latest generation of biomedical surgery equipment, at Intuitive Surgical in Mountain View, California. They were looking for a number of top senior design engineers. I asked, "What does an engineer need to do in the first six months for every person here to agree that the engineer hired is truly outstanding?" We converted required skills into SMARTe performance objectives. We benchmarked some existing top engineers to better define competencies and how problems are solved. We came up with about six deliverables around technology, quality, creativity, and team dynamics. I received a call the next day from their recruiter, thanking me. He was very excited about one candidate who was initially excluded because he didn't quite meet the skills-based profile. As a result of our meeting, the candidate was being reconsidered. I later learned that an offer was extended, accepted, and now this previously excluded candidate is a top performer. How many top people have you excluded for the wrong reasons?

Here's a similar example from an earlier time and a different industry. A few years ago, Wendy Wimmer-Ross, former Director of Human Resources at Ruby's Restaurants in Southern California, described to me how using POWER Hiring impacted her company's sourcing efforts. Ruby's, a chain of 1940s-themed diners, has always had difficulty staffing its restaurants with enough managers and serving staff. We had recently conducted a hiring seminar for their management team. During the program, we

stressed that they could broaden their pool of qualified applicants by reducing the emphasis on restaurant experience and
highlighting the performance requirements of the job. These
had to do with team and organizational issues, the need to be
proactive with respect to dealing with people, and an ability to
deal with the physical demands of the job, among others.

As a result of these changes, within six months the company was able to fully staff each of their 40 restaurants, including store and regional managers, by going outside the industry,
primarily into retail. This is the first time in five years the
company had been fully staffed. Wendy said that no compromises were made on the quality of the people hired. All met
the existing high performance standards of the company. To
ensure that the emotional control component was neutralized,
she conducted a phone interview before each candidate was invited in for a personal interview. At each first interview, she led
a panel interview with the store management. By controlling
emotions and changing the focus to performance instead of experience, Ruby's was able to overcome an artificial sourcing
problem very quickly.

Sourcing problems are cut in half when you focus on the performance needs of a job instead of skills and experience.

■ THE MESSAGE IS KING—GOOD SOURCING STARTS WITH A COMPELLING OFFER

A compelling ad is the foundation of every good sourcing program. Whether the ad is posted on a job board, the company
Web site, or used as a verbal pitch to explain the opportunity, it
must be compelling. This is the first time a prospective candidate will hear about the job; therefore, you want it to appeal to
the right audience—the top candidates. Top candidates will explore career opportunities if the underlying message appeals
to their motivating needs. These have to do with the opportunity inherent in the job—what the person will do, what the
person can become, and what the person will learn.

Traditional skills and experience-based advertising is too
narrow. The best candidates are excluded from applying because

the ads are overly restrictive. Those who do meet the qualifications won't apply unless they're desperate because the jobs appear boring. The best candidates are not interested in doing the same job again, even for more money. If the ad is compelling enough, you'll attract more high-potential candidates and those great applicants sitting on the fence, waiting for just that right opportunity to present itself.

➤ How to Write a Compelling Career-Oriented Ad

Here's my favorite ad of all time. This one has it all—a great title, enticing copy, and a focus on the motivating needs of top talent—the learning, doing, and becoming. This type of ad might turn out to be the only thing you'll need to get your sourcing

---

Director Software Development — Back to the Future

Fast Forward One Year—We'd like to thank you for doing a remarkable job for getting us on the final list of the *Forbes Best Web Sites of the Year.* To get our new eCommerce platform up and running quickly we thought it would require at least 5 to 10 years software experience and a background in ASP, SQL Server, MS, Java, XHTML, and a BS degree, but you proved us wrong. You showed us it was your desire, commitment, and ability to build an outstanding team of developers who wouldn't quit that was the key to success. Everyone in the company would like to thank you for a tremendous effort, and for the camaraderie and respect you showed everyone.

Back to Today—If you'd like this story to be yours, send us your resume with a half-page write-up of your most significant technical management accomplishment. While we're less concerned with your skills and qualifications, we won't compromise on your ability to deliver team results. We'll be back to you in 24 hours if you have what it takes to achieve something special.

You might even want to check out our Web site—www.POWERHiring.com—for some insight into what we're doing. We think you'll be excited as much as by where we are today, and the challenge to get us where we're going.

programs into high gear. With this ad, we hired an outstanding software development manager who was too young and didn't have all of the skills or qualifications, but who was an A+ employee who consistently delivered high-quality results.

A great sourcing program requires a compelling message targeted to the right audience. Underlying this, you must have a great job and a filtering and assessment process based on performance, not skills and qualifications. Sourcing can take multiple forms: advertising, career fairs, referral and network programs, web mining, and calling potential candidates. But regardless of the medium, it's the attraction piece that's most important. You need to get a top candidate interested enough in your job opening to endure the subsequent interview and assessment process. Advertising and sourcing programs need to offer more than just another job. They must offer better jobs. They must offer careers. Most don't. A typical example of 95 percent of the ads found on job boards appears on the facing page.

➤ The Traditional (and Not Very Effective) Ad

Ads are written mostly for people looking for work. The following ad appeared on monster.com:

Associate Marketing Manager— Consumer Direct Channels

We rank as one of the top 10 banks in the country. We're staffing our Home Loans Marketing Department to support the myriad of marketing initiatives that will help strengthen and grow our position in the marketplace.

Position is responsible for facilitating the development and production of all marketing materials Internet Lending, Loan Servicing, Corporate Relocation and Employee Lending. Individual will facilitate the production of consumer direct paper-based materials and electronic marketing initiatives from inception to fulfillment, including: identifying, defining, and recommending materials to support business strategies, creative and copy direction, editing and proofreading, along with all aspects of

---

**Associate Marketing Manager—
Consumer Direct Channels** *(continued)*

print production. Position reports to Assistant Vice President, Senior Marketing Manager.

Strong project management, organizational, oral and written communications, independent judgment, problem-solving and negotiation skills required. A degree in marketing or related field and 3 to 5 years experience required. Mortgage banking experience a plus. Working knowledge of Microsoft Office and Excel required; some knowledge of PhotoShop, Illustrator, PageMaker, and Adobe Acrobat is favored. Portfolio presentation required.

This style of ad is representative of 90 percent of the one million plus new jobs posted every month. It was difficult to find and not very interesting. This type of traditional ad attracts only people who need jobs—the underemployed or unemployed. If a person needs a job, he or she will find the ad and apply. If a person wants a better job, this type of ad won't cut it. If you're using job boards or other traditional advertising, write ads that attract those who want a better job. This can reduce your cost per hire without sacrificing candidate quality.

If you want to attract the best people, write your ads from a different perspective. Start by treating candidates as customers, not vendors. An ad is a marketing tool. Prepare it with this in mind. Strong people who already have jobs need a persuasive reason to leave their current positions. There are just too many options available today; therefore, your ad must be targeted to strong candidates.

Great ads must meet these criteria:

1. Use a compelling title that's quickly seen on the list of open opportunities. "HR Wizard Required" is much more effective than "HR Director." We recently used this one with great results.

2. Focus the copy on what the candidate will learn, do, and become. "Use your HR magic to rebuild a department,

which has just endured six years of neglect, in six months" appeals to the candidate's underlying motivating needs.

3. Describe the most critical skills in the context of how they're used. For example, don't say that 5 to 10 years of training and employment are essential. Something like this is a much better approach: "One of the biggest challenges you'll face is to use your training and employment expertise to set up a companywide effort to reduce turnover and improve customer service at our 350 locations."

Remember, an ad needs to overcome the inertia of not responding, or the pull of dozens of similar sounding ads. The job and the ad must be different, interesting, and compelling. You want to attract as diverse a group of responses as possible. The best-case scenario for ads that emphasize skills and qualifications, as most do, is hiring candidates who are competent, but unmotivated. The best candidates are looking for something more than another job. Your ads must focus on the motivating needs of top performers. For most, the need is a challenge or opportunity. For some, it's better working conditions. For all, it's an opportunity to excel and be recognized for doing outstanding work. Make sure your ads capture this aspect.

Review a few of your most recent ads. Which group of candidates do they attract—those needing work or those open to explore new opportunities? I learned this fundamental rule about management from one of my candidates, who said: "If something isn't working right, don't keep on doing it. Keep on changing it until it works right." You might want to try this technique with your ads if they're not pulling as effectively as they should.

When you use performance criteria to write ads, you've come full circle. This is the same performance criteria you'll use to write job descriptions, assess competency, transition new employees into the company, monitor progress, write reviews, and reward and promote. This is what performance management is all about. At its core is the prioritized list of deliverables, the P in POWER, and the SMARTe objectives created in Chapter 2.

➤ Filtering, Positioning, and Other Ideas for Maximizing the Effectiveness of Job Boards

The Internet promised high-quality candidates and low cost. It didn't deliver. Well-written ads dramatically improve the effectiveness of job boards. However, even a great ad that doesn't appear until the fourth or fifth page of the job listings will get poor response. You might need to run the ad more frequently to make sure it's always on the first page or two. It's worth paying this premium if you're getting good response.

In your ad, ask the candidate to submit a one- to two-paragraph write-up of a comparable accomplishment. This is a great way to minimize the number of unqualified candidates responding to your ads. Only those motivated by the ad will respond, and the good ones will be readily apparent by their write-ups. You can do something similar using an autoresponder and your e-mail system. Most e-mail programs allow users to reply with a standard e-mail message based on the subject or other keyword. In the outbound e-mail, describe the job again in compelling terms and request a write-up of a significant comparable accomplishment. This allows the staffing department to better prioritize and manage the incoming flow of resumes.

By including some type of performance-based filter in the outbound e-mail, you'll be able to further qualify candidates. One of our clients was getting too many candidates for sales representative positions. This was a hot company in a slow economy and its name alone drew the attention of thousands. We devised a simple program to manage the data flood. In addition to the request for an accomplishment write-up, the outbound e-mail asked for quantitative data in the following categories:

1. Number of years of quota-based commission sales.
2. Percent of time meeting or exceeding quota.
3. Percent of time sales awards were won.
4. Overall ranking in the sales team.
5. Type of selling environment, either solution-oriented or transactional.

This proved to be a useful means to rank order the resumes to determine whom to call first. The Wonderlic Company in Chicago developed this system into an online product. Monster also automates this in their HQ Office product.

Job boards are the first place to start finding candidates, but be careful. When you find a great candidate from one of these job boards, move quickly. The best candidates always have multiple opportunities. If a candidate is responding to ads or has posted a resume, be assured other companies will discover this great candidate, too. Contact the candidate within 24 hours. Conduct a phone interview within 48 hours. Invite the candidate to a personal meeting within 72 hours. If you're using POWER Hiring, you'll be in even better shape. All of your interviewers, including the hiring manager, will be on the same page in assessing competency and in describing the job opportunity. This is one of the best means to hire a great person once you've found one.

Job boards work better for lower level and mid-level manager positions. They're less effective for more senior level positions because more personal consulting is required to attract, assess, and close these candidates. Consider how many of your company's executives were hired through job boards. With good ads, you'll have better luck attracting staff and mid-level managers. Effectiveness declines the higher the position, although we've seen some positive results at the director and VP levels during the economic slowdown. It's possible that job boards will be more readily accepted over time, but their impersonal nature makes it unlikely that they'll be the primary means to hire executives. During strong economic times, they'll be less effective for hiring top people at any management level.

■ MULTILEVEL SOURCING—DON'T PUT ALL YOUR EGGS IN ONE BASKET

You always need to be looking, and you need to be looking everywhere. If you're going to run an ad only on a job board, you're limiting yourself. Unless they're having a bad day, the best people generally don't look at job boards for jobs. They do glance at their trade magazines, business journals, and trade newspapers. They might attend a career fair. And they'll take a professional call from a recruiter or listen to a pitch from a friend as part of a referral program. The key is to try many different channels concurrently. This increases your odds that the best people will hear about the opportunity. In addition, you need more than one finalist to protect yourself. Expect things to go wrong. There's always lots of competition for the best, in both weak and in strong economies.

➤ Employee Referral Programs

This is better than advertising as a means to find top talent. Company after company will tell you that their internal employee referral program has produced more top people than all other methods combined. In the past few years, we have spoken with representatives from Microsoft, Cisco, Verizon, Tricon, Cardinal Health, Hallmark, J&J, Amgen, 3M, and dozens of mid-size companies. All indicated that internal referral programs were by far the number one source for top candidates. Your best employees know other great employees, so you need to tap into this network in an aggressive way. This should also be the primary means to accelerate your diversity hiring efforts. At POWER Hiring, we expanded our diversity hiring programs with great people just by getting referrals from our diverse staff. The best way to drive up candidate quality and reduce cost and time to hire is through a sophisticated, well-run employee referral program.

The requirements of an employee referral program include the following:

1. Make it a formal, professional program heavily promoted throughout the organization.

2. Provide a bounty for referrals. This can range from $500 to $3,000 for recommending candidates who are ultimately hired. Generally, the new employee needs to stay at least six months for the referring person to earn this fee.

3. It's best that the current employee provide only names of good people. It's better to let the staffing department present the job and do the recruiting.

4. Make sure you follow up quickly with every referred person.

Pam Ferrell, the Director of Staffing at Texas Instruments (TI), recognizes the importance of a strong employee referral program. She and her team proactively ask for names of top people from all employees. She does not wait for candidate leads to be submitted. This internal lead generation program significantly increases the quality and quantity of potential candidates. Someone on the recruiting team is then responsible for following up with the referred person to convince him or her to explore an opportunity with TI. The referrer still gets the bounty for giving the name. TI also uses this same lead generation approach to improve its diversity hiring efforts. Diverse employees know other diverse employees, so this is a great way to develop this important pool of candidates. About 50 percent of the company's new hires come from employee referrals, a remarkable performance that attests to the importance of a strong employee referral program.

➤ Networking

If enough candidates are not coming to you, you'll need to reach out to them. This is called *direct sourcing,* and it is one of the best means to find top people. Calling many potential candidates and then screening them until you find an outstanding candidate is too labor intensive and time-consuming. After a few weeks of little luck, your standards will drop and you'll wind up settling on a compromise candidate. Getting names of high-quality people from these candidates is the best way to rapidly expand the number of top candidates you're seeing. This is called *networking,* and it's how the best internal and third-party recruiters spend most of their time. My suggestion: Don't spend much time on the Internet looking for names. Instead, get on the phone with just a few top candidates, get names from these candidates, and then get more names. In a few days, you'll have more than enough top quality candidates.

Here's how it's done. You need to create instant interest when you first connect on the phone. Don't describe the job first, or ask how the person is doing. Instead ask, "Would you be open to explore a situation that's clearly superior to what you're doing today?" If the answer is yes (which it is most of the time), ask the candidate for a quick overview of his or her background, and then give a quick summary of the job. With this quick phone screen, you'll be able to determine if the candidate is even a possibility before the person has a chance to say he or she is not interested. This is a very critical step. Getting the candidate to respond first establishes credibility and leaves the recruiter in the driver's seat. Don't discuss the job first other than in vague terms. For example, "We're looking to fill a senior project position in marketing." One other critical point—never discuss your compensation range, but always ask about the candidate's. Then, even if the candidate is unqualified or uninterested, the initial five- to ten-minute dialogue increases the likelihood of obtaining a good referral.

Networking starts by then asking this person for names of other people you can call. Just ask if he or she knows somebody in the industry who might know somebody else. Never ask who's looking or might be interested in exploring a job. Instead, get names of previous coworkers in the same department, or a previous boss or subordinate who the person thought was great. From each person you talk with, try to get three names of potential candidates or others in the same field. During the initial 10-minute phone screen, I also ask the person to describe his or her work team and get names. As I ask for referrals, I go back to this list and ask who would be best to call.

Once you have the name, ask the candidate to describe the person. Find out why he or she considers the person highly qualified. Asking questions allows you to prequalify the candidate. When you do this consistently, you'll be able to develop a small pool of highly qualified candidates in days. You can save time when you call only top people. If you can systematize this process, you can maximize your candidate quality while dramatically reducing your cost and time to hire.

➤ Expand Your Network with Backtracking—A Creative Way to Find More Candidates

If you can't find enough good candidates with traditional networking, it's time to get creative. One way is by backtracking.

This is the formal process of identifying who would know the candidate and then connecting with these people at the start of the search. This is the concept of one-degree-of-separation. To begin, ask yourself who would know the candidate in a nonwork, professional, customer-vendor relationship, or via some special interest. This type of networking is quite effective because people will more openly refer a good person to you if they're not working in the same company, or if they know of the person in a nonwork-related way. To obtain many ideas on where to network, conduct a brainstorming session with all members of the hiring team. Start with this target list of categories:

➤ **Targeted Groups to Develop Network Connections with Candidates**

1. Competitive and source companies.
2. Customers.
3. Vendors.
4. Trade and professional associations.
5. Academic relationships.
6. Potential social connections including hobbies.
7. Online discussion groups.
8. Conference presenters.

Once you have actual names, you'll need to contact these people directly. A professional letter describing the job is a good first step. Make sure the job is compelling. No one will refer a person to a boring job. One of our clients, a large chain of furniture stores, advertised in their stores for salespeople, directly asking parents to refer their 16- to 22-year-old children. We got the names of good medical device salespeople by calling local clinics and asking for the best sales reps who visited them. To find salespeople in retail, we called the buyers at a large club store to get the names of top salespeople.

Don't forget to include in your network your suppliers, professional service providers, and even your customers. Find people who work with the types of people you want to hire. Suppliers know experts in their fields; and if you need someone with special skills, they're a good source to tap into. A lot of companies ask their accounting firms for leads when they want to hire financial people. Expand this to include your bankers, legal advisors, consultants, and business associates. Make the approach formal. I've asked many of my search clients for names of top people they've worked with in the past.

Call or join the trade associations of people you want to attract. Material Control people belong to the American Production and Inventory Control Society (APICS). For electrical engineers, it's the Institute of Electronics and Electrical Engineering (IEEE). Financial managers belong to the Financial Executives Institute and the CPA Society. Property Managers belong to the Institute for Real Estate Management (IREM). Get in touch with the local chapters and start spreading the word. Send letters to the officers of these groups. We've discovered that these are some of the best people. Ask them for referrals.

The Encyclopedia of Associations is a great place to start to get the names of appropriate trade groups and professional societies. You can also get these names from the resumes you receive from your ads. We often run highly specific ads for the primary purpose of getting these kinds of leads. We then call the trade group headquarters to get rosters, officer lists, and a list of members open to explore new opportunities. Outplacement firms are also a good place to start to look for mid- and upper-management personnel. Some of the larger outplacement firms have databases of all the candidates in their system, so they're easy to find.

One way to narrow down the list quickly is to target industry-specific trade conferences as a source of names. Once you find the conference, contact the presenters. These people are already recognized as experts in their fields, so it's a terrific way to network with top people. While getting a name of a potential candidate is an important step in the recruiting process, it's still only the first step. How you contact these people and develop the leads will have the biggest impact on the quality of your sourcing programs.

➤ Internet Datamining and Resume Databanks

You can find many of the trade groups online. There is even a mini-industry of Internet name-generating gurus. Getting names is different from networking, and there are now many advanced search techniques available to find more targeted names. Some of them are great. Try AIRS (www.airsdirectory.com) for the latest happenings in this area. They lead the industry with seminars and tools to find names. However, there is a downside—too many names. It takes a great amount of work to sort through and call all of the names available. Getting a few great names and then networking is a much better approach.

Searching through resume databases is even more time-consuming than name generation. Unless you find a candidate immediately after the resume is posted, it's not worth sorting through hundreds of resumes. The time it takes to call and qualify these candidates is just not worth it. The best are picked over in the first week; therefore, if you can't get in early, you don't have a chance to find a good candidate. On important searches, we monitor the incoming resume flow on resume databases such as monster.com on a daily basis. Occasionally, we'll find a good candidate, but it's not a replacement for great advertising, referral programs, and networking.

One way to make better use of resume databases and other name-generating approaches is direct e-mail contact. This is similar to opt-in e-mail direct marketing. Because people have made their names available, you can contact them via e-mail. Rather than calling these people, send them an enticing e-mail. Describe the challenges of the job. Include your compelling ad in the copy. Then invite the candidate to respond if interested. Ask for the half-page write-up and include the pre-qualification screening checklist. If the job is captivating enough, you might find a few good candidates. Be sure to include a request for referrals. Regular mail might work better if you're not getting enough e-mail action. Keep this chain-letter mail or e-mail approach going. It's a great secondary means to source top candidates. Be sure to ask the person if he or she would like to be notified about future opportunities. This is one way to build a strong nurturing program.

➤ Career Fairs and Other Events

A career fair is a very good way to find many candidates quickly. It's especially useful for high tech. Companies like

BrassRing and HotJobs actively promote career fairs, so check out their sites for the latest schedules. If you participate in career fairs, use the following important tips. Because you're competing with other employers, how you interact with potential candidates on the floor is essential.

Tips for Managing Career Fairs

1. Put your desk in the back and the people in the front. You must mingle. Don't put up barriers. Talk to everyone who comes by.

2. Have an attention-getting device. You want people to flock to your booth. Try singing, dancing, and even juggling.

3. Advertise ahead of time. Invite all of those people who have contacted you in the past to visit you at the fair. Send e-mail to resume databases describing your exciting jobs.

4. Have a few hiring managers staff the booth. This is a great way to quickly screen and attract top performers.

When you corral someone, use a prescripted ten-minute interview to screen him or her. Find out the candidate's name, company, and area of expertise in the first minute. Then give a two-minute targeted pitch to the potential candidate. Include an interesting concept about the company as it directly relates to the candidate's area of interest. Ask if something like this is worth exploring. Conduct a quick screen for six minutes. Using the candidate's resume as a guide, specifically review the last two jobs for titles and progression. Quickly look at academics and certifications. Most importantly, ask the candidate to describe his or her favorite work experience in the past year or two. Find out why he or she liked it, and obtain a quick overview of the accomplishment and results. Ask the person what's important in a new job and why. This line of questioning validates the candidate. For the last two minutes, schedule the next meeting if the person seems qualified. Before you end the meeting, ask the candidate for other people you should contact. This is a quick way to generate more names. Ask the person to invite his or her friends over to your booth immediately. Before you know it, you'll have a line outside your booth and be the envy of every company nearby.

You must be extremely proactive when networking, both on the phone and in person. You'll use your personal energy to excite a candidate about your company and career opportunities. You'll then be able to use the candidate's energy to help generate other names.

As an alternative to career fairs, consider sponsoring a booth at professional association meetings. We met a number of great human resources managers and executives at one of their annual meetings. At a recent local state-of-the-Internet affair, the three sponsoring companies had booths. Each had a dozen potential candidates lined up to talk. If you're looking for a targeted audience, this is a great way to find candidates.

Sponsor your own career fair, and invite a few experts in to discuss various career topics. Advertise it on your Web site. Consider a joint program with a local chapter of an engineering society, or with one of the major outplacement or employee service firms. They sometimes have experts who can draw talent to the event. These kinds of events are more proactive than advertising because you are going into the field to find people who are actively looking. Career fairs and other events should be part of an ongoing sourcing program.

➤ External Recruiters

If you need a top person and can't find or attract one, you should consider a recruiter or headhunter. They use all of these techniques and charge anywhere from 20 percent to 35 percent of total compensation. As a headhunter, I'd like to offer a basic principle that covers every position: Only pay a search fee for a B+ or better candidate. Search fees should be an investment, not an expense. A strong candidate pays for himself or herself quickly—an A+ candidate, within six months; a B+, within a year or so. You can find B candidates easily enough on your own, so don't waste your money if all you need is a solid performer. Stronger candidates need to be pried out of their current situations, and that's how the fee is justified.

This brings me to a second principle: You must use a recruiter for every strategic position if you don't have a few great leads firmly in hand. These are the game-breaker positions you must fill with a top candidate. Don't compromise on these positions. The cost to acquire this expertise is insignificant if the person needs to achieve a major business objective. It doesn't matter whether it's a senior engineer or a vice president of marketing. When the success of the company rides on this person's shoulders, go all out. Don't nitpick on the compensation, either.

If you decide to use a recruiter, use a retained recruiter[2] for every critical position over $125,000 per year, a contingency recruiter in the $50,000 to $125,000 per year category, and temporary to permanent for all administrative positions. Top people expect to get their next job through a recruiter. They often go out of their way to cultivate these relationships because the expectation is that recruiters are the source of the best jobs.

In the mid-1990s, the Internet was advertised as the great recruiter buster. The hope was that the Internet would transform the recruiting process by making the best candidates easy to find and hire. Recruiters and their elevated fees would be eliminated. It didn't happen, and it won't. The best candidates are not actively looking for jobs. While they're willing to explore new opportunities, they still require more time and more counseling before they'll move on to greener fields. The Internet is better suited for a more transactional approach to hiring. It works well for those candidates who need another job, not those who want a better job. While some of the techniques in finding candidates are similar, the process used to evaluate and close top candidates is totally different. Internal recruiters who use all of the techniques will be able to obtain results similar to headhunters' results. But it will be a result of their ability to network, write compelling ads, and interact professionally with top candidates, not their ability to work the Internet.

■ WEB TOOLS—FROM RESUME TRACKING SYSTEMS TO CAREER WEB SITES

Many new Internet-based hiring tools have been introduced over the past five years. Some have been useful and are still here. In addition to job boards, three other software applications are important for you to know about as you design sourcing programs. Each of these will have some impact on the quality of candidates you find:

1. Applicant tracking systems to manage all phases of the hiring process.
2. Filtering systems to better manage incoming resumes.
3. The career section of company Web sites for candidates to directly apply for open positions.

Applicant tracking systems come in a variety of sizes and shapes designed for the individual recruiter or for the complete hiring team at a Fortune 100 company. Their prime function is to manage the data involved in the hiring process, from completing a job requisition to posting ads and tracking the status of all the resumes received. They are not designed to hire better people; they automate existing hiring processes. So, if you're not hiring great people, don't expect to see improvements with an applicant tracking system. You should see better reporting and better data management, though; and through better organization, you should be able to focus more of your efforts on improving your hiring processes. Some even include POWER Hiring tips to help you along the way.

Where applicant tracking systems can help in sourcing is through metaposting of ads and rank-order filtering of resumes. *Metaposting* means writing one ad and putting it up on hundreds of sites. This is a distinct advantage if you write compelling ads. If not, it means only that you'll be dealing with more average candidates. Some tracking systems have built-in filtering systems that review the resumes and put them in some type of quality order. Most current filtering is based on keywords; therefore, skills are emphasized, not performance. Regardless, it does help better manage the recruiter's workload. Resume filtering is one area of automation where new advances are coming. If you include a test or questionnaire, make sure the questions you ask do not inadvertently exclude the best. For example, it's okay to ask if the candidate has experience with a complex CRM system. It's not okay to ask first if he or she would be willing to take a drug test or relocate. These questions are okay only after the candidate has agreed to go forward. Some of the best candidates are only casually looking, so you want to keep them interested each step of the way. Some of the hurdles you put candidates through are designed to keep the unqualified ones from applying. Unfortunately, in the process, you make it too hard for some of the best to apply.

At POWER Hiring, we're working with a few companies to develop filtering based on performance traits. For example, with one client, we're filtering resumes based on the number of years the person achieved quota, sales awards won, and the type of selling process used. The objective of this filtering is to automatically screen and rank order all resumes. The objective is similar to the prequalification questionnaire sent out with the e-mail program mentioned earlier; but, with automatic filtering, the candidate isn't required to do anything. In some cases, a top candidate, regardless of the compelling offer, might not be willing to take an online test or return a form. Better filtering can eliminate this problem. If you're looking for new sourcing tools, explore this area.

A company career Web site is a critical component of a company's sourcing program, especially for positions below the senior management level. Candidates will explore a company's Web site not only to find jobs, but also to learn about its products, financial performance, benefits, and culture. Remember that top candidates are looking for more than just a job, so it's important to include this information on your company Web site. Most applicant tracking systems include some type of front-end Web site feature, but don't compromise on this. Monster.com and Hire.com both offer this career Web site component. BrassRing, a great applicant tracking system, is putting a great deal of effort into strengthening their Talent Gateway offering, their career Web site. It fits well into their positioning as a talent management relationship system.

The primary objective of the career portion of a company's Web site is to provide quick access to jobs for interested candidates. Secondarily, the Web site is a means for candidates to stay connected to this company even if no current job is available. Scott Biggerstaff is leading the effort developing Sprint's career site. Here candidates can quickly find jobs, create search agents to learn about future jobs, and opt-in to be on the company's career newsletter. Kirk Santos, the former site development manager at Phillip Morris, credits their BrassRing-powered site with allowing them to handle the huge influx of resumes—from 10,000 per month in the late 1990s to almost 40,000 per month in 2002. He told me it would have been impossible to handle this volume of resumes without the BrassRing resume filtering system. The system allows them to sort through resumes in less than two hours versus a full day. Patty Shanley, the technical recruiting manager at Unisys, sings similar praises for their BrassRing system. Without it, they would not have been able to create their global requisition system and improve all aspects of their online recruiting efforts. A career Web site is the critical hub of a company's hiring efforts. Don't skimp here. A survey we took a few years ago of over 500 candidates showed that 65 percent to 70 percent of all candidates explore a company's Web site before applying for a job they found at one of the job boards. Half of these declined to apply because the site's career section was weak.

Following are basic rules to follow as you evaluate and design your company's career Web site:

Basic Requirements of the Career Section of a Company Web Site

1. Make it easy to find. Candidates should be able to go from the home page directly to the career section.

2. Give direct access to the specific job of interest with very few clicks. The best candidates opt out if they can't quickly read about the position.

3. Write the job description in a compelling manner, focusing on the challenges and opportunities, describing what the candidate will learn, do, and become. The listings for skills and qualifications should never have the phrase "must have" nearby. The focus needs to be on the future, not the past.

4. Make the application process quick and easy. Try to make it two minutes or less. Cut-and-paste resumes are

great, but don't require them. Get more information as the candidate moves into the application process.

5. Provide reasons to come back. Provide games, quizzes, newsletters, and other important information.

6. Include an easy-to-use job search agent. This allows candidates to learn about future opportunities as they become available without having to return to the site.

If you receive too many resumes, you'll need to automate the site. Most applicant tracking systems include automation as part of their offerings, but effectiveness varies. That's why it's important to balance all of your needs. Trade-offs occur as you compare features. Don't get seduced by better reporting and improved resume management. The key to these systems should be in helping a company hire top people. Vendors providing these tools are now moving to incorporate this capability, but it's not easy to automate a process that requires a great deal of handholding. This is where the talent relationship aspect becomes more important.

➤ The Effectiveness of Job Boards

I recently spoke with Jerry Crispin, who, along with Mark Mahler, wrote the remarkable book *CareerXRoads*.[3] Jerry and Mark are experts in understanding the impact job boards have on sourcing programs.

Jerry described two recent private studies involving more than 50 companies and thousands of candidates to determine their sources. Both studies concluded the same thing: Internet job boards are directly responsible for only about 10 percent of all hires. According to Jerry, and I agree, "Job boards are no big deal—especially if no single job board represents more than 1.5 percent to 2 percent of any company's hires!" Most companies get 5 percent to 15 percent of their hires from job boards, but they're far less important than employee referrals and the company's career Web site.

Jerry's underlying message is: Instead of using the job board as your primary sourcing tool, use it as part of an overall sourcing strategy. A job board's primary function is to act as an advertising medium to deliver an employment message. And it does it differently than the radio, the television, the newspaper, the trade journal, the electronic monitor on the wall of the college book store, the 20-foot by 40-foot billboard on the side of the highway, or the employment kiosks in the malls and fast-food franchises. It is also different from a personalized invitation to meet with a prospective employer that is handwritten on quality stock and delivered by messenger.

Job boards do serve an important function. They are an inexpensive and excellent means to deliver a message to a targeted audience. They can operate with a sense of urgency to reach the candidate through an opt-in "agent" that matches interests or skills with requirements and delivers an instant e-mail. Use them for part of your sourcing and for getting the word out.

A great ad with a compelling title is the first step in using the boards properly. In Crispin and Mahler's *CareerXRoads,* you'll find some great targeted sites to post these ads. Make sure your ads are always on the first two to three pages of the listing of jobs. Pay to run the ad again to keep it near the top. Because most of your candidates first explore your company's Web site, the same job must be easy to find there. The best lose interest quickly if the process for applying gets bogged down, or if the message on the company Web site does not enhance the job. The two largest sources of hires are employee referrals and the company Web site. Even referrals check out the Web site first, so invest time and money in developing a first-class online career center. This will be a critical hub in all of your recruiting activities.

DirectEmployer.com provides an interesting twist on the job board concept. Bill Warren, the site's executive director, told me that major companies want to ensure that their career sites are the dominant portals for new candidates, not the job boards. At DirectEmployer, candidates search for any type of job and then are sent directly to the company's career Web site to see the actual listing. Jobs are posted only once, on the company's career site. For a fixed annual fee, companies have a central location for candidates to quickly find all of their openings. This siphons jobs away from the job boards, so consider this as an alternative as you plan your advertising strategy.

■ THE EMPLOYER OF CHOICE OR "JOB OF CHOICE"

Sourcing the best candidates is much easier if you're an employer of choice. In good economic times, fast-growing, highly visible companies attract a disproportionate share of the top candidates. In slower economic times, solid, stable companies with a more secure future act in this role. Cisco was the star of the Internet boom as people flocked to apply. Microsoft lost its luster to Cisco during the dot-com bust, but it reemerged as the new long-term employer of choice. Microsoft now has the best developers and product managers and marketers in the country trying to get in. With this rich talent pool, they're bound to hire the best. Consistent great hiring eventually becomes a competitive advantage. It starts with great sourcing. If you aren't an employer of choice, you have to double your efforts to make sure each open position is a job of choice.

Even if you are an employer of choice, you need to describe each job in compelling fashion. You still want to offer top people great jobs when they apply. If you're not an employer of choice, don't despair. You can still hire outstanding people. This foundation will be the cornerstone to begin upgrading your talent pool. One of our clients, a large Southern California services company, recently lost its luster as an employer of choice. Now candidates are reluctant to apply. Despite this cloud, by making each job critically important and implementing the process described, the company is still able to hire top people. They're working harder now to rope them in. Once candidates see the career opportunity firsthand, the lure of the employer-of-choice banner is neutralized.

➤ Employer Branding

Although Cisco has had its problems, we can learn much about their sourcing efforts during the boom of the late 1990s. Much of what they did was groundbreaking and still very applicable. In a September 29, 1997, *Fortune* magazine article, "Cisco's Recruiting Edge," some very innovative sourcing approaches were described in action. It started at the top with CEO John Chamber's strategy of hiring only the top 10 percent to 15 percent. This created the talent-driven culture focus necessary to launch an aggressive sourcing program. Michael McNeil, Cisco's former director of global staffing, is a leading-edge sourcing practitioner and was responsible for implementing this strategy. Following is a sampling of some of their more creative sourcing techniques:

➤ Enticing newspaper ads advertise the company's Web site, not specific jobs. At the Web site, the job seeker can review hundreds of open positions. This is what employer branding is all about. Sell the company first, the job second. You can do this if you're a hot company.

➤ Meeting prospective candidates at unusual congregating places. For example, representatives of the company go to the local home and garden show to meet young home-owners. The up-and-comers typically go to these types of events, and Cisco contacts them in this unusual setting.

➤ Matching potential candidates with current employees to learn firsthand about the company. Candidates learn more about the company before they get heavily involved in the interviewing process. They hear about this "friends" program through local movie theatre advertising, at career fairs, and on a very attractive and advanced Web site.

➤ The company launched the first online nurturing program. Interested candidates submit a quick resume and hear about openings as they became available.

The key to all of Cisco's efforts is in developing new techniques to go after the best people who aren't aggressively looking for new jobs. Most people are willing to explore an exciting career opportunity, even if they are currently happy with their existing position. Cisco took networking and referral programs to another level. While any company can do this, a commitment from senior management that hiring the best is important should start the process. This is the only way you'll get buy-in from all those involved. This is the best way to make sourcing top people a top priority.

■ MANPOWER PLANNING AND JUST-IN-TIME SOURCING

Developing a repeatable means to hire the best requires a longer time horizon than usual. Most sourcing programs are reactive. For many companies, new hiring requisitions are the result of someone's quitting or the approval of a new project. In these cases, hiring must begin immediately. This gives little time to source top talent. You have fewer options, generally job boards or recruiters. Standards fall because the need to fill the position overrides quality. The best generally take longer to find, and they take longer to decide. Therefore, if your hiring process is primarily reactive, you have little chance to consistently hire top people. Forward-looking manpower planning minimizes these problems and gives you the time you need to hire the best.

The essence of manpower planning is to forecast your hiring needs at least four to six months in advance. This provides time to implement all of the sourcing programs described in this chapter. Hiring the best requires preplanning. If you must hire people yesterday, you'll compromise your standards. If you need to hire 20 design engineers in six months, start the planning today. In six months when you need to hire these people, they'll be waiting at the door.

One aspect of manpower planning is recurring hiring—the people you consistently hire with some regularity because of both turnover and growth. These could be engineers, salespeople, or call center associates. For these positions, develop ongoing sourcing programs that create a constant flow of good candidates. I call this just-in-time sourcing. This should be a combination of companywide and individual manager efforts.

In 1975, when I worked for a living and early in my career, this is how I got an important job. I was Director of Business Planning with Rockwell's Consumer Electronics operations (one of the companies that originated the hand-held calculator). Our business dropped from $10 million per month to $5 million in a matter of months and losses were mounting. It was time to think about leaving.

Just a month before, a group president of another company I had met at a business meeting the prior year called and asked if I was interested in another opportunity. We had met for lunch a few times during the year, so it was not an unexpected call. He had been keeping me informed of opportunities at his company regularly, and now the timing was right for me. I called him back, met with him, and started with his firm a few weeks later in a similar position. Within two years, I was a vice president and business unit manager. After starting, the group president told me this contact program was something he had been doing his whole career. He said he was able to fill about 50 percent of his open positions this way. He developed a career plan for all his staff and could roughly predict when open positions would become available for these people.

Always be on the lookout for good people. Keep a database of people you know who could be potential team members. The timing for people is never exactly right. A great person you know is rarely available exactly when you need him or her. However, if you know three or four people, you'll often find one when the timing is right for both of you. This is what recruiters do. We're always on the lookout for top people. We cultivate and maintain these relationships. When a great situation arises, these are the first people we call.

Don't leave sourcing exclusively to the human resources department. Line managers need to develop their own sources of top candidates. Get each member of your current team to give you three to four names of top associates from prior companies. Start meeting these people. When the need arises, you won't need to make a desperate call to human resources or your friendly headhunter. Line managers can help themselves when they take personal responsibility for finding and hiring top talent. Hiring top people is one sure way to ensure long-term career success.

One of my former contingency search clients is a top senior executive at one of the large entertainment companies. I met him early in my search career when he established an unusual relationship with some of the search firms in the area. Because he wanted to have his pulse on the Los Angeles employment market, he agreed to meet any strong candidate even if he didn't have a position currently open. Over a period of two years, he was able to fill more than 20 mid-management positions using this just-in-time hiring and nurturing program. Every person was top-notch. Line managers at every level need to have this same talent mind-set. Building a great team is one of the performance objectives of every manager. It will not happen if you leave it exclusively to the human resources department.

■ SOURCING—IT'S THE STRATEGIES, NOT THE TACTICS, THAT ULTIMATELY DETERMINE YOUR SUCCESS

A number of sourcing tactics have been presented in this chapter, but it's the strategies that really matter. And the most important is the need to create a proactive talent-driven culture. This mind-set is essential to hire top people. If the senior management group doesn't buy into this concept, all the best tactics in the world have little impact. Jim Collins, in *Good to Great*,[4] indicated that building a top team was the first step for every company that eventually became great. In *The War for Talent*, the McKinsey team underscores the need for top talent to remain competitive in a changing and challenging world. It was clear in *Jack*[5] that setting up a methodology and culture that focused on hiring and developing outstanding managers was Jack Welch's true legacy at General Electric. These three books look at the landscape of American business over the past 20 years. Although each person took a different path, each came to the same conclusion—hiring the best is not an activity that can be talked about but really ignored, or delegated to human resources.

Aggressive and proactive sourcing is essential. The best aren't looking. You have to go after them. Planning, a prerequisite, buys the time needed to do it right. If you treat candidates as potential customers rather than future subordinates, a whole shift in attitude takes place. This impacts advertising, priorities, the time spent on the process, the allocation of resources, and the quality of the interviewing and recruiting process. Hiring a great team starts with great sourcing.

Compensation can't be excluded from your sourcing strategies either. Don't expect to hire top candidates if your overall compensation package is below average. You might be able to sneak one or two people in this way, but it won't work as a long-term strategy. Candidates get to know very quickly which companies don't pay well and which ones do. If you have a reputation as a low-paying company, you won't be given the opportunity to see some of the best people. They won't even consider applying. As Catherine Meek, the well-known compensation expert, once told me, "Over the long term, an aggressive compensation program based on performance is essential if you want to build a world-class company with world-class people."

The strategies and tactics presented in this chapter will help increase the flow of top candidates to your company Web site. With a focus on performance instead of skills, you'll quickly discover that many top candidates are inadvertently excluded. When you switch to compelling, performance-based advertising and filtering, the number of top candidates applying will increase. If you can move quickly, you can hire some of these top candidates who are actively looking. While this approach won't fulfill all of your hiring needs, it's a great start. Longer range networking and employer referral programs need to be expanded and formalized. A company career Web site needs to be the hub of all of this new activity. Sourcing is the critical make-or-break component of the hiring process. When you evaluate your sourcing programs from this perspective, everything changes.

POWER HIRING HOT TIPS: SOURCING— HOW TO FIND THE BEST

✔ Offer careers, not jobs. Great advertising, employee referral programs, and networking should form the bulk of an effective sourcing program.

✔ Go after only the best. Understanding candidate motivation is critical to sourcing success. The best candidates explore a situation based on what they'll be doing, learning, and becoming, not by emphasizing skills.

✔ Design sourcing programs around quality per hire. This has a bigger impact than cost per hire or time per hire.

✔ Skills-based advertising and weak interviewing skills eliminate too many top candidates from consideration. POWER Hiring advertising and interviewing tools will quickly eliminate 50 percent of your sourcing problems with little effort.

(continued)

✔ Build your sourcing program around the "treat candidates as customers" concept. You want these great candidates to "buy" your company. This requires enticing ads, personal contact, and attention.

✔ Make your ads compelling with some sizzle created around the top one or two SMARTe objectives. It's better to focus on the opportunity and challenge to draw the best candidates in. Minimize passive verbs like "having" and "responsible for" unless you want to attract the average candidate.

✔ Formalize your employee referral program. You'll find more top candidates this way than from any other means.

✔ Use aggressive networking to expand your pool of top candidates. This is what recruiters do, and it works. Use your employees, vendors, customers, trade associations, and professional service corporations to get names of top people *not* looking. Then go after them with a personal pitch and ask for more top names.

✔ Use recruiters if you can't find a top person through a referral network. The fee is worth it if you get a top candidate. Make sure that recruiters are going after people who are not aggressively looking. Half your fee is going to finding people you can't find on your own. The other half is for keeping the deal together.

✔ A career-oriented Web site is an essential component of a sourcing program. This is the hub for all of your sourcing efforts. It must be easy to find, describe compelling jobs, include a great company overview, and be easy for the candidate to apply online.

✔ Every manager needs to take a personal leadership role in hiring the best. Start looking now for top people to add to your staff. Build your own personal network of potential team members when you don't need to hire anyone. This group will be on call when you do.

✔ Sourcing must be a high-priority strategic process with forward-looking manpower plans and a well-thought out compensation program. This gives you the opportunity to anticipate staffing needs, rather than having to react to surprises.

Chapter 10

Implementing POWER Hiring

There are no secrets to success: Don't waste time looking for them. Success is the result of perfection, hard work, learning from failure, loyalty to those for whom you work, and persistence.

—Colin Powell

■ CREATING A TALENT-DRIVEN CULTURE

Hiring should be a proactive process—not a reactive event. For many companies, hiring starts when someone quits or a requisition for a new employee is approved. The next step is to call a recruiter or post an ad, and hope you find a reasonably good person to start within 30 days. Unless you have a strong employee referral program, an effective networking process in place, and a database of great candidates ready to sign on, you'll settle for a compromise candidate. Traditional hiring is too reactive—it doesn't give you enough options to do it right. Instead, you need to look out at least three to six months. This gives you the time to set up the networking, referral, and nurturing programs needed to find top candidates. Preparing a workforce plan is the first step to improving your company's hiring effectiveness.

Over the past ten years, business conditions have profoundly affected every aspect of managing. The link connecting strategy,

270

structure, and hiring has tightened. The pace of change has accelerated, and those companies wanting to remain competitive must stay current. Flexible teams, employee leasing, virtual corporations, and outsourcing of anything but core competencies are now commonplace. Few major electronics companies now do any of their own manufacturing. Major companies are now outsourcing key components of their human resources departments; some, the whole department. The restructuring of the corporate infrastructure has begun, replaced by fast, responsive, and customer service-oriented organizations.

The impact on hiring and recruiting has been equally profound. Tenure-based promotions are now part of history. Lifetime employment has been replaced by three- to five-year assignments. Teams are rebuilt and replaced by new teams every few years. Management layers have been removed, and every employee is expected to work harder and smarter. In the face of this constant change, the manager's job is more challenging. Hiring top people has become more important. Every hiring decision has a bigger impact than before and there are more decisions to be made. If asked individually, most managers would say that building their team is one of the most important contributors to their personal and company success. Despite this, few companies have formalized the hiring process to meet the challenging needs of a competitive economy. Hiring one great person is worth celebrating. Knowing you can hire a team of great people whenever you need them is worth rejoicing.

Hiring top people is too important to rely on ineffective, and, at times, conflicting processes. A more formalized business process is essential. Throughout this book, many of the pieces have been discussed. In this final chapter, we show how to put the pieces together using POWER Hiring as the foundation. The result is a talent-driven culture that is focused on building top teams and hiring top people at every stage of the

---

Hiring one great person is worth celebrating. Knowing you can hire a team of great people whenever you need them is worth rejoicing.

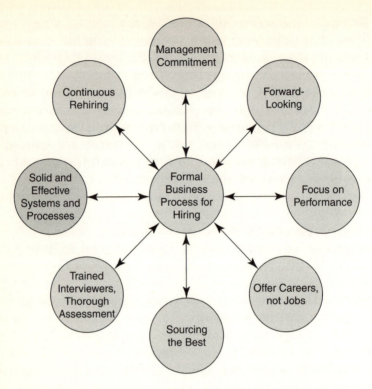

Figure 10.1 How to create a talent-driven culture.

economic cycle. Figure 10.1 shows the components of this type of process.

As you read this section, rank your company's existing processes against each of these standards. This serves as a quick gap analysis on what you need to do to create a talent-driven culture in your company.

➤ Management Commitment

It takes more than hype and hope; it takes focus and effort. I recently spoke to a Young Presidents Organization (YPO) group of 35 CEOs. Each one believed that hiring is a critical function, essential to their company's future growth. Yet, when I asked for examples of company initiatives underway to prove the claim, there was little in the way of process or practice in place.

For example, one was using a personality test to screen candidates, another was trying to get all managers to use a structured interviewing process that some managers used, and a third was starting to launch a company Web site for posting jobs. This was about it. This surprising state of affairs is representative of the 60 mid-size and Fortune 500 companies POWER Hiring works with every year. The Fortune 500s have more systems in place; but when examined in depth, many are not much more effective. It's still difficult for some to find top candidates and close them quickly, some of their internal systems and processes compete with each other, some processes are overbearing and hard to use, some are ignored, and many line managers still do their own thing despite the constant chastising from the human resources department. They call their pet recruiters, ask their pet questions, and everyone wonders why it's so hard to hire top talent.

Public or private, big or small, hiring top talent is essential for long-term success. I recently met with the engineering team at Intuitive Surgical in Mountain View, California, the company building the new Da Vinci robotic surgeon. We're helping them establish a performance-based hiring process. It didn't take long to figure out this is a world-class product being built by world-class people, who have set the hiring of top talent as the foundation for growing their company. At a training session we conducted last year at Microsoft, it was obvious that hiring the best is at the core of Microsoft's domination of the personal computer software market. At the nation's most beloved burger chain, In-N-Out Burger, the company has set its sights on hiring only the best young adults to serve its fanatic customers. Having had the privilege to work with these people, I know it's their talented team that has made their burgers a California icon. The YMCA already has a professional hiring process in place, but they asked us to overhaul it and train their 60-member volunteer board of directors. They know that by striving to ensure that the best people run their operations, they will achieve their aggressive community service goals. The message is clear: Hiring the best requires a dedicated executive management team who recognizes its importance as a core business process, who is willing to commit whatever resources it takes to create it, and who spends the time and effort to keep it going. Hiring the best must be a process, not an event.

➤ Forward-Looking Workforce Planning

If you want to hire someone for an important position six months from now, you need to start the sourcing process today. Otherwise, you'll be left with just a few short-term options. That's why a workforce plan is essential. How to do this was discussed in the chapter on sourcing. This is the demand forecast. It takes into account company growth plans, attrition, and restructuring for every department. This provides you with a month-by-month look at your hiring needs at least six months out.

One of our alliance partners, Kevin Wheeler, the developer of Xtreme® recruiting, is an expert in developing recruiting strategies. He suggests that before you go outside to bring in talent, consider the supply side. Before anything else, determine your bench strength—all of your employees now working hard hoping to get a bigger and better job. Do you have a formal program that gives you the ability to plug them into critical spots as they become available? A program like this is similar to a succession plan, but it requires an internal talent database showing the skills and abilities of all your best people. When a position becomes available, you'll then have instant access to this pool of top employees. With a workforce plan in place, you can even begin grooming some of them for spots coming up six to twelve months from now.

Hiring processes need to be proactive and forward-looking. This gives you the time to find the best candidates available. If your hiring is reactive or short-term, you have fewer options to find good candidates, and you'll lower your standards as you succumb to business pressures.

➤ Focus on Performance

Performance management is the core component of a talent-driven culture. Clarifying performance expectations has been shown as the key to motivating people to perform at peak levels[1] This is the P in POWER, the performance profile. Clarifying expectations by defining the deliverables is the way to hire, manage, review, motivate, reward, and promote people. Clarification starts with defining performance for every new job by writing a clear statement of what the person must do to be successful. It's not a list of skills, experiences, and academics. By clarifying performance expectations, you'll be able to attract more top people and more accurately assess their competency. The basis for a complete performance management system is in place when these performance measures are tied to the company vision and assigned to individual functions and departments, with a performance profile prepared for every job.

➤ Offer Careers, Not Jobs

The best candidates, even those who are actively looking, always have multiple opportunities. They want the best job available, or one better than the one they now have. Most jobs advertised on the major boards describe skills, duties, and responsibilities, certainly not exciting career challenges. This precludes the best from even applying. The best are looking for career opportunities, not just another job. Writing performance profiles rather than job descriptions and using them to advertise for candidates is the way to turn jobs into careers. It's what people do with their skills, not the skills themselves, that excites and motivates them to perform at peak levels. It's how you reduce turnover and improve productivity in the bargain.

To quickly test how your company is doing, read one of your posted ads for a senior manager or staff person. Does the ad overemphasize skills and experience? If it does, you're excluding the best from even applying. It's better if you include just a few skills, with more attention devoted to the challenges. The best candidates generally have 70 percent to 80 percent of the skills, but 125 percent of the motivation. You exclude this audience if you demand 100 percent of the skills.

➤ Sourcing the Best

If you want to build effective sourcing programs, you need to target those candidates who want a better job, not those who want just another job. Everyone knows that the best people are generally not found on job boards. In fact, these boards represented only about 10 percent of all hires in 2001. While there are some good candidates available on the job boards, this shouldn't be your primary source of top candidates. At best, job boards should be a secondary means. In an economic slowdown, more top people use job boards, but it's hard work to filter out the best from all the rest applying. In a recovery, the best can find jobs quickly on their own through other means. Over the long term, you'll find many more top candidates through a formalized employee referral program, strong networking, and a candidate nurturing program centered around your company's career Web site. That's why a formal workforce plan is essential. A workforce plan gives you the time to build a multi-pronged sourcing program using a combination of the best short- and long-term sourcing methods.

Here's a quick way to determine the effectiveness of your current sourcing programs. For the last few positions, obtain the following information:

1. Quality of the person hired.
2. Source of the candidates who applied.
3. Length of time to fill the positions.

This is a useful snapshot. If you didn't hire great people for each position quickly enough, you need to make some changes.

➤ Professional Interviewing, Assessment, and Recruiting Process

If you want to hire top people, it's essential that you have a professional interviewing and recruiting process in place designed around the specific needs of top people. The little bit of behavioral interview training that a few managers use when they feel like is not a substitute for a professional hiring process. The best can recognize an unprofessional team during

---

If you want to build effective sourcing programs, you need to target those candidates who want a better job, not those that just want another job.

the first round of interviews, and it drives them away. Some clues of an unprofessional team are everyone describing a different job, nobody asking challenging questions, everyone selling, and no one listening. Interviewing is as much about career management and consultative selling as it is about assessing competency. The best interviewers allow the best candidates to talk more than they do. They create an opportunity gap and make candidates jump across. This is how you make a job a career. The best candidates accept offers based on what they'll be doing, learning, accomplishing, and becoming, not on the level of their skills. To gain an immediate picture of how well your company is doing in this area, call a few candidates who have recently turned you down and find out why.

Hiring the best requires a well-trained management team that knows how to use the performance profile as the basis for assessing competency and closing the deal. Without this step in place, everything else will fall apart.

➤ Effective Systems and Processes

Whether you're a small firm tracking hiring needs on an Excel spreadsheet or a Fortune 1000 using some type of high-end employee and candidate management system, managing the data is critical. It becomes a major problem, though, when managing the data and the system causes the management and hiring team to lose focus on the real prize—hiring top talent. I've seen this happen too often. Balance is essential. Hiring great people has more to do with the people involved in the process than the process itself. You need to consider the personal and human needs of hiring managers, recruiters, candidates, other interviewers, and company executives every step of the way. Effort must be spent on architecting the total people and data systems before the components will work as promised.

One component essential to an effective hiring program is the company career Web site. How to put this together was described in the chapter on sourcing. A career Web site is the hub of all of your sourcing and hiring activities. Everything comes together here. It's where potential candidates can explore career opportunities or sign up to be contacted when a great job develops. It allows all of the potential candidates you started looking for six months ago as part of your long-term referral and networking efforts to hear about a job today. If you want to quickly see how good your systems are, check your company Web site now. Can you find your job of choice quickly? Is the description more like a window sticker on a car or a career opportunity? If there's nothing for you right now, can you sign up to be contacted in case something else exciting comes along later on? Now conduct a quick check of your other hiring systems using the following list:

1. Can job requisitions be completed and approved online?
2. Are resumes, assessment forms, and interview questions readily available on your system?
3. Are candidates applying for open positions presented in rank order based on some performance measurement system other than skills?
4. Do your systems make hiring top people easier, or do you spend too much time feeding and maintaining the systems?

Data management systems are essential, but they sometimes lead the process and can get in the way of hiring top people. If you address all of the people issues first, adequate systems are all you need to hire the best.

➤ Continuous Rehiring

While most hiring takes place in an upturn, it doesn't begin or end there. At the peak of the boom, realignment needs to take place. Those who shouldn't have been hired need to be weeded out and replaced by top performers. In a downturn, reductions in force should be made by matching critical business needs with the abilities of top performers, not based on across-the-board percentages. At the trough, restructuring is essential. The bottom 15 percent should be eliminated, replaced by top people who can lead the next recovery. Whatever the stage of the economy, do you have the right team in place today that can lead your company forward?

Try this quick way to determine how well you and your company are doing. Rank each of your team members on an A-B-C scale. The A players are your current and future leaders. The B players form the backbone of your company, and require nurturing and investment. The C players require too much time and attention, yielding only marginal results. At the personal level, are you doing everything you can to ensure you have a team of A and B players? This is what effective management is all about. Does your company have a formal program in place to make sure that it's building an employee base of only A and B players? This is a talent-driven culture.

■ RANKING YOUR HIRING PROCESSES

The eight factors in the table that follows form the foundation of an effective hiring process. Use the table to rank yourself on

Category	Description of the Best	1–5
Management commitment	Management is totally committed to hiring the best, including whatever time and resources it takes to make it happen.	
Long-term and forward-looking, not short-term and reactive	A workforce plan is in place describing all hiring needs for at least the next six months. This is matched with an updated talent pool of current employees to determine external needs.	
Focus on performance, not skills and experience	All new positions are described using a performance profile. Managers use performance measures to manage, motivate, and reward existing team.	
Offer careers, not jobs	New jobs clearly define challenging career opportunities, with an emphasis on performance, not skills and experience.	

(continued)

Category	Description of the Best	1–5
Target the best—those that want a better job, not those looking for another job	Sourcing plans are designed for hiring top people, not just filling positions. The emphasis is on long-term programs like employee referrals, networking, and nurturing potential candidates, rather than just job boards. Employer branding and employer-of-choice programs are in place.	
Professional interviewing and recruiting process	All managers are thoroughly trained in interviewing, assessing competency, and consultative career-management recruiting techniques. They listen more than talk and make objective assessments, minimizing first impressions and emotions.	
Solid systems and processes	A great career Web site that allows candidates to quickly find great challenging jobs, not lists of skills and requirements. Data management systems need to make the lives of recruiters and hiring managers easier.	
Continuous rehiring	A formal process is in place, whereby all managers are constantly rebuilding their teams to ensure that it's comprised of "A" and "B" players only. Hiring and restructuring is a continuous top-down-driven process at every phase of the economy.	

a scale of 1 to 5 on each of the eight measures. You don't need to be great at every stage; you just need to be doing all of the steps, all of the time, reasonably well. This is enough to provide a great system.

How do your company's hiring processes rank against this standard? A 40 is a perfect score. A 32 or more, with no holes such as managers who are incompetent interviewers, is what it takes to build a talent-driven culture. A 24 or more, with no holes, puts your company in the top third, based on what I've seen. It takes at least a 2 on each factor to make sure you don't have an obvious gap. These gaps can completely wipe out outstanding performance somewhere else in the process. If top candidates can't quickly find your open jobs, then everything else is a waste of time, even if you have a great employer branding program. If the jobs are boring and focus too much on skills rather than challenges, the best won't even bother to apply.

Building a talent-driven culture won't happen by chance. It requires management commitment and effort. This is how good companies become great, and it's how great companies like General Electric and Microsoft strengthen themselves and thrive in any stage of the economic cycle. The cost to implement this type of process is insignificant compared to the cost of doing business as usual.

POWER Hiring can serve as the foundation for developing a talent-driven culture. It's the underlying operating system that links the people, systems, and processes in an effective formal business process. In the rest of this chapter, we describe how POWER Hiring can be used in this capacity. We also introduce you to a 20-step action plan to guide you there.

■ THE POWER HIRING SYSTEM—THE FOUNDATION FOR CREATING A TALENT-DRIVEN CULTURE

The POWER Hiring system addresses all aspects of hiring— defining the job, sourcing candidates, assessing competency, determining best fit, and recruiting and closing. This five-step performance-based system links every component of effective hiring into a system that can increase effectiveness into the 80 percent to 90 percent range. As you've seen, none of the steps are hard to understand or difficult to use. The challenge is doing them all together. While each step is practical and easy to grasp, the process is severely weakened if any step is eliminated or compromised. It's the integration of these five steps that makes the process so effective. Following is a quick review of each of the POWER Hiring components, explaining how each component fits into the framework of building a complete hiring system.

Performance Profile: Define superior performance by writing out the top five to six deliverables or SMARTe objectives for each position. By emphasizing the challenges in the job rather than skills, the performance profile improves the effectiveness of every aspect of sourcing and recruiting. It's much easier to attract and hire top people when jobs are challenging. The performance profile is the benchmark used to interview and assess candidate competency. Job needs change as companies cycle through growth and retrenchment. The performance profile changes with it by focusing on success, rather than skills.

Objective Interview and Evaluation Process: Along with trained interviewers, preplanned interviews and written assessments are prerequisites to accurate hiring. Past performance is the best predictor of future performance. Make sure everyone on the hiring team obtains detailed examples of a candidate's accomplishments to determine true capabilities. Compare the results achieved, the process used to achieve the results, and the environment in which these results took place to the objectives in the performance profile. Combine this with cognitive and skills testing, detailed reference checking, and a complete background check. These steps alone will prevent many unnecessary hiring errors.

Wide-Ranging Sourcing: Sourcing is marketing, not advertising. Don't wait for candidates to call you. Target them and reel them in. You have to see good people before you can hire them. Good sourcing starts with compelling ads based on performance needs, not experience. You'll use these great ads to advertise careers, not jobs. They will be seen on every job board and on your career Web site, so make them outstanding. Your employee referral and networking programs will become more effective and self-sustaining as you create these "jobs of choice." It's much easier to recommend an associate to an exciting and challenging career position than to just another typical job.

Emotional Control: More errors are made in the first 30 minutes of an interview than at any other time. To control the impact of first impressions and personality, wait 30 minutes and measure first impression again. To stay objective, ask tougher questions if you like the person, and go easy on those you don't care for. While true personality is critical to job success, interviewing personality isn't the same as true personality. You'll see these differences emerge after 30 minutes. You'll discover that about a third of the people you thought were very good are really pretty average, and a third you thought were weak are significantly better. Emotions are the cause of more hiring mistakes than all other causes combined. If you don't get this part right, everything else is reduced to window dressing and legal compliance.

Recruiting Right: Recruiting is consulting, not selling. Most managers think they can convince a hot prospect to accept an offer through persuasion and personal appeal. This is demeaning to the candidate and often drives the best away or raises the price. Top candidates always view a new job from a strategic perspective. Managers need to be able to offer career management advice to their top candidates every step of the way. This requires consultative solution selling techniques that match career needs with job opportunities. Many recruiters and hiring managers lose great candidates because of unsophisticated and overbearing selling practices. It's easy to "sell" a candidate who needs a job. It requires a pro to close a deal with a top performer who has multiple job opportunities. Few companies would send their salespeople out to their customers without training. Yet, most send their managers and recruiters to call on top candidates without the skills needed to present and manage career opportunities.

▣ THE POWER HIRING 20-STEP IMPLEMENTATION PLAN

The following 20-step action plan describes everything you need to create a talent-driven culture. The first eight are basic steps that provide a good foundation. Once these are in place, start adding other key features. You'll soon have all the talent you need to take you and your company anywhere you want to go.

1. **BASIC: Use Performance Profiles for all new job openings.** Define the deliverables for every new job. Make sure everyone on the interviewing team agrees to the deliverables and the priority list before meeting any candidates.

2. **BASIC: Conduct structured interviews.** Make sure everyone on the interviewing team uses the basic eight-question interview as the standard structure for all interviews and for all candidates. Measure first impressions after 30 minutes. This increases objectivity and accuracy.

3. **BASIC: Write compelling ads.** Use outrageous titles and write great copy focusing on learning, doing, and becoming. Reduce skills to the absolute minimum. Post your ads everywhere.

4. **BASIC: Build and use a basic career Web site.** If you're hiring more than ten people per year in the $30,000 to $100,000 range, make sure the job section of your company Web site is first class. Candidates must be able to find jobs quickly, the descriptions must be compelling, and candidates should be quickly notified of their status.

5. **BASIC: Always conduct testing and background checking.** Never hire another person without some type of intelligence test, a complete reference check, and a thorough background check. Add a skills test if the job requires some level of competency. Use a personality style test only to help confirm the interview assessment. Collectively, these measures will prevent a third of all future hiring mistakes.

6. **BASIC: Provide interview and recruiting training for all managers and recruiters.** You don't need training if you're hiring average candidates; and without training, that's all you'll hire.

7. **BASIC: Assess competency using the Ten-Factor Candidate Assessment form.** Formalize the assessment. Balance candidate strengths and weaknesses across all job measures. Have the hiring team assess candidates in a group setting. It's harder to hide emotions and prejudices this way.

8. **BASIC: Establish the standards of excellence with formally written guidelines.** Make hiring a formal business process with high standards. These first eight steps are the foundation of a very good talent-building system. The executive management team must lead the effort with focus, attention, time, and resources.

9. **Develop a six-month workforce plan.** Be proactive, not reactive. You need to use both long- and short-term sourcing techniques to hire the best. If you're not looking out far enough, you're left with fewer options, and you're likely to reduce your standards as business pressures mount to fill a seat.

10. **Set up an employee talent database system for internal moves.** Your first source of top people should be internal. Start building a database of every employee's skills, abilities, and performance record. Tap into this group before going outside.

11. **Conduct an employee satisfaction survey.** How do your employees feel now about your company? Are they willing to participate in an employee referral program? If your existing employees are unsatisfied with their jobs, you'll have a difficult time using them as a source of new employees. You need to uncover and address any fundamental problems here before you can build a talent-driven culture.

12. **Formalize the employee referral program.** About 30 percent to 40 percent of your entire outside hires should be from employee referrals. This is your most

effective and least expensive means to find top talent. Formalize the process, market it aggressively, and give hefty bounties. It will pay for itself in months.

13. **Establish direct sourcing and networking programs.** Make sure your recruiters and hiring managers are building their own networks of contacts. They should spend time on the phone working the network, rather than looking for more names on the Internet. Have them join associations, participate in discussion groups, and contact conference presenters. Make sure every manager and recruiter is developing a personal network of potential candidates. This is just-in-time hiring. You'll have two or three candidates ready at a moment's notice for any important job.

14. **Develop an enhanced company career Web site.** Make this an exciting hub of activity for short- and long-term hiring. Every job hunter will check out your Web site. Make sure the best find what they're looking for quickly; and if not, make sure they want to come back again. Require only a two-minute profile to apply for a job.

15. **Create a great recruiting department.** Provide the necessary resources and staff your recruiting department with A players. This is the best investment you can make. Recruiting is not the same as human resources. Recruiters are solution salespeople who know how to find great people and then are able to coach the hiring managers through the process. How well you staff and organize your recruiting department determines the success of your top talent hiring efforts.

16. **Implement applicant tracking and data management systems.** Upgrade your systems if you're spending too much time on managing the data. You need a place to collect all of the information, and a good tracking system is important. However, don't overinvest in a system or commit too much time to get it up and running. These systems won't replace the hard work needed to hire top people.

17. **Use advanced interviewing techniques including panel interviews and take-home projects.** For the

second round of interviews, add some pizzazz. Panel interviews are a great way to shorten the interview process and get others involved. Have candidates present a mini-case study on a real problem. This is a great way to test for both interest and competency.

18. **Implement an employer branding program.** Market the company, not just the job. The best candidates accept offers largely on the job opportunity and the team they'll be working with. The best are more open to explore opportunities if they've heard about the company or some major new project. Develop generic public relations programs highlighting these projects and put them on job boards, sponsor forums, and association meetings.

19. **Establish a continuous rehiring program.** Hiring is a process, not an event. Don't stop hiring when the recovery stalls. At the peak of the recovery, replace those you shouldn't have hired with top performers. During the slowdown, use the performance profile to realign your workforce. At the trough as you get ready for the next recovery, replace the C players with top A players, who are now more plentiful.

20. **Institute a companywide performance management system.** Begin this process once the candidate starts. Review the performance profile to make sure the candidate is very clear regarding the expectations. After 30 days, renegotiate the deliverables and the priorities. This is a great way to communicate real job needs and improve performance. Expand the use of the performance profile by creating performance objectives for each function, department, and job that tie to the company vision and strategy. Use these SMARTe performance objectives to manage, review, reward, and promote your team members. Great management starts with great hiring, but it doesn't end there.

You must do the first eight basic steps. This is the absolute minimum to get you started. Give yourself no more than 90 days to get them implemented. You're probably doing many of them anyway. In this case, complete the basic steps in 30 days. If you have a strong company, above-average compensation, and a strong labor pool, doing just these basics will improve your hiring right away and provide a solid foundation to build on.

Wherever you are in this hiring process, you don't need to do everything on the top 20 list to see significant improvement. You'll start seeing more top candidates, improve hiring accuracy, and reduce errors with each addition.

Lantronix, a Southern California high-tech company, is starting to see great hiring results using the POWER Hiring principles. They've trained every manager (about 100) over the past two years. They've formalized their hiring process into a simple handbook providing guidance on preparing performance profiles and conducting the fact-finding interviews with a ten-factor assessment. Linda Duffy, their human resources director, told me that since they began using the performance profile as their baseline for hiring, they have not made one hiring mistake, out of more than ten mid- and senior-management hires. However, the few times they got lazy and didn't prepare a performance profile for new openings, they made mistakes. In one case, they hired someone who was unmotivated to do the work and left within a few months. In another case, they almost hired someone too weak to handle an important technical assignment. The hiring team couldn't come to agreement on this candidate until they prepared a performance profile. Then they realized the candidate was ill suited for the task.

Jack Lantz, the president of Unitek Miyachi, a southern California industrial products company with heavy international operations, has been using POWER Hiring since 1993. When I started working with Jack, the company had revenues of less than $20 million per year. Now revenues are almost $100 million. At a recent meeting, he told me that the company has added more than 40 management-level positions with only two or three modest hiring mistakes.

Jack has formalized the hiring process around the performance profile. He requires that every new management position list the top six to eight performance objectives before he'll give approval to hire the person. These objectives must be agreed on by the hiring team beforehand. Thus, everyone involved in the interviewing process clearly understands the performance needs of the position before interviewing candidates. The evaluation assessments are conducted in a group session using a modified form of the Ten-Factor Candidate Assessment. This helps keep everyone honest by requiring examples to prove a high or low ranking.

The company also uses the Wonderlic Comprehensive Personality Profile and Wonderlic Personnel Test during the interview process. Further evaluation is conducted if these tests reveal any inconsistencies with the performance-based interview. The use of these tests as a confirming indicator helps Jack and his management team pinpoint potential performance problems before hiring a new employee. As Jack told me, the personality issues become less important when everyone knows and agrees to the performance criteria of the position. Background verifications, including reference checking and drug screening, are the final part of the pre-employment screening and evaluation process.

The Lantronix and Unitek Miyachi examples send a clear message: A basic performance-based hiring process that's formalized and used for every new hire has a profound effect on company performance. It doesn't take magic to hire top people; it takes discipline, management focus, and a set of principles designed around the theme of hiring top talent.

Verizon Information Services is the $4 billion advertising services arm of Verizon Corporation. They're now using POWER Hiring to hire salespeople for their SuperPages®and SuperPages .com®offerings. Their division sales managers are very excited about using an assessment process that helps them quickly assess a candidate's ability to meet their high standards. The recruiting department is equally excited. They're gaining more cooperation with their line manager clients, and they feel more confident when presenting candidates. On the sourcing side, they're attracting more top candidates using compelling advertising. The company's overall objective in launching POWER Hiring is to reduce turnover, increase motivation, expand diversity hiring, and improve bottom-line company performance. While results are only preliminary, POWER Hiring seems to be having a positive impact on all of these initiatives. Monique Love, the company's senior staffing manager leading this project, recently told me that POWER Hiring is the first sourcing and selection process she has seen that has the potential to virtually eliminate every major hiring concern she has faced in her career.

Whether Fortune 100 or start-up, or those in between, we've found that everyone using POWER Hiring gets better results. The key is preparation of the performance profile. The first time will take over an hour or two to get it right. After a few tries, your time will drop to about 45 minutes for new positions. Updating an existing position takes only 20 to 30 minutes. Once the process used to achieve success is clearly defined, interviewing becomes a natural process of fact-finding and benchmarking performance. Then, there is no need to substitute biases, emotions, and stereotypes as the selection criteria.

■ THE IMPORTANCE OF CREATING A TALENT-DRIVEN CULTURE

Bottom line, good hiring is no more than changing the selection criteria from assessing a candidate's ability to *get* the job to assessing the person's ability to *do* the job. Everything changes when this switch is made. We stop hiring people that are great at interviewing, but weak on substance. We also reconsider those great candidates reduced to temporary nervousness by the glare of the spotlights. It's substance, not style, that counts. As Red Scott said, "Hire smart, or manage tough," and you can never manage tough enough to overcome a hiring mistake that you could have prevented.

The cost of bad hiring decisions and weak hiring systems is staggering. It impacts the organization from top to bottom including lost productivity, excessive management time spent on marginal employees, and the onerous costs of negligent hiring lawsuits. The cost of one bad hire at the staff level has been estimated at two to three times the person's annual salary. It's five to ten times salary for a manager. This is a staggering amount when applied across the organization.

A process like POWER Hiring that seamlessly links systems, processes, people, and practices can serve as the framework for getting hiring under control. The performance profile is the first step. Never hire another person until every member of the hiring team agrees to what the candidate needs to do to be considered successful. This step alone will change everything. By defining job success up front, managers have a relevant benchmark to assess competency rather than relying on their own biases and perceptions. From the candidate's perspective, the performance profile is what attracted him or her to the job opening in the first place and why he or she decided to accept an offer, even though there were multiple opportunities. This now represents a career opportunity, not just another job. Most hiring systems are designed to fill positions, not hire the best. If you want to hire the best, start by defining what the best need to do. You'll reduce turnover, minimize legal problems, and increase the quality of top people joining your firm.

Do you have the right team in place today that can lead your company forward in any phase of the economy? If not, now is the time to create a talent-driven culture. The cost to implement this type of process is insignificant compared to the cost of ignoring the warning flags. It starts with a commitment by the executive management team to hire top people, an action plan to get it started, and the resources to make it happen.

POWER HIRING HOT TIPS: IMPLEMENTING BEST PRACTICES FOR HIRING TOP TALENT

Following is a quick summary of the best POWER Hiring tips by chapter.

Prepare Performance Profiles for Every Job (Chapter 2)

✔ Define success, not skills. Create six to eight SMARTe objectives (**S**pecific, **M**easurable, **A**ction, **R**esult, **T**ime, **e**nvironment) that best describe superior performance. This is what the candidate must do to be successful.

✔ These SMARTe performance objectives represent the DOING, not the HAVING; they cover all critical aspects of the job, including major and interim objectives, problems, needed changes, and technical and management issues.

(continued)

(continued)

✔ Make sure everyone on the hiring team understands and agrees to these objectives, including priorities, before interviewing any candidate. Otherwise, emotions and perceptions will dominate the assessment.

✔ Using SMARTe objectives improves understanding and communications, clarifies expectations, allows candidates to self-select, is more fair and legally sound, and acts as a great transition program for the new employee. This is what performance management is all about.

Controlling Emotions (Chapter 3)

✔ Wait 30 minutes before judging competency. Instead, measure first impression at the end of the interview.

✔ Performance and personality are both important, but measure performance first.

✔ Recognize your hot buttons. Note when you make the hiring decision and then fight to stay objective. If you're relaxed or bored within fifteen minutes, you've made an emotional decision.

✔ Stay the buyer as long as possible. If you decide too soon, new data has less value than older data.

✔ Change your frame of reference. Ask tougher questions for those you like, and go easier on those you don't.

Interviewing and Assessment (Chapters 4–7)

✔ Don't compromise on personal energy and team skills. They represent the core traits of all top performers. Evaluate the trend of individual and team accomplishments over time to see the trend of these two core traits of success.

✔ Fact-finding is critical. Peel away the onion and probe deeply. Clearly understand the results achieved for every accomplishment, the process used to achieve the results, and the environment in which they took place.

✔ Anchor and visualize each SMARTe objective. A candidate's ability to anticipate the needs of a task before starting it, plus a track record of comparable accomplishments, is a great predictor of subsequent performance.

(continued)

✔ Ask for examples of everything. This is how you turn generalities and exaggeration into specifics.

✔ Use panel interviews and take-home tests to make the interview more representative of real work.

✔ To prevent classic mismatches (great candidate, but wrong job), assign the candidate's major accomplishments into work-type categories and compare to the SMARTe objective profile.

Recruiting (Chapter 8)

✔ Offer career counseling and advice. Recruiting is more like consultative needs analysis than transactional selling.

✔ Create a compelling vision of the job and an opportunity gap. This represents the opportunity for growth. If the gap is big enough, the candidate will then sell you, rather than your having to sell the candidate.

✔ Stay the buyer from beginning to end. This way new data has the same value as old data. Don't stop gathering information until you have complete details about five or six major accomplishments.

✔ A job has more value when it's earned rather than given away. Don't move too fast. Make the candidate earn the position.

✔ Break long recruiting pitches describing the company into one-minute sound bites. Use these at the beginning of each question to describe the importance of the job. This is marketing.

✔ Never make an official offer until you're 100 percent sure it will be accepted. Test each component throughout the interviewing process. Don't wait until the end. Ask, "What do you think about . . . ?"

Sourcing (Chapter 9)

✔ The best candidates want a better job or the best job among competing alternatives. Average candidates are looking for

(continued)

(continued)

another job. Target your sourcing efforts toward the motivating needs of the best candidates.

✔ The prime sources of top external candidates are employee referrals, strong direct networking by the recruiting team, and compelling advertising. This requires a balanced combination of short- and long-term sourcing programs.

✔ Great ads are the key to attracting top people. Write compelling ads with outrageous titles. Focus on what the new employee will do, learn, and become. Reduce skills to the absolute minimum. Make it easy to apply.

✔ Be proactive, rather than reactive. Anticipate hiring needs by preparing a workforce plan of all hiring needs at least three to six months out. Before you go outside to find candidates, make sure you first compare these needs against your internal team. This is a key to high internal satisfaction and essential if the employee referral program has any chance of working.

✔ Make sure you have a compelling career-oriented web site. All candidates explore this first. Make sure the jobs are easy to find, and make sure you're offering careers, not just jobs.

Afterword

The methodology developed by Lou Adler in *Hire with Your Head: A Rational Way to Make a Gut Decision* represents not only a significant breakthrough for employers trying to identify the optimal candidate from a given pool of job seekers, but also a legally sound defense to hiring decisions which are routinely challenged in today's litigious society.

Employers have long recognized that the key to avoiding a problem employee is to hire the right person for the job. Theoretically, that seems simple and straightforward. In practice, however, the vast majority of employers rely more on instinct than intellect in hiring employees. Consequently, most employers don't have the proper screening methodology in place to adequately avoid the problem employee. For employers, this often means playing a litigation lottery that pays employees two-thirds of the time.

Several different employment laws are responsible for the astonishing 250 percent increase in employment discrimination claims filed by employees since 1992. At the federal level, Title VII of the Civil Rights Act of 1964, the Americans with Disabilities Act, the Age Discrimination in Employment Act, and the Rehabilitation Act all provide stringent protections for employees who claim they were discriminated against. Moreover, several states have enacted companion legislation that in most cases increase the legal protections an employee already enjoys under the federal antidiscrimination regime.

In addition, the federal Fair Credit Reporting Act, as well as other laws regulating background checks, provide still more protections to employees when potential employers base employment decisions at least in part on background checks.

Finally, the courts have been more willing than ever to extend protections to workers in the employment arena. The most recent incarnation in this trend is the negligent hiring claim, which is premised on the theory that an employer knew or should have known that an employee would engage in criminal, violent, or other harmful acts against a third party. The third party may be a co-employee, customer, or just a visitor to the employer. Most disturbing, however, is the court's willingness to impose liability on employers for employee acts clearly committed outside the course of their employment.

Lou Adler's POWER Hiring protocol helps employers navigate the legal minefield of employment law by focusing like a laser an employer's attention on hiring. Lou Adler accomplishes this by focusing on the steps an employer should take to avoid the problem employee. These steps include: (1) identifying the needs of the position to be filled; (2) evaluating the best recruiting options; (3) conducting proper interviews; and (4) checking all personal and professional references.

In addition to these critical steps, the POWER Hiring protocol also provides excellent guidance on the use of effective job applications and help with the critical task of checking personal and professional references.

In sum, from a legal perspective, *Hire with Your Head* and POWER Hiring represent an important breakthrough in the art and science of hiring employees. By following Lou Adler's approach, employers are equipped with the tools they need to hire the right job candidate and legally defend that critical employment decision. Our extensive legal experience has shown us that most plaintiffs in employment lawsuits are problem employees who should not have been hired in the first place. Using the POWER Hiring protocol in the workplace should significantly reduce an employer's exposure to litigation and provide the solution to hiring productive, successful employees.

ROBERT J. BEKKEN
Partner, Fisher & Phillips

Appendix A

The Legality of the POWER Hiring Protocol

Robert J. Bekken

We have had the opportunity to review *Hire with Your Head: A Rational Way to Make a Gut Decision* by Lou Adler. The methodology developed by Lou Adler not only represents a significant breakthrough for employers in identifying the optimal candidate from a given pool of job seekers, but POWER Hiring also creates a legally sound defense to hiring decisions that are routinely challenged in today's litigious society.

Robert J. Bekken is a partner in the Irvine office of Fisher & Phillips LLP. He received his law degree from Emory University in 1976 and his undergraduate degree from Albion College in 1973. He has authored various publications on employment law and is a frequent lecturer to various business groups around the country on labor and employment law issues. He has conducted over 1000 workshops and seminars and spoken to numerous conventions and groups. He is a member of the California and Georgia Bars.

Fisher & Phillips LLP is a national law firm engaged exclusively in the practice of labor and employment law representing management. Founded in 1943, the firm has grown to more than 150 attorneys, with offices in Atlanta, Chicago, Fort Lauderdale, Las Vegas, New Orleans, Oakland, Orlando, Irvine, and San Diego.

Fisher & Phillips LLP practices in all areas of labor and employment law, including wrongful discharge litigation, employment discrimination, sexual harassment, union avoidance, collective bargaining and arbitration, employee benefits, wage and hour matters, occupational safety and health and employment-related immigration matters. While Fisher & Phillips LLP takes a highly aggressive and creative approach to the litigation of employment disputes, the firm also emphasizes preventive maintenance strategies to help clients avoid litigation altogether.

Our Firm has represented management in labor and employment law since 1943. Over the years, Fisher & Phillips has represented employers in literally thousands of cases. Statistically, employees who file these lawsuits have one thing in common—they never should have been hired in the first place. In 70 percent of cases, a lawsuit could have been prevented if proper hiring protocol were followed. In lawsuits involving allegations of discrimination in hiring, employers can successfully defend the actions if objective criteria are used to reject the applicant.

This is why *Hire with Your Head* represents a revolutionary breakthrough in terms of providing employers with a methodology to avoid litigation by not hiring the litigious applicant and providing a defense in the event the employer's hiring decision is challenged. In essence, the POWER Hiring protocol is the "missing link" in the hiring process. It is both the practical and legal component of the hiring process most employers overlook.

Employers have long recognized that the key to avoiding employee problems is to hire the right person for the job. In theory, that seems simple enough. In practice, unfortunately, most employers do not have the proper screening methodology in place to adequately predict a successful employee. Instead, employers tend to rely on instinct, rather than focusing on lawful, objective criteria that will predict a successful candidate. Employers can easily fix this problem by implementing Lou Adler's POWER Hiring protocol. Employers who opt to make this initial investment avoid not only potential legal exposure, but more importantly, hire the best employees who will enhance their business and reduce employee turnover.

The scary reality is that employment discrimination cases have increased nearly 250 percent since 1992. Not only has there been a litigation explosion, but employees who get their cases before a jury end up winning an astonishing two-thirds of the time. The payoff for spinning the lottery wheel of justice is that winning plaintiffs are now walking away with an average jury award of over $600,000.

Two factors explain this litigation explosion. The first factor is the several statutes passed to prohibit discrimination in the workplace, as well as the evolution of common law tort claims such as negligent hiring. As discussed next, there are simply more employment laws in today's workplace. Legislators, both federal and state, in concert with the courts, have given employees more and stronger protections regarding their employment status.

The second factor is the attorney's fees provisions contained in these new laws. This provides an incentive for plaintiffs' attorneys to shift from personal injury work to employment litigation. Unfortunately, this also increases an employer's potential liability if it decides to risk a jury verdict.

Initially, employers must understand the legal landscape that they face in the employment arena today. By understanding this landscape, employers can better understand the importance of implementing an objective hiring protocol.

■ WHAT LAWS ARE CAUSING EMPLOYMENT LITIGATION TODAY?

➤ Statutes

As discussed, several statutes exist to protect employees from certain actions taken by employers. The following are just a *few* of the many major laws regulating the workplace.

Discrimination

Federal, state, and local laws prohibit employment discrimination based on enumerated categories, including race, color, ancestry, religion, sex, medical condition, physical or mental disability, national origin, age (40 and above), citizenship, sexual orientation, or marital status. Title VII of the Civil Rights Act of 1964 is the principal federal antidiscrimination statute, but there are many other federal and state sources of equal employment opportunity rights.

Individuals with a disability are protected by the Americans with Disabilities Act (ADA) and the Rehabilitation Act, both federal laws, as well as additional state laws. Generally speaking, the ADA and the Rehabilitation Act prohibit discrimination against a qualified individual with a disability with regard to job application procedures, the hiring, advancement or discharge of employees, employee compensation, job training, and other terms, condition, and privileges of employment.

Harassment

Under most federal and state antidiscrimination acts, employers, labor organizations, apprenticeship and employment training programs, other persons, agents, and supervisors can be civilly liable for harassment of an employee, applicant for employment, or a person providing services under a contract. Harassment, like discrimination, can be on the basis of race, religious creed, color, national origin, ancestry, physical disability, mental disability, medical condition, marital status, sex, age, or sexual orientation.

The Fair Credit Reporting Act (FCRA) and Other Laws Regulating Background Checks

The Fair Credit Reporting Act (FCRA) applies to employment-related decisions if the employer bases that decision on a consumer report or investigative consumer report obtained from a consumer reporting agency. Consumer reports generally include motor vehicle reports, criminal background checks, and credit history reports obtained from third parties. Investigative consumer reports generally include reference checks and other types of personal interviews. It is strongly recommended that all employers utilize background checks. In order to comply with the Fair Credit Reporting Act, however, the employer must have all applicants sign a separate form acknowledging that a report may be obtained. See the end of this Appendix for a sample disclosure form.

Federal and state laws also prohibit certain forms of background checks. For instance, the ADA prohibits employers from denying job opportunities to applicants who: (1) are rehabilitated drug users, (2) are currently participating in a supervised drug rehabilitation program and are no longer using drugs, or (3) are erroneously believed to be illegal drug users. Additionally, disqualification for employment based on past criminal behavior can violate federal law when the disqualifying criterion has a disproportionate impact on a protected class or has a tenuous or insubstantial relation to job qualifications. Also, employers may not ask disability related questions and may not conduct medical examinations until after they make a conditional job offer to an applicant.

➤ Common Law

Although most employers are aware of the exposure under common law claims of defamation, assault and battery, and infliction of emotional distress, most employers are unaware of the potential liability for negligent hiring. Negligent hiring claims are premised on the theory that an employer knew or should have known that an employee would engage in criminal, violent, or other harmful acts against a third party. The third party may be a co-employee, customer, or just a visitor to the employer.

The most astonishing aspect of a negligent hiring claim is that liability can even arise when an employee's acts are outside the scope of employment. Traditionally, the employer is only responsible for acts of its employees that occur during the course and scope of employment—meaning while in the employer's control. In negligent hiring cases, though, employers may be liable for acts where the employer did not exercise control over the employee. For example, if an employee follows a customer home and assaults that person, the employer will be liable if the customer can: (1) prove that the employee was unfit, incompetent, or dangerous; and (2) that the employer failed to protect the employee.

➤ Eliminating the Problem Employees before They Become the Problem Employees

As discussed, many lawsuits can be avoided by focusing on the crucial stage of the employment process that is often overlooked by employers—hiring. Employers need to dedicate more resources toward a proper hiring process, because the manner in which an employer conducts the hiring of its employees drastically impacts on the time an employer finds itself in court.

It is essential that employers implement several measures for the proper selection of a new employee. After all, the employer will be liable for almost anything that employees do within the scope of their employment—and even beyond. The measures an employer should take include: (1) identifying the needs of the position to be filled, (2) evaluating the best recruiting options, (3) conducting proper interviews, and (4) checking all personal and professional references.

Hire with Your Head and the POWER Hiring selection method effectively encompass all the elements and measures needed to significantly reduce an employer's exposure to future employment litigation. The principles behind this methodology represent the ideal manner in which an employer should hire future employees. Unfortunately, a significant number of employers fail to incorporate all of these elements into its employment process. As a result, the wrong employee is hired, turnover increases, and the potential for litigation is created.

Another fundamental mistake employers make is to use a deficient employment application that fails to force applicants to truly reveal their weaknesses and strengths. The profile of the problem employee is easily identifiable and can be revealed if a proper application is utilized.

➤ Using an Effective Application

By requiring all candidates to complete an application, you can focus on the characteristics you are looking for in filling the position, as well as discover any negative characteristics about the candidate. For instance, by requiring candidates to list the reasons for leaving past employment positions, you may be able to discover a pattern of poor work performance. Employers can also see if candidates have criminal histories that may present potential problems related to negligent hiring. It is important that employers do not accept resumes as substitutes for applications. They should only be used as a supplement since they generally list the characteristics that hold the employee in the best light while failing to disclose anything that may be negative.

Throughout *Hire with Your Head* and POWER Hiring, excellent advice is given concerning the application. For example, it is suggested that employers make it clear to candidates on the application that a background check will be conducted. This minimizes applicant claims of fraud. Additionally, it is recommended that employers ask candidates to reconfirm that everything on the application and all statements that are made during the interview are true and correct. The following language should be utilized:

> *I hereby state that all the information that I provided on this application or any other documents filled out in connection with my employment, and in any interview is true and correct. I have withheld nothing that would, if disclosed, affect this application unfavorably. I understand that if I am employed and any such information is later found to be false or incomplete in any respect, I may be dismissed.*

This way, employers will be able to easily eliminate candidates whose applications conflict with statements made during interviews.

The application should also establish that any disputes regarding the applicant's hiring or subsequent employment are governed by binding arbitration. This allows the employer to avoid the legal system and to eliminate the potential for a jury verdict. The language must be modified on a state-by-state basis. See the end of this Appendix for a sample arbitration agreement.

Finally, the application should include a statement that if employed, the employee is employed on an at-will basis. See the end of this Appendix for a sample at-will employment statement.

➤ Checking All Personal and Professional References

"If you are serious about a candidate, you need to conduct reference checks" (*Hire with Your Head,* p. 159). Checking all personal and professional references is crucial and must be incorporated into the hiring process. Reference checks allow an employer to get experience-based opinions about the candidate's abilities and are an important way to determine a candidate's potential future liability to the business.

A perfect place to collect references is on the application. Candidates should be required to list a reference for each of their previous positions, such as a supervisor, as well as personal references. Personal and professional references are an excellent source of good information regarding a candidate. Checking these references will verify the candidate's application and give the employer an idea of the candidate's past job performance. For some candidates, it may even reveal important reasons not to hire that candidate.

The final step in the hiring process is to check references. *Hire with Your Head* and POWER Hiring provides an extensive procedure for checking references, as well as other tips and techniques that occur after the initial interview. Once again, utilization of these procedures provides a legally defensible basis for not hiring an individual. These techniques all focus on conducting your hiring process using lawful, objective selection criteria that comply with the myriad employment laws and agency guidelines that regulate the hiring process.

➤ Compliance with Applicable Law and Agency Guidelines

The techniques espoused in *Hire with Your Head* and POWER Hiring not only represent an effective and practical means of hiring and recruiting personnel, but are also compliant with federal laws like the Fair Credit Reporting Act and guidelines issued by federal agencies such as the Equal Employment Opportunity Commission and the Office of Federal Contract Compliance. The following chart highlights important legal guidelines and how the *Hire with Your Head* and POWER Hiring protocol complies with these guidelines.

Identifying the Needs of the Position to be Filled: Identify the critical success factors of every job, and generate a performance-based job description that incorporates S.M.A.R.T. objectives (Specific, Measurable, Action-oriented, Result, and Time-based. Make these objectives the dominant selection criterion so decisions are based on a candidate's ability to meet the objectives rather than on other, subjective factors. Consider a performance objective of increasing workforce diversity. *See Hire with Your Head,* Ch. 2.	**Selection criteria may be "objective" or "subjective."** *"Objective"* criteria must be specific, clearly delineated, quantitative, objectively verified, and mechanically applied. *See Zahorik v. Cornell University,* 729 F.2d 85 (2d Cir. 1984). *"Subjective"* criteria are permissible but *disfavored* by the courts because they may mask the influence of impermissible bias in making hiring decisions. *See Atonio v. Wards Cove Packing Co., Inc.,* 827 F.2d 439 (9th Cir. 1987).
Evaluating the Best Recruiting Options: When advertising, develop a marketing-driven performance-based advertisement that effectively describes a challenging position with a strong company that has growth opportunity. The advertisement should *only* focus on the performance needs of the job rather than experience or other requirements. *See Hire with Your Head,* pages 253–54.	Title VII and Age Discrimination in Employment Act proscribe employment advertisements that indicate any preference, limitation, specification, or discrimination based on a protected classification (race, color, religion, sex, national origin, age), unless the classification is a bona fide occupational qualification. *See* 42 U.S.C. § 2000e et seq.; 29 U.S.C. § 623(e); 29 C.F.R. § 1604 et seq.
Using an Effective Application: Employers should make it clear to job candidates on the application that a background check will be conducted. Employers should also ask job candidates to reconfirm that everything on the application and all statements that are made during the interview are true and correct. *See Hire with Your Head,* page 176.	State agency and federal EEOC regulations place strict express limitations on inquiries that attempt to identify protected characteristics such as race, religion, sex, sexual orientation, political affiliation, disability, national origin, and age. Inquiries relating to facially neutral criteria such as education, experience, height, weight, veteran status and military discharge, and financial status, are not impermissible per se. *See* 29 C.F.R. § 1625 et seq.
Conducting Proper Interviews: Questions should focus on fact-finding information about the candidate's past performance, team leadership ability, job competency, character and values, and professional accomplishments. *See Hire with Your Head,* pages 97–98. Use a telephone interview as a first stage to minimize personal bias. *See Hire with Your Head,* page 123.	
Checking All References and Conducting Background Checks: Conduct a thorough background check on every finalist for any position in your organization. *See Hire with Your Head,* page 175.	The Fair Credit Reporting Act permits an employer to obtain a credit report on a prospective employee from a consumer reporting agency. *See* 15 U.S.C. § 1681b(a)(3)(B)

■ CONCLUSION

Hire with Your Head and POWER Hiring represents an important breakthrough from both a practical and legal standpoint. By using this approach, employers are now equipped with the tools to hire the right employee and to legally defend that decision. Since our experience has shown that most plaintiffs should not have been hired in the first place, using the POWER Hiring program in your workplace should significantly reduce an employer's exposure to litigation and provide the solution to hiring employees who have the skill sets to be successful.

■ DISCLOSURE OF INTENT TO OBTAIN CONSUMER REPORTS OR INVESTIGATIVE CONSUMER REPORTS

For employment purposes, the Company may obtain consumer reports on you as an applicant or from time to time during employment. "Consumer reports" are reports from consumer reporting agencies and may include driving records, criminal records, and so on.

For such employment purposes, the Company may also obtain investigative consumer reports. An "investigative consumer report" is a consumer report in which information as to character, general reputation, personal characteristics, or mode of living is obtained through personal interviews with neighbors, friends, associates, acquaintances, or others. You have a right to request disclosure of the nature and scope of an investigation and to request a written summary of consumer rights.

AUTHORIZATION

I authorize the Company to obtain consumer reports and/or investigative consumer reports regarding me from time to time for employment purposes.

Signature: _____ Date: _____

Print Name: _____

Driver's License Number: _____ State: _____

Other Driver's Licenses Held in Past Five Years: _____

Print Maiden or Other Names under Which Records May
Be Listed

_____

Date of Birth (to be used only for proper identification):

_____

SAMPLE ARBITRATION AGREEMENT

I also acknowledge that the Company utilizes a system of alternative dispute resolution that involves binding arbitration to resolve all disputes that may arise out of the employment context.
Because of the mutual benefits (such as reduced expense and increased efficiency), which private binding arbitration can provide both the Company and myself, both the Company and I
agree that any claim, dispute, and/or controversy (including,
but not limited to, any claims of discrimination and harassment, whether they be based on the California Fair Employment and Housing Act, Title VII of the Civil Rights Act of 1964,
as amended, as well as all other state or federal laws or regula-
tions) that either I or the Company (or its owners, directors, officers, managers, employees, agents, and parties affiliated with
its employee benefit and health plans) may have against the
other which would otherwise require or allow resort to any court
or other governmental dispute resolution forum arising from,
related to, or having any relationship or connection whatsoever
with my seeking employment with, employment by, or other association with the Company, whether based on tort, contract,
statutory, or equitable law, or otherwise (with the sole exception
of claims arising under the National Labor Relations Act which
are brought before the National Labor Relations Board, claims
for medical and disability benefits under the California Workers' Compensation Act, and Employment Development Department claims) shall be submitted to and determined exclusively
by binding arbitration under the Federal Arbitration Act, in

conformity with the procedures of the California Arbitration Act (Cal. Code Civ. Proc. sec 1280 et seq., including section 1283.05 and all of the Act's other mandatory and permissive rights to discovery). However, nothing herein shall prevent me from filing and pursuing administrative proceedings only before the California Department of Fair Employment and Housing, or the U.S. Equal Opportunity Commission. In addition to requirements imposed by law, any arbitrator herein shall be a retired California Superior Court Judge and shall be subject to disqualification on the same grounds as would apply to a judge of such court. To the extent applicable in civil actions in California courts, the following shall apply and be observed: all rules of pleading (including the right of demurrer), all rules of evidence, all rights to resolution of the dispute by means of motions for summary judgment, judgment on the pleadings, and judgment under Code of Civil Procedure Section 631.8. Resolution of the dispute shall be based solely upon the law governing the claims and defenses pleaded, and the arbitrator may not invoke any basis (including but not limited to, notions of "just cause") other than such controlling law. The arbitrator shall have the immunity of a judicial officer from civil liability when acting in the capacity of an arbitrator, which immunity supplements any other existing immunity. Likewise, all communications during or in connection with the arbitration proceedings are privileged in accordance with Cal. Civil Code Section 47(b). As reasonably required to allow full use and benefit of this agreement's modifications to the Act's procedures, the arbitrator shall extend the times set by the Act for the giving of notices and setting of hearings. Awards shall include the arbitrator's written reasoned opinion and, at either party's written request within 10 days after issuance of the award, shall be subject to affirmation, reversal or modification, following review of the record and arguments of the parties by a second arbitrator who shall, as far as practicable, proceed according to the law and procedures applicable to appellate review by the California Court of Appeal of a civil judgment following court trial. Should any term or provision, or portion thereof, be declared void or unenforceable it shall be severed and the remainder of this agreement shall be enforceable.

I UNDERSTAND BY VOLUNTARILY AGREEING TO THIS BIND-
ING ARBITRATION PROVISION, BOTH I AND THE COMPANY
GIVE UP OUR RIGHTS TO TRIAL BY JURY OF ANY CLAIM I
OR THE COMPANY MAY HAVE AGAINST EACH OTHER.

I further understand that this voluntary alternative dispute resolution program covers claims of discrimination or harassment under Title VII of the Civil Rights Act of 1964, as
amended. By marking the box to the right, I elect to give up the
benefits of arbitrating Title VII claims.   [ ]

■ SAMPLE AT-WILL EMPLOYMENT STATEMENT

If hired, I agree as follows: My employment and compensation is
terminable at-will, is for no definite period, and my employment and compensation may be terminated by the Company
(employer) at any time and for any reason whatsoever, with or
without good cause at the option of either the Company or myself. No implied, oral, or written agreements contrary to the express language of this agreement are valid unless they are in
writing and signed by the President of the Company (or majority owner or owners if Company is not a corporation). No supervisor or representative of the Company, other than the President
of the Company (or majority owner or owners if Company is not
a corporation), has any authority to make any agreements contrary to the foregoing. This agreement is the entire agreement
between the Company and the employee regarding the rights of
the Company or employee to terminate employment with or
without good cause, and this agreement takes the place of all
prior and contemporaneous agreements, representations, and
understandings of the employee and the Company.

Appendix B

A Discussion of the Validity of the Structured Interviews Used in the POWER Hiring Process

Charles A. Handler, PhD

The purpose of this Appendix is to document the validity of the interviews used in the POWER Hiring system. This goal is accomplished via the presentation of three specific types of information:

1. Information about Content Validity (Section 1).
2. A summary of the research literature investigating the validity of structured interviews (Section 2).
3. Information summarizing best practices for structured interviews (Section 3).

The following sections provide an overview of each of these types of information as well as a description of the relevance of this information for demonstrating the validity of POWER Hiring interviews.

■ SECTION 1: CONTENT VALIDITY

The information in this section provides evidence that the process used to construct the interviews used in the POWER Hiring system is consistent with established requirements for demonstrating Content Validity.

➤ Content Validity Defined

Content Validity exists when it can be demonstrated that the content of a selection measure is related to the job for which it is being used.

➤ Requirements for Content Validity

The *Uniform Guidelines on Employee Selection Procedures* present a set of standards for ensuring that selection procedures are Content Valid. The Guidelines suggest that there are 2 critical aspects to constructing Content Valid selection measures:

1. The development of a clear definition of job performance.
2. The documentation of a clear link between job performance and the content of selection measures.

➤ POWER Hiring Content Validity

This Appendix provides evidence that the process used to develop the interviews used in the POWER Hiring is consistent with the specifications outlined in the Uniform Guidelines because it:

1. Utilizes job experts to develop a clear definition of job performance by
    ➤ Establishing job related performance objectives for a given position.
    ➤ Ranking various aspects of job performance in terms of their relative importance.

➤ Linking all aspects of job performance to an underlying competency model.

2. Links interview content directly to the definition of job performance by using job experts to develop interview questions that are based on concrete examples of job performance.

➤ Using examples of job performance to develop detailed rating scales for each interview question.

➤ Using both examples of job performance and a competency model to create an overall form for rating each candidate's job performance.

➤ Further Evidence of Content Validity

This Appendix also suggests that consistency with the Uniform Guidelines requires that an empirical validation study be conducted to support each implementation of POWER Hiring structured interviews.

■ SECTION 2: OVERVIEW OF INTERVIEW LITERATURE

The information in this section summarizes literature providing evidence that interviews can be valid predictors of job performance. The implications of this information for the validity of POWER Hiring interviews is also discussed.

➤ Interview Validity Levels

Recent research has demonstrated that interviews used for the purpose of employee selection have shown validity coefficients that approach .60. This research also suggests that that there are two major determinants of interview validity:

1. The addition of structure to the interview process.
2. The use of job-related interview questions that examine an applicant's past job performance.

The interviews used in the POWER Hiring process incorporate both of these major determinants of interview validity. POWER Hiring interviews contain a high degree of structure and make extensive use of questions requiring interviewees to discuss their past job performance.

➤ Additional Validity Information

Interview validation research also provides information that structured interviews such as those used in the POWER Hiring process:

- ➤ Provide Incremental Validity—this means that these interviews predict a component of job performance not measured by cognitive ability and personality tests.
- ➤ Are unlikely to demonstrate differences in score based on race or sex.
- ➤ Will demonstrate validity in a wide variety of situations.

■ SECTION 3: THE BENEFITS OF STRUCTURE

This section provides a more detailed look at the impact of structure on interview validities by summarizing best practices in two critical areas: (1) structure related to Interview *process*, and (2) structure related to interview *content*. This section also provides information demonstrating that the interviews used in the POWER Hiring process are consistent with best practices in both of these areas.

➤ Content Issues

Content issues refer to anything related to the creation of questions used in the interview process. The interview literature outlines three major content issues that may contribute to increased levels of interview validity:

1. The use of formal techniques such as job analysis to define job performance.

2. Asking the same questions to each interviewee.

3. Using questions that require interviewees to discuss their past performance in situations that are similar to those they will face while performing the job for which they are interviewing.

➤ Process Issues

Process issues refer to all aspects of the process in which the interview itself is embedded. The interview literature outlines five major process areas that may contribute to increased levels of interview validity:

1. Rating each interview question individually and combining information from multiple questions when making final ratings.

2. Using rating scales that provide clear, job-related anchors.

3. Requiring interviewers to take detailed notes for each interview question.

4. Using multiple interviews to assess each candidate.

5. Providing extensive interviewer training.

The interviews used in the POWER Hiring process are consistent with best practices identified for both process and content, a fact that should contribute significantly to their validity.

■ CONCLUSION

The information summarized in this Appendix supports the fact that the interviews used in the POWER Hiring process are content valid, are representative of the most effective type of interviews available, and are consistent with best practices identified in the interview literature.

■ REFERENCES

Campion, M. A., Campion, J. E., & Hudson, J. P. (1994). Structured Interviewing: A note on incremental validity and alternate question types. *Journal of Applied Psychology, 79*(6), 998–1002.

Campion, M. A., Palmer, D. K., & Campion, J. E. (1997). A review of structure in the selection interview. *Personnel Psychology, 50*(2), 655–703).

Cortina, J. M., Goldstein, N. B., Payne, S. C., Davison, H. K., & Gilliland, S. W. (2001). The incremental validity of interview scores over and above cognitive ability and conscientiousness scores. *Personnel Psychology, 53,* 325–318.

Huffcutt, A. I., & Arthur, W. (1994). Hunter and Hunter (1984). Revisited: Interview validity for entry level jobs. *Journal of Applied Psychology, 79*(2), 184–190.

Hunter, J. E., & Hunter, R. F. (1984). Validity and utility of alternate predictors of job performance. *Psychological Bulletin, 96,* 72–98.

Janz, T. (1982). Initial comparisons of patterned behavior description interviews versus unstructured interviews. *Journal of Applied Psychology, 67,* 577–580.

McDaniel, M. A., Whetzel, D. L., Schmidt, F. L., & Maurer, S. D. (1994). The validity of employment interviews: A comprehensive review and Meta-Analysis. *Journal of Applied Psychology, 79*(4), 599–616.

Motowidlo, S. J., Carter, G. C., Dunnette, M. D., Tippins, N., Werner, S., Burnett, J. R., & Vaughn, M. J. (1992). Studies of the structured behavioral interview. *Journal of Applied Psychology, 77,* 571–587.

Orphen, C. (1985). Patterned behavior description interviews versus unstructured interviews: A comparative validity study. *Journal of Applied Psychology, 70,* 774–776.

Weisner, W. H., & Cronshaw, S. F., (1988). A meta-analytic investigation of the impact of interview format and degree of structure on the validity of the employment interview. *Journal of Occupational Psychology, 61,* 275–290.

Appendix C

Templates

POWERhiring® SMARTe Objectives
Best Practices for Hiring Top Talent

Define the Job, not the Person — Create SMARTe Performance Objectives

Position:	Department:	Hiring Manger:	Date:

Instructions for Creating the Performance Criteria for Any Position

- Every job has six to eight major things that need to get done (performance objectives) for the new employee to be successful.
- Make all objectives **SMART** - **S**pecific, **M**easurable, **A**ction Oriented, **R**esult-based, **T**ime Bound, describe **e**nvironment.
- Ignore job spec. Use macro approach to develop performance objective for each major area of job. Follow template below.
- Use micro approach (over) to convert traditional experience/skill spec to performance. Find out what's done with each criterion.
- Use benchmark approach (over) by finding traits and capability of people now in the job known to be competent.
- Prioritize the top 6-8 performance objectives and include on performance-based job description.
- ANCHOR and VISUALIZE each SMART objective to determine competency (over and Fact-Finding Worksheet).

Determine Performance Objectives using the Macro Approach

Job Factor	Example of HAVING vs. DOING	Comments and Descriptions	SMARTe Objectives
Major Functional Objectives	Misleading: Have 10 years OEM sales experience. BETTER: Increase OEM sales by 15% in year 1 and build new team.	Objectives need action verb (e.g., increase, change, improve) and measurable objective (e.g., 10% in 90 days).	
Subordinate Objectives	Misleading: Have good planning skills. BETTER: In 90 days submit plan and hire 3 people.	Include the sub-steps necessary to achieve key objectives. Ask for examples.	
Management & Organizational Issues	Misleading: Have good management skills. BETTER: Assess and rebuild the team within 120 days.	Provide measurable objectives to determine quality of management skills needed.	
Changes and Improvements Necessary	Misleading: Be an agent of change. Better: Upgrade the client contact tracking system before the next promo.	Be specific regarding the needed changes and upgrades. It's easier to compare applicant's accomplishments this way.	
Problems to Be Solved	Misleading: Be a problem solver. BETTER: Work with IS to eliminate customer service bottleneck before May.	Describe actual problems needing work and then ask applicants how they would solve them.	
Technical Skills in Actual Situation	Misleading: Have good PC skills. BETTER: Develop PC-based tracking system by June.	Provide specific example of how technical skills will be used. It's better to have open discussion of real work	
Team Skills in Actual Situation	Misleading: Have good team skills. BETTER: Jointly develop inventory reduction plan with sales and manufacturing.	Describe situations that demonstrate good interpersonal/team skills and get similar examples from the applicant.	
Long Range, Planning, Strategic, & Creative	Misleading: Have good strategic thinking and planning skills. BETTER: Develop a long range product plan.	Cover anything that hasn't been addressed above. Also describe actual examples of creative and strategic projects.	

The performance profile template.

POWERhiring
Best Practices for Hiring Top Talent

SMARTe Objectives Part II

Creating SMARTe Performance Objectives

Create Performance Objectives with the Micro Approach | **Benchmark the Best**

Traditional Job Spec Skills and Experiences	Performance Criteria What's the outcome of each skill?	What do the best people do who have held this position? Create performance objectives by comparing to the "best in class."
		Advice: This is a great technique for process oriented jobs. Think about what the best people in this job do that makes them best. Seek these traits. Reverse this and avoid those traits of the weaker people. Some examples, "handle angry customers," "accurately input data for 6 hours per day."

Advice: Convert each skill, experience, responsibility or trait into a measurable objective. Ask "What will the person do with this that determines competency?" For example, for strong PC skills, indicate what they'll do with the PC skills, e.g., "Set up detailed project tracking system."

Prioritize the Objectives

Use this Checklist to Prioritize the Top 6-8 Objectives and Transfer to the Performance Profile
Check those objectives that must get done.

☐ Rank the impact on the company on ABC scale.
☐ Are there any alternatives? If so you might want to eliminate an objective or lower its priority.
☐ Don't duplicate. Be broad. Make sure final list covers all important job criteria.
☐ Get appropriate balance between management and individual contributor.
☐ Are technical objectives properly placed?
☐ Have interpersonal and culture issues been covered in the objectives?
☐ Make sure there's a balance on the technical, tactical and conceptual (strategic) level.
☐ Include thinking and intellectual skills in one of the objectives.

The Preliminary List - Top 6-8 Performance (SMARTe) Objectives

Summarize Major Objectives from Macro, Micro and Benchmark Approach Here

Objective (Summarized)	Check if a Must Have	ABC Ranking of Importance	Eliminate Duplicates	Management or Individual	Balanced Thinking	Priority Ranking

The 4-Question Interview

Best Practices for Hiring Top Talent

Develop a Trend Line of Accomplishments Over Time			
Candidate:	**Position:**	**Interviewer:**	**Date:**

Part 1 - Ask About Team and Individual Accomplishments for Each Past Job		Fact-finding Checklist
#1: Overview and Impact - Give me a quick overview of your job, the company, and describe your most significant accomplishment. (You can also ask for examples of initiative or accomplishment you're proud of.)	**#2: Organization Chart and Team Project** - Have candidate draw an org chart and describe a team or management project and specific role. (If a manager find out how candidate built and developed the team.)	Get this info for each accomplishment to validate it. Follow-up each previous answer with a related question to peel the onion. Spend 8-10 minutes on each accomplishment. ❑ Overview of the accomplishment.
Title Most Recent: _____ Dates: ____	Titles of Direct Reports or Team Members:	❑ Describe complete team - titles, names ❑ What was bottom line, business impact? ❑ When: dates, how long? ❑ Why: what was the problem? ❑ What was your actual role? ❑ How did you develop the plan? ❑ Why were you chosen for this role? ❑ What were the biggest challenges? ❑ What do you consider the most significant work you did in this job? ❑ What were the major deliverables involved in accomplishing the task? ❑ Get details of implementation steps ❑ Get three examples of initiative ❑ What did you change or improve?
Title Prior #1: _____ Dates: ____	Titles of Direct Reports or Team Members:	❑ How did you grow or change as a result of this effort? ❑ Was it completed on time, on budget? ❑ Find out how the candidate ranks the overall success of the task and why. ❑ What aspects did you enjoy (dislike) the most and why? ❑ How would others describe you? ❑ What would you do differently? **Team Issues** ❑ Get details about the team - names and titles. Find out the reporting relationships. Who was in-charge? ❑ Rank each team member's ability.
Title Prior #2: _____ Dates: ____	Titles of Direct Reports or Team Members:	❑ How did you build the team? ❑ Was team as strong as it could be? ❑ Describe how group decisions were made and get examples. ❑ Ask "Describe the people challenges and give me some examples." ❑ Get examples of persuading others. ❑ Get examples of handling conflict. ❑ Get examples of developing people. ❑ How did you change as team leader? ❑ How could you have improved your team accomplishment?

The four-question interview template.

The 4-Question Interview

Benchmark Performance - Determining Ability to Meet SMARTe Objectives		
ANCHOR	**VISUALIZE**	**SMARTe Objectives**
State the performance (SMART) objective and ask the candidate to describe their most comparable accomplishment. Use the Fact-finding Checklist to validate each accomplishment.	Ask the candidate how they would achieve the objective if they had the job. First ask the candidate what information they would need. Then how they would organize and implement the task.	Prioritize the top 5-6 deliverables or performance objectives for the position. Make them SMARTe. For example, "Within 6 months improve factory performance by 3%."
SMARTe Objective 1:		• Specific • Measurable • Action Oriented • Result-based • Time Bound • environment
SMARTe Objective 2:		Consider all the job factors as you prepare these performance objectives - major objectives, interim objectives, team and management issues, problems, technical issues, changes needed, and interpersonal problems.
		ANCHOR
		It's important to get a comparable past accomplishment to determine a candidate's ability to achieve the SMART objective. Use the fact-finding techniques on the front. Keep notes on this page under the specific objective.
SMARTe Objective 3:		**VISUALIZE**
		All good candidates can anticipate the needs of the job before starting. Get into a give-and-take discussion with the candidate by asking how they would implement the task. You only need to do this for two or three SMART objectives. Here's some additional questions to ask.
SMART Objective 4:		❑ What are the critical issues involved? ❑ Is the time schedule realistic? ❑ What other resources would be needed? ❑ What other information would you need to obtain before beginning? ❑ What would you do in the first week or two? ❑ What types of people would you need to complete the task on time? ❑ What's the critical success factor?
SMART Objective 5:		Look for these important clues: • the quality of the questions • the depth of insight • organizational skills • alone or with a team • ability to identify critical issues
		The ability to ANCHOR and VISUALIZE is a strong predictor of success. Be careful of good ANCHORS only. These people are too structured. Good VISUALIZERS only are good consultants, but have never done it.

POWERhiring®
Best Practices for Hiring Top Talent

The Basic 8-Question Interview

A Complete Performance-based Interview

Candidate:	Position:	Interviewer:	Date:

Use This Interview When the SMARTe Performance Objectives Are Known

The Deliverables - SMARTe Performance Objectives	Hot Tips and Fact-Finding Checklist
List SMART Objectives (Specific, Measurable, Action verb, Result, Time-bound) Example: *Improve product margins by 5% within 6 months.* 1. .... 2. .... 3. .... 4. .... Work-Type: ___ Technical ___ Organizer ___ Entrepreneur ___ Strategist/Creative Assign SMARTe Objectives to Work-Type and Indicate Dominant (1) and Secondary (2)	1. Be inquisitive. Get examples to turn generalities into specific responses. 2. Get trend of personal growth, energy, and team/management skills over time. 3. Listen 4X More Than Talk! Get this info for each accomplishment to validate it. - Get overview of the accomplishment. - Get actual title, size of team, titles of supervisor and subordinates, dates and duration of task.

Opening Question (Recruiting and Setting Performance Tone of Interview)

(First provide 1-2 minute overview of company and importance of job, and then ask...) Please give me a quick overview of how your background and experience has prepared you for this type of leadership position.

		Hot Tips (cont.)
Benchmark Experience Question Pattern (ask these two questions for the past 2-3		- Ask for bottom line, business impact. - Ask the candidate what his/her leadership role was - how did he/she develop program and implement it. - Find out the biggest challenges or most difficult aspects of the task. Ask "What constraints needed to be overcome?"
Please give me a quick overview of your (current/prior) position and describe the biggest impact (change) you made (or when you took the initiative).	*Describe your organization (draw org chart) and tell me how you developed, and managed your team (or tell me about some team project and describe your role).*	- Ask "Why do you consider this a significant accomplishment?" - "What were the key steps and major deliverables involved in accomplishing the task?"
Current/Most Recent Position - Title:	**Yrs:**	- Ask "Describe the people challenges and give me some examples." - Get names and titles of staff and rank their performance. Get examples of how people were developed. - Get some examples when the candidate had to change the opinion of others and in dealing with conflict. - Ask "Was the task completed on time, and was this difficult?"
Prior Position #1 - Title:	**Yrs:**	- Ask "Why were you chosen for this role?" - "How would others (peers, subordinates, supervisors) describe you and your style?" - "How would you rank the overall success of the task and why?" - Ask "What was your real contribution or value-added to this project?"
Prior Position #2 - Title:	**Yrs:**	- "If you had a chance to do it over, what would you change?" - Ask "How did you grow or change as a result of this effort?"

The eight-question interview template.

The Basic 8-Question Interview

Best Practices for Hiring Top Talent

A Complete Performance-based Interview

Candidate:	Position:	Interviewer:	Date:

Benchmark Performance (ask these two questions for each SMARTe objective)		Hot Tips - Assessing the Answers
ANCHOR: (State objective) *Describe your most similar past accomplishment.* Objective 1: Objective 2: Objective 3: Objective 4:	**VISUALIZE:** *How would you accomplish this task?* (O.K. for just top two objectives) Objective 1: Objective 2:	**Key:** Use fact-finding to learn everything about top 4-6 accomplishments and then use these tips to evaluate answers. **Work-Types:** Assign responses to these categories and compare to job needs: - **Creative/Strategist:** long range, visionary, new ideas, concepts, strategy. - **Entrepreneur/Builder:** risk taker, fast-pace, persuasive, energetic. - **Improver/Organizer:** manager, upgrades, improves people and process. - **Technical/Producer:** analytical, detailed, quality, executes process. **Team and Management - ABC Rule:** Assign responses to **A**lone (individual contributor); **B**elonging (part of team); or in-**C**harge (as manager). Determine patterns and compare to job needs.
Character and Values (if not already answered) *Tell me about a time you were totally committed to a task.*		**Scope and Size - The 6S Rule:** During fact-finding evaluate companies and jobs according to - **S**pan of control, **S**peed (pace of change), **S**ophistication, **S**tandards of performance, **S**ize, **S**cope and complexity of the work. **Focus - Internal or External:** Assign major accomplishments according to Building the Business - External, or Running the Business - Internal.
Personality and Cultural Fit *What three or four adjectives best describe your personality? Give me examples of when these have aided in the performance of your job and when they have hurt.*		**Breadth of Thinking:** Assign major accomplishments into Strategic (long range), Tactical (current), or Technical (process). **Functional or Project Focus:** Assign responses to task, department, function, multi-function, or total business. **Personality:** Look for honesty, self-awareness.
Closing - Use this to create supply and determine interest *Although we're seeing some other fine candidates, I think you have a very strong background. We'll get back to you in a few days, but what are your thoughts now about this position?*		**Close:** Don't go too fast. Make the job worth earning. Create competition to test true interest.

Summary and Assessment Notes

Trend of Impact, Energy and Initiative - Up, Flat or Down	
ABC Rule for Team/Management Skills - Alone, Belonging, in-Charge	
Technical Competency and Ability to Learn - Strong, Adequate, or Weak	
Work-Type Fit - Dominant and Secondary Match, Partial, or None	
The 6S Rule Scope and Size of Prior Jobs - Comparable, too big, too	
Focus - Internal (Running the Business) or External (Building the	
Breadth of Thinking - Strategic, Tactical, Technical	
Functional or Project Focus - Task, department, function, multi-function	
Personality - Self-aware and open or misleading	

The Ten-Factor Performance-Based Assessment Template

Trait/Factor	Scale—Weak (1) to Strong (5)					Score
	1	2	3	4	5	
1. Energy, Drive, Initiative	Little energy shown in any previous job. Passive work performance.	Generally consistent performance, but never exceeds expectations.	Consistent level of performance with some periods of high levels of energy.	Generally highly motivated, but a few periods of average performance.	Consistent self-starter. Always delivers more than expected.	
2. Trend of Performance over Time	Growth trend is spotty and inconsistent with the needs of the position.	Trend of growth down, but canidate meets the basic needs of the position.	Trend of growth has flattened, but still consistent with needs of position.	Trend of growth is upward and/or direct hit with needs of position.	Upward pattern of growth and increasing track record of performance.	
3 Comparability of Past Accomplishments (Anchor SMARTe Objectives)	No position needs are directly met. The gap is too wide to overcome.	Only one or two SMARTe objectives are met, with too many voids to handle.	Key SMARTe objectives are met with few voids that can be addressed.	Most SMARTe objectives are met with little compromise needed.	Past accomplishments directly compare to all SMARTe objectives.	
4. Experience, Education, and Industry Background	Weak fit on all standard measures: not enough experience or education.	Adequate experience and education. A stretch to meet minimum standards.	Solid education and experience, consistent with needs of position.	Direct education and experience exceeds current position needs.	Very strong comparable experience with good industry and educational fit.	
5. Problem-Solving and Thinking Skills (Visualize Objectives)	Structured thinking. Inability to adapt knowledge to new situations.	Some ability to upgrade and modify existing methods and processes.	Able to understand issues. Can develop some alternative solutions.	Has ability to understands most issues and can develop new solutions.	Understands all issues and can develop and communicate solutions.	
6. Overall Talent, Technical Competency, and Potential	Little direct technical competence and inability to learn within reasonable time.	Some technical ability and talent, but might take too long to come up to standard.	Technically competent. Reasonable ability to learn. Narrow focus on job only.	Technically strong, smart, ability to learn quickly. Broader focus. Sees related issues.	Very talented, learns quickly, strategic, tactical, and technically focused. Broad perspective.	
7. Management and Organizational Ability	Little relevant management experience or unable to organize similar projects.	Some management ability, but insufficient to make contribution soon.	Reasonable management experience consistent with needs of position.	Solid manager and organizer. Exceeds the needs of the position.	Outstanding ability to manage and organize groups of similar size and staff.	

(continued)

Trait/Factor	Scale—Weak (1) to Strong (5)					Score
	1	2	3	4	5	
8. Team Leadership—Persuade/Motivate Others	Little evidence of persuading or leading others. Tends to be more individualistic.	Some evidence of team skills, but inconclusive. Generally more individualistic.	Solid team leadership skills or potential. Consistent with needs.	Seems to have very strong team leadership. Exceeds needs.	Strong track record. Clearly the ability to motivate and develop others.	
9. Character—Values, Commitment, Goals	Questionable values and integrity. Self-serving. Misleading.	Reasonably solid values and ethics, but some questions remain unclear.	Appropriate values and ethics. No significant problems observed.	A committed person. Good character, values, and attitude.	High integrity, committed person with strong values and ethics.	
10. Personality and Cultural Fit	Fatal flaw or some imbalance or poor attitude and fit with existing team.	Adequate fit, but could cause some conflict or negative impact.	All around solid person. Will fit with group without causing much conflict.	Generally positive attitude. Personality will help in performance of job.	Has balanced ego, positive attitude, flexible, and can work with others.	
Total Point Score	Rank each trait on a 0–5 scale. Reinterview the candidate if insufficient information is available for any of these categories. Multiply total score by two (× 2) to compare with 100.					

Notes

Chapter 1

1. Michaels, Handfield-Jones, Axelrod. *The War for Talent* (Cambridge, MA: Harvard Business School Press, 2001).
2. Jerry Crispin and Mark Mahler, *CareerXRoads*, 2001.
3. Hunter and Schmidt. The Validity and Utility of Selection Methods in Personnel Psychology. *Psychological Bulletin, 124,* 1988.

Chapter 3

1. A $50,000 salary plus direct overhead and actual benefits is about $80,000 per year. If the employee stays an average of three years plus, the total amount is over $250,000.

Chapter 5

1. If you'd like to learn more about this topic, read Ichak Adizes' *Corporate Lifecycles* (Englewood Cliffs, NJ: Prentice Hall, 1988) and Kathy Kolbe's *The Conative Connection* (Lexington, MA: Addison Wesley, 1990). We each came at this similar concept independently, but you'll notice the common theme of the work-related life cycles. *Work-types* is our own term, but it represents a common-sense way to categorize work into different activities. Failing to categorize jobs into work-types is a big cause of hiring errors, and one easily prevented.

Chapter 6

1. These documents describe in detail the marketing needs of a specific product. The layout of a keyboard would be an example for a new handheld computer.
2. Hunter and Schmidt. The Validity and Utility of Selection Methods in Personnel Psychology. *Psychology Bulletin, 124,* 1998.
3. Don Riso, *Personality Types* (Boston, MA: Houghton Mifflin, 1987).

Chapter 7

1. The book *Emotional Intelligence,* by Daniel Goleman, addresses this issue to some degree, by describing a variety of different types of intelligence.

Chapter 9

1. Ed Michaels et al., *The War for Talent* (Cambridge, MA: Harvard Business School Press, 2001).
2. Retained recruiters sign a contract to find a person and get paid during the course of the search.
3. Jerry Crispin and Mark Mahler, *CareerXRoads,* 2001.
4. Jim Collins, *Good to Great* (New York: HarperCollins, 2001).
5. Jack Welch, *Jack, Straight from the Gut* (New York: Warner Books, 2001).

Chapter 10

1. Buckingham and Coffman, *First, Break All of the Rules* (New York: Simon & Schuster, 1999).

Index